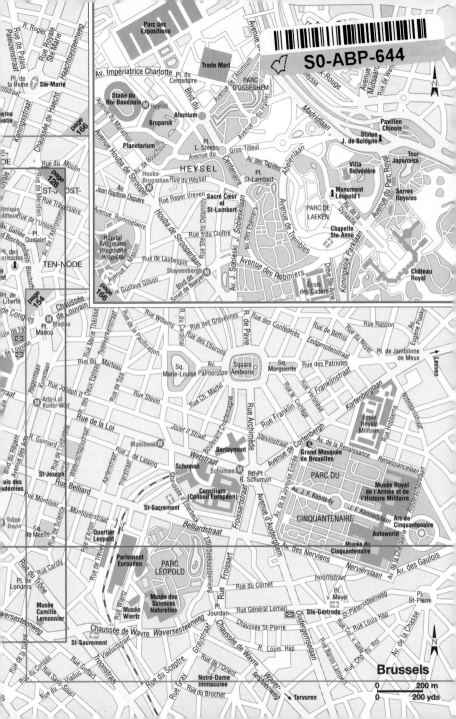

Brussels

S0-ABP-644

INSIGHT CITY GUIDE

BRUSSELS

APA PUBLICATIONS
Part of the Langenscheidt Publishing Group

✳ INSIGHT GUIDE

BRUSSELS

Editor
Cathy Muscat
Updating Editor
George McDonald
Editorial Director
Brian Bell
Art Director
Klaus Geisler
Picture Editor
Hilary Genin
Production
Kenneth Chan
Cartography Editor
Zoë Goodwin

Distribution

UK & Ireland
GeoCenter International Ltd
The Viables Centre, Harrow Way
Basingstoke, Hants RG22 4BJ
Fax: (44) 1256-817988

United States
Langenscheidt Publishers, Inc.
36–36 33rd Street 4th Floor
Long Island City, New York 11106
Fax: (1) 718 784-0640

Canada
Thomas Allen & Son Ltd
390 Steelcase Road East
Markham, Ontario L3R 1G2
Fax: (1) 905 475 6747

Australia
Universal Publishers
1 Waterloo Road
Macquarie Park, NSW 2113
Fax: (61) 2 9888 9074

New Zealand
Hema Maps New Zealand Ltd (HNZ)
Unit D, 24 Ra ORA Drive
East Tamaki, Auckland
Fax: (64) 9 273 6479

Worldwide
**Apa Publications GmbH & Co.
Verlag KG (Singapore branch)**
38 Joo Koon Road, Singapore 628990
Tel: (65) 6865-1600. Fax: (65) 6861-6438

Printing

Insight Print Services (Pte) Ltd
38 Joo Koon Road, Singapore 628990
Tel: (65) 6865-1600. Fax: (65) 6861-6438

ABOUT THIS BOOK

This guidebook combines the interests and enthusiasms of two of the world's best-known information providers: Insight Guides, whose titles have set the standard for visual travel guides since 1970, and Discovery Channel, the world's premier source of non-fiction television programming.

The editors of Insight Guides provide both practical advice and general understanding about a destination. Discovery Channel and its Web site, www.discovery.com, help millions of viewers explore their world from the comfort of their own home.

How to use this book

The book is carefully structured to convey an understanding of the city:

◆ To understand Brussels today, you need to know something of its past. The first section covers the city's people, history and culture in lively essays written by specialists.

◆ The main Places section provides a full run-down of all the attractions worth seeing. The main places of interest are coordinated by number with full-colour maps.

◆ Photographic features show readers around major attractions such as the city's parks and the Royal Museums of Fine Arts, and identify the highlights.

◆ Photographs are chosen not only to illustrate geography and buildings but also to convey the moods of the city and the life of its people.

◆ The Travel Tips listings section provides a point of reference for information on travel, hotels, shops and festivals. Information may be located quickly by using the index printed on the back-cover flap – and the flaps are designed to serve as bookmarks.

the restaurant map were written and selected by him. He also researched and wrote the new Travel Tips section packed with information and recommendations.

The principal contributor for the original chapters in the features section was **Lisa Gerard-Sharpe**, another Insight regular, who got to explore the underbelly of Brussels while working as a journalist in the city and also running training courses for Eurocrats and Nato personnel.

Contributors to the original guide include **Susanne Urban, Hartmut Dierks, Kirsten Kehret, Rosine de Dijn, Joseph Lehnen, Gisela Decker, Helmut Müller-Kleinsorge, Wolfgang Schmerfeld, Edgar Goedleven** and **Dr Barbara Beuys**.

The face of Brussels is constantly changing, with old buildings being restored, run-down areas being gentrified and new buildings under construction to accommodate the increasing number of Eurocrats. Thanks to dynamic photographs by **John Brunton, Anne and Philippe Croquet-Zouridakis, Alex Kouprianoff, Mark Read, Georgie Scott** and **Neil Setchfield**, this new edition presents a true picture of an ever-changing city, including its lesser-known corners. Thanks go also to **Hilary Genin** and **Jenny Kraus** for sourcing so many of the images.

The guide was proofread by **Neil Titman** and indexed by **Isobel McLean**.

The contributors

This major revision of *Insight Guide: Brussels* was put together by Insight Guides editor **Cathy Muscat** and builds on the original edition produced by **Kristiane Müller** and **Eberhard Urban**. This edition has been thoroughly updated by Brussels expert, **George McDonald**. McDonald also wrote the *Insight Pocket Guide to Brussels* and the *Insight Compact Guide to Bruges*, and is author and co-author of other Insight Guides covering Belgium, the Netherlands and Cyprus. He is now based in Germany, but spent many years living and working as a journalist in Brussels, and visits the city on regular assignments. He provided a variety of additional material and interesting information for the update and expansion of the existing chapters. The restaurant reviews that appear in the book and

CONTACTING THE EDITORS
We would appreciate it if readers would alert us to errors or outdated information by writing to:
Insight Guides, PO Box 7910, London SE1 1WE, United Kingdom. Fax: (44) 207 403-0290. insight@apaguide.co.uk

NO part of this book may be reproduced, stored in a retrieval system or transmitted in any form or means electronic, mechanical, photocopying, recording or otherwise, without prior written permission of *Apa Publications*. Brief text quotations with use of photographs are exempted for book review purposes only. Information has been obtained from sources believed to be reliable, but its accuracy and completeness, and the opinions based thereon, are not guaranteed.

www.insightguides.com

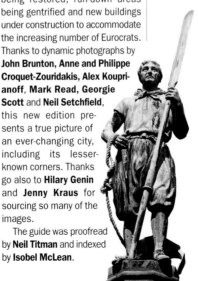

Contents

Travel Tips

THE BEST OF BRUSSELS

Setting priorities, saving money, unique attractions...
here, at a glance, are our recommendations, plus tips
and tricks even the Bruxellois won't always know

ONLY IN BRUSSELS...

- **The Grand-Place** It is a comforting thought that a capital city which is by no means the world's most handsome should possess one of its most beautiful squares. *See page 85.*
- **Manneken-Pis** As symbolic of Brussels as chocolate and chips is this old fountain in the shape of a cheeky little boy peeing. *See page 101.*
- **Comic Culture** *La Bande Dessinée*, the comic strip, is a cult in Brussels, celebrated in shops, museums, metro stations and on city walls. *See page 108.*
- **Mussels in Brussels** *Moules-frites* is the classic national dish. A call for *"un complet"* brings mussels, chips and a beer to your table. *See page 54.*
- **Surrealism** Brussels is the "capital of Surrealism" and Magritte and Delvaux were masters of the movement. *See page 69.*
- **Toone Theatre** The long tradition of bawdy puppet plays is kept alive in this little theatre. *See page 113.*

- **Waterloo** Stroll over the battlefield of Waterloo, south of Brussels, where in 1815 Europe's destiny was decided. *See page 188.*
- **European Quarter** The urban chaos of Europe's Parliament is best experienced on an organised tour. *See page 154.*
- **Chocolate** For heavenly chocolate head for Neuhaus in the Galeries Royales St-Hubert *(see page 112)* or Wittamer and Pierre Marcolini on the place du Grand Sablon *(see page 134).*
- **The Marolles** Catch Brussels' old working-class district, before gentrification sets in. *See page 119.*

BRUSSELS FOR FAMILIES

- **Mini-Europe** Tour Europe's icons in miniature: Big Ben, the Brandenburg Gate, Brussels' own Grand-Place, even an erupting Vesuvius are among the many scale-model attractions. *See page 175.*
- **The Atomium** The iron crystal magnified 165 billion times is an impressive sight. *Page 173.*
- **Centre Belge de la Bande Dessinée** The Belgian Comic Strip Centre dedicated to Tintin, the Smurfs, Charlie Brown et al. *See page 109*

- **Chez Léon** This vast down-to-earth restaurant, known for its Belgian classics, is central, family-friendly and has menus for children. *See page 116.*
- **Park Life** One of Brussels' big selling points is its profusion of parks. There are plenty of green spaces in and around the city for strolling, relaxing, picnicking and for the kids to let off steam. *See page 46.*
- **Museums** The Musée des Enfants in Ixelles *(see page 145)* is a wonderland for young children while the Scientastic Museum *(see page 225)* and the Natural History Museum *(see page 158)* have plenty to keep the eight-to-twelves amused.

LEFT: Hôtel de Ville's openwork spire is topped with a statue of St Michael.
ABOVE: the Grand-Place.

BEST ART NOUVEAU

- **Horta Museum** Influential Art Nouveau architect Victor Horta's home and studio is a stellar example of the genre. *See page 147.*
- **Old England Department Store**. The bold and beautiful old department store, now houses a delightful musical instrument museum. *See page 132.*
- **Magasins Waucquez** Another former department store that narrowly escaped demolition, is now home to the Centre Belge de la Bande Dessinée. *See page 109.*
- **Isabelle de Baecker** the only Art Nouveau shopfront in Brussels. *See page 128.*
- **St-Gilles** this commune has a wealth of Art Nouveau architecture. *See page 148.*
- **Maison Saint-Cyr** A riot of swirling wrought iron and intricate woodwork. *See page 156.*
- **De Ultieme Hallucinatie** This old Masonic temple is now a fine restaurant and bar. *See page 127.*

ABOVE: Maison Saint-Cyr (left) and the Isabelle de Baecker florist (right). **ABOVE RIGHT:** the Marolles flea market.

BEST MARKETS

- **Vieux Marché** Everything and anything you can imagine that's old and tatty makes its way onto the stalls of this popular flea market on Place du Jeu de Balle in the Marolles district. *See page 122.*
- **Marché du Midi** The best general street market in the city, covering food, clothes and many other items, ranges through streets close to the Gare du Midi. *See page 115.*
- **Sablon Antiques Market** With heirlooms that have more than a touch of class, but at prices that are somewhat less than keen, this weekend market adds cachet to the already chic Place du Grand Sablon. *See page 134.*
- **Flower Market** Every day except Monday, from March to October, the Grand-Place is filled with the sight and smell of beautiful blooms. *See page 86.*
- **Christmas Market** In the run-up to Christmas the flowers disappear and the Grand-Place becomes a festive market place where arts and crafts from all EU member states are sold. *See page 86.*

MONEY-SAVING TIPS

Brussels Card Valid for 3 days, the pass affords free public transport, free entry to nearly all major museums and discounted entry to other major attractions. Card carriers can also get discounts from participating shops, restaurants and bars. It is available from museums, tourist information centres and some hotels. www.brusselscard.be

Bus and Tram Card For short-term, intermittent use of public transport around the centre over several days, invest in a 10-trip card which is better value than single tickets or day passes. *See page 218*

Hotels Many Brussels hotels depend on business visitors. At times when business travel is reduced, particularly in high summer and at weekends, these hotels are likely to offer deals aimed at tourists. Three-, four- and five-star hotels may drop their rates by one or even two levels. Booking through the hotel website is often, but not always, cheaper. It is always a good idea to compare rates posted on the net with rates quoted by phone before committing. *See page 213*

Restaurants If you are on a tight budget but still want to experience the local cuisine, look out for the magic words *plat du jour* (dish of the day) and *menu du jour* (menu of the day). In many places they will be perfectly acceptable. Less certain is the *menu touristique* (tourist menu), which is more likely to be a sub-standard concoction. Even expensive establishments offer cut-price lunch menus that make desirable venues affordable.

8

RIGHT: Le Dixseptième
Hotel, one of the best
central options.
BELOW RIGHT: A La Mort
Subite, a traditional wood-
and-mirrors bar, complete
with surly bar staff and a
great choice of beers.

BEST MUSEUMS

- **Musées Royaux des
Beaux-Arts de
Belgique**
Belgium's finest art mu-
seum has great works
by Old Masters like
Brueghel, van Dyck and
Rubens, and modern
masterpieces by the
likes of Ensor, Magritte,
Delvaux and Matisse.
See page 132.
- **Musée du
Cinquantenaire**
The monumental
Arc du Cinquantenaire,
a majestic architectural
paean of praise to
national glory, houses
three museums in its
colonnades. The
Cinquantenaire museum
of art and civilisation at
its heart is the best.
See page 159.

- **Musée Royal de
l'Afrique Central**
Having belatedly
abandoned its original
colonial glory and
"white man's burden"
approach in favour of
African ethnology and
environment, the
Central Africa Museum
is a memorable explor-
ation of the Continent.
See page 181.
- **Musée des
Instruments de
Musique**
A wonderful sight-and-
sound museum in an
old Art Nouveau
department store.
Donning headphones,
you can hear what the
instruments on display
sound like as you pass
them by. *See page 132.*

BEST SMALL HOTELS

- **Welcome** The exotic
decor of each room is
inspired by a different
country in this truly
welcoming hotel.
See page 214.
- **Le Dixseptième** Com-
fort and elegance are

the hallmarks of this
small boutique hotel
just off the Grand-
Place. *See page 214.*
- **Les Bluets** A quirky,
homely budget hotel
close to Avenue Louise.
See page 216.

BEST BARS

- **A La Mort Subite**
An earthy bar named
after a fruity beer.
See pages 112 and 117.
- **Le Roy d'Espagne**
Traditional *estaminet*
occupying a prime spot
on the Grand-Place.
See pages 96 and 97.
- **Le 19ième** The Hôtel
Métropole bar offers a
touch of class.
See page 214.

- **Le Cirio** A slightly
scruffy but atmospheric
fin de siècle bar. *See
pages 104 and 117.*
- **Chez Moeder Lambic**
Temple of Belgian beers
with over 1,000
varieties on the menu.
See page 151.
- **L'Archiduc** American-
style Art Deco bar on
fashionable rue
Dansaert. *See page 117.*

RIGHT: *La Voix
Publique* by Paul
Delvaux (1897–
1994), one of
many master-
pieces by the
Belgian Surrealists
on display in the
Modern Art
Museum.

FREE BRUSSELS

- **Free light show** Summer evenings on the Grand-Place are livened up with a *son-et-lumière* show. *See page 87.*
- **Free art** The Brussels underground is a showcase of modern art. *See page 133.*
- **Free museums** Some museums offer free admission on the first Wednesday afternoon of the month. *See page 226.*
- **Free concerts** In summer free classical music concerts are performed in the Bois de la Cambre and on Sundays in Park Josaphat (*see pages 146 and 178*). Many of the live acts staged during the May Jazz Marathon are free. *See page 75.*

LEFT: Parc du Petit Sablon. **BELOW:** the Ommegang festival.
BELOW LEFT: autumn in Bois de la Cambre.

BEST PARKS

- **Parc de Bruxelles** Bruxellois love to stroll, jog, relax and snack in their city's central park. Though not especially big, it has been cleverly laid out to combine wide avenues with leafy trails. A spectacular firework display is held here on 21 July to celebrate National Day. *See page 128.*
- **Bois de la Cambre** For fresh air and a place of escape from the crowds, head out to this large park on the city's southern edge. *See page 146.*
- **Forêt de Soignes** When even the Bois de la Cambre just won't do as a place of escape, you can head further south to this dense and tangled treescape, a remnant of the ancient forest that once covered much of Belgium. *See page 184.*
- **Parc Josaphat** Less sophisticated, but more typically Bruxellois, is the Schaerbeek district's pretty 19th-century park. *See page 178.*
- **Place du Petit Sablon** This tiny, well-tended garden, dedicated to the memory of freedom fighters. Egmont and Hoorn, is a lovely spot to take a breather between sights. *See page 135.*

BEST FESTIVALS AND EVENTS

- **The Ommegang** A costumed procession that wends its way to the Grand-Place. July. *See page 87.*
- **Tapis des Fleurs** When the Grand-Place is carpeted with flowers. Every other August. *See page 87.*
- **Meiboom** Planting of a "Maypole" to celebrate summer. August. *See page 75.*
- **Couleur Café** Loud and lively festival of World Music featuring live acts from Africa to the Caribbean. June. *See page 75.*
- **Brussels Jazz Marathon** For three days in May the city centre becomes a stage for jazz from Dixieland and trad to acid jazz chill out played in bars and squares across town. Many performances are free. *See page 75.*
- **KunstenFESTIVAL des Arts** The prestigious festival focuses on the performing arts, notably ballet, contemporary dance, theatre and opera, at various locations. May. *See page 75.*

A CITY OF SURPRISES

Brussels is often said to lack an identity. The truth is it has many identities – and no shortage of hidden charms

Impressions of Brussels have always varied. The 19th-century English poet Matthew Arnold called it a "white sparkling, cheerful, wicked little place". His American contemporary, Herman Melville, on the other hand, sourly remarked: "a more dull, humdrum place I never saw." Opinions about the city remain as divided as ever, but the "boring Brussels" cliché is becoming increasingly hard to justify. This is an understated city full of underrated charms.

Essentially, Brussels is a city of curious quarters and atmospheric trails rather than a city of specific sights. It comprises a patchwork of 19 distinctive districts, known as *communes*. Their diversity is one of Brussels' most striking features. Designer neighbourhoods are cheek-by-jowl with bohemian districts, or a stone's throw from the bureaucratic business quarter. In the centre alone, there is the aristocratic Sablon; the working-class Marolles; arty Ixelles; fashionable St-Gilles; and the gourmet Ilot Sacré. The city also has ethnic neighbourhoods, dominated by African, Turkish and Mediterranean communities.

While it is true to say that, in the past, great art and architecture have been destroyed in equal measure (historic buildings, from pinnacled gables to Art Nouveau interiors, have been bulldozed to create space for ugly new blocks), a new civic spirit coupled with better promotion of the city mean that historic quarters are finally being preserved.

For a city this size, the variety and number of museums and galleries is astounding. Most of these are concentrated in the city centre, from the world-class ancient and modern art collections to the quirky Comic Strip Museum and captivating Horta Museum.

Art and culture aside, shopping, eating and drinking are three very good reasons for coming here. The city is a maze of luxurious shopping arcades where you can splash out on French *haute couture* and precious jewels or stock up on beer and chocolate. Every day is market day, and you can trawl through colourful stalls across town for anything from books, bric-a-brac and antiques to lobster and exotic spices. You can eat better here than almost anywhere else in the world – the variety of restaurants is as wide as the price range – and beer drinkers are spoilt for choice, with a bar around every corner and a bewildering 400 varieties of ale available.

Brussels may not have the glamour of Paris or the romance of Rome – but, when approached with an open mind and a spirit of adventure, it turns out to be a city full of pleasant surprises. ❑

LEFT: Lower City mural by François Schuiten, Belgium's number one comic-strip artist.

THE MAKING OF BRUSSELS

The city grew from a "village in the swamp" into a prosperous centre of commerce, but Belgium became a battlefield as empires wrestled for control of its trade routes and industries

According to legend, Brussels was founded by St Géry, the Bishop of Cambrai and Arras (586–625), who carried the seed of the city in his mitre to the Senne valley, where he planted it like a flower. A more plausible version of events is that some time around 600 the bishop had a chapel built on one of the islands in the Senne around which a settlement developed.

The first recorded mention of Brussels occurs in 966, when the settlement was referred to as *Bruocsella* – "the village in the swamp". In 977, Charles Duke of Lower Lorraine built a fortress on St-Géry island. Two years later he made it his residence. For this reason, 979 is regarded as the year in which the city was officially founded.

With the Senne river (now completely built over) providing additional protection, craftsmen and merchants began to settle around the castle. The town spread from the marshy valley to the slopes of the surrounding hills, whose forests provided wood for fuel and construction. In 1041, Count Lambert II of Leuven moved into a new fortress on higher ground at Coudenberg. In an unprecedented move, he built a rampart to separate the classes. His knights, stewards and merchants built their homes within its walls while craftsmen and peasants remained outside. This segregation was to sow the seeds for many a future conflict.

The weaving industry

Brussels became increasingly prosperous, thanks to its location on the trade route between Cologne and Bruges. From the 12th century, these commercial cities developed into important centres of power, and the blossoming trade between the Continent and England resulted in their rapid growth. Artefacts of wrought gold and silver from Brussels became valuable trading items. The weaving industry – which relied upon a steady supply of wool from England – flourished, and the quality of Belgian textiles was unmatched anywhere else in Europe. Colourful fabrics from Flanders and finely woven material from Brabant were in demand as far

LEFT: St Géry preaching a sermon, with the cathedral visible in the background, c.1470–90.
RIGHT: intricate tapestry; Belgian textiles were highly prized in Europe.

away as the Orient, but the beneficiaries were the cloth merchants rather than the weavers, dyers and fullers, who earned pitiful wages.

Brussels' burgeoning prosperity began to express itself in fine buildings. The construction of a great church (later a cathedral) in honour of St Michael and St Gudula, the town's patron saints, was begun in 1225. This remarkable building with twin towers was not completed until the 16th century, and incorporates features of several different architectural styles.

At the end of the 13th century the craftsmen revolted. Tired of having to labour on behalf of the privileged merchants and cloth manufacturers, while they lived in poverty and without

civic rights, they joined forces to improve their lot. Initially their efforts backfired, and their right to form a guild was made subject to the agreement of the town council. Their second offensive was more successful. In 1303, the oppressed masses of Brussels rose up against those in power, and the ruling minority of noblemen were forced to address their demands. The guild of weavers, fullers and dyers was awarded representation on the town council.

But the peace following their hard-won victory was short-lived. In 1306, Duke Jean II, backed by the nobles, took up arms against the plebeians. The rebels were defeated in a bloody battle at Vilvoorde and their leaders buried alive

CIVIC SPLENDOUR

Trades and guilds gained their independence in the 14th century and functioned as political forces until the 17th century. They played an important role in shaping the cities of Flanders. Flemish wealth was effectively spun from fine cloth as English wool was transformed by skilled Flemish weavers into furnishings, clothing and tapestries.

During this period, Europe was criss-crossed with trade routes established between major centres of commerce and industry. Flanders was pivotal to trade between Germany, the Low Countries and Britain. The success of the mercantile Flemish cities, most notably Bruges and Antwerp, was reflected in the architecture. As civic pride

burgeoned, the prosperous burghers and guilds built town halls, guild houses, cloth halls and Gothic mansions. These major public buildings were clustered around the main square – the *grand-place* or *grote markt* – the finest of which is undoubtedly Brussels' Grand-Place *(see page 85)*.

The town hall *(hôtel de ville* in French, *stadhuis* in Flemish)* was the most obvious symbol of civic pride. The Bruges *stadhuis,* dating from 1376, formed the Flemish model for such buildings, inspiring those in Leuven, Ghent and Brussels. The building of Brussels' magnificent Hôtel de Ville, begun in 1402, marked the beginning of a new stage in the city's development.

before the city gates. From then on, craftsmen were forbidden to carry weapons, and weavers and fullers, who had been at the forefront of the unrest, were subjected to a curfew and forbidden to leave their homes after nightfall. Nonetheless, the forces of change had been set in motion, and the grim determination of the guildsmen enabled them to win progressively more civil rights.

The Burgundian era

The Burgundian Empire came into existence during the Hundred Years War, a conflict waged spasmodically between England and France from 1337 to 1453. Burgundy consisted

of two regions separated from one another geographically. The southern region, in eastern France, stretched from Dijon to Basle. The other sector, of greater strategic importance, consisted of today's Belgium and Luxembourg, plus the French territory near the border and a large portion of what is now the Netherlands.

The Burgundians increased their power and sphere of influence by diplomacy, military

LEFT: Philip the Bold, Duke of Burgundy (1363–1404), leads his army.
ABOVE: Philip the Good, third of the four "great dukes" of Burgundy, and his wife, Isabella of Portugal.

endeavours and cleverly arranged marriages. The fortunes of this powerful, though short-lived, empire were moulded by the four "great dukes", who between them were in power for just over a century (1364–1477).

In 1369, King Charles the Wise (Charles V of France) commanded his younger brother Philip the Bold, the Duke of Burgundy, to marry Margaret, daughter and heiress of the Count of Flanders. Thus in 1385, after the death of the count, Flanders and other territories were incorporated into the Burgundian duchy of Philip the Bold, who died in 1404.

Philip was succeeded by his son, John the Fearless. This second Duke of Burgundy was

pitted directly against his uncle, Louis of Orléans, and the unpredictable Mad King Charles VI of France. John had Louis assassinated, defending his action as the necessary removal of a tyrant. What goes around comes around, and in 1419, during a conference with representatives of the new Count of Orléans, John in turn was assassinated. The Burgundian title was inherited by his son, Philip the Good.

By the middle of the 15th century Philip's territories included Brussels, Brabant, Flanders, Limburg, Holland, Zeeland, Hainaut, Namur and Luxembourg as well as Burgundy. The court moved between the ducal palace in Dijon and residences in Lille, Bruges and

Charles V

When he wasn't standing on the creaking deck of a ship, Charles V, Holy Roman Emperor and King of Spain, would most likely be found in the saddle of a fast horse. His territories were vast, his responsibilities huge and his travels wide. Despite a sickly constitution, the last emperor of the Middle Ages made nine journeys to Germany, seven to Italy, six to Spain, four to France, two to England and two to Africa.

Charles was born on 20 February 1500 in Ghent, the son of Philip the Handsome,

King of Castile, and Joanna the Mad. His father died in 1506, and his mother, a chronic melancholic, was confined for the rest of her life, while her father, Ferdinand the Catholic, took control of Castile.

Charles's childhood was spent in Mechelen under the guardianship of his aunt, Archduchess Margaret of Austria. On the death of his maternal grandfather, Ferdinand the Catholic, Charles was ceremonially declared of age in Brussels, being nominated Duke of Brabant and King of Spain (as Charles I) in 1516. He returned again and again to his native land, and at heart he remained a Netherlander all his

life. He shared with his compatriots a love of good food, riotous feasting and fine art. His life of travelling began when he was only 17, shortly after the death of his grandfather. He sailed to Spain in order to take up the reins of government there. Charles had been in Spain for just two years when his paternal grandfather, Maximilian I, died, leaving open the title of Holy Roman Emperor. And so, in the summer of 1519, before he had a chance to win over the proud southerners to his cause, Charles had to return to northern Europe to receive the Holy Roman Emperor's crown. At the age of 20, Charles had become the most powerful monarch in Europe.

During his lengthy reign, Charles had little chance to settle down. The Spanish and Habsburg Empire he had inherited extended across Europe from Spain and the Netherlands to Austria and the Kingdom of Naples, stretching across the Atlantic Ocean to Spanish America. Time and again he was forced to take up arms – to put down his arch rival, François I of France, or to quash the infidels (Turks and Protestants). In the final analysis, he failed on both these counts. By the end of his life he had managed to prevent neither the schism within the Christian Church nor the fragmentation of his empire. Charles's fortunes waxed and waned as Henry VIII of England and the popes in Rome transferred their allegiance between his cause and that of François I.

In 1553, old, sick and disillusioned after a lifetime of almost continuous war, he returned to the Netherlands. It was here that he made his last public appearance, in October 1555. In a moving speech before the assembled estates of the 17 provinces in the Great Hall of his castle in Brussels, Charles V renounced the throne of the Netherlands in favour of his son Philip.

At the beginning of 1556, he also relinquished the Spanish crown; and shortly after that he abdicated as Holy Roman Emperor in favour of his brother Ferdinand. Divested of power, he left the Netherlands for ever, retiring to a Spanish monastery in Estremadura; he died there in 1558. ❏

LEFT: a contemporary portrait of Charles V.

Brussels. But by 1459, Brussels had become the favoured residential city in what was by now a powerful kingdom.

The Dukes of Burgundy were great patrons of the arts, intent on nurturing a court culture in the Low Countries to match that of France and demonstrate their power and wealth. At the height of his power, Philip the Good was the richest man in Europe. He had a fondness for ostentation, luxury and elitism. The glittering lifestyle of his Brussels court attracted large numbers of famous artists and craftsmen, and it became a focal point of European civilisation and culture. Great Flemish painters were employed in its service: Jan van Eyck painted

today as Notre-Dame du Sablon) was built by the city's crossbowmen. The magnificent Hôtel de Ville (Town Hall) on the Grand-Place, started in 1402, was completed in 1455, and prosperous burghers surrounded the market square with dignified guild houses reflecting the ruler's love of pomp.

Decline and fall

The fall of the House of Burgundy was ultimately due to its overweening ambition. Philip the Good died in 1467. His successor was Charles the Bold, the last "great duke". Charles's attempt to create an extensive, independent Kingdom of Burgundy, at the expense

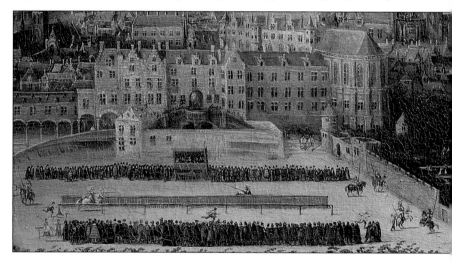

the portrait of Philip's future wife, Princess Isabella of Portugal, and Rogier van der Weyden worked for many years as Brussels' official court artist.

The city became the arena for magnificent jousting tournaments, pageants and festivals, and an ambitious building programme was embarked upon. The Church of Notre-Dame de la Chapelle, which had been destroyed by fire, was promptly rebuilt. The remarkable Church of Notre-Dame des Victoires (better known

ABOVE: view of Brussels with the Ducal Palace, the Town Hall and St Gudule, by Lucas I van Valckenborch (1535–97).

of his arch rival, the King of France, foundered in 1477 at the Battle of Nancy where he himself was killed.

His daughter and heir, Mary of Burgundy, was forced to fight the French for control of her territory. Her marriage to the Habsburg Maximilian I, son of the Holy Roman Emperor, Frederick III, saved the Burgundian possessions in the Low Countries from French attack. But the price was acceptance of Habsburg rule.

In 1494, Maximilian handed over the Netherlands to his son, Philip the Handsome. By virtue of his marriage in 1496 to the Spanish princess Joanna of Castile, daughter of King Ferdinand and Queen Isabella of Spain, Philip laid the foundations for what would in the future become the world empire of their son and heir, Charles V *(see page 20)*.

King and emperor

At the age of 15, Charles V took up residence in the Coudenberg Palace (centre of power until 1731 when it was destroyed by fire). Although he spent little time in the Low Countries, travelling constantly in his capacity as King of Spain and Holy Roman Emperor (from 1519), he always regarded Flanders and Brabant as his home. In 1531, Brussels was declared capital of the Low Countries. The city owes to Charles its cultural and political importance in 16th-century Europe. No other city within his vast empire profited more from his reign.

Brabant's cultural boom, centred around Brussels and Antwerp, was still in full flow. Dukes and nobles continued to build palaces, and trade in luxury goods flourished. Brussels lace achieved world fame and became the height of fashion in Paris. Equally coveted were weapons forged by the city's smiths. With the completion of the Willebroek Canal between Brussels and the Scheldt in 1561, the city acquired a direct link to the North Sea.

Poets and philosophers, artists and merchants all revelled in the city's lively atmosphere. The great philosopher Erasmus acted

FALL AND RISE OF THE GRAND-PLACE

In 1695 Brussels was drawn into the continuing conflict between France and Spain, which had flared up at intervals throughout the century. Louis XIV's French army bombarded the city for two days. Thousands of buildings were destroyed and the Grand-Place was reduced to rubble; only the tower of the Town Hall miraculously escaped destruction.

It took the citizens of Brussels just a few years to completely rebuild their city and some of the architectural masterpieces on the Grand-Place – redesigned as a harmonious fusion of Gothic, Renaissance and baroque elements – date from this period.

as an adviser to the young Charles. Pieter Brueghel the Elder, the most famous 16th-century artist in the Netherlands, left Antwerp in 1563 and settled in Brussels.

Science also flourished in the city. Charles V's personal physician, Andreas Vesalius, who was born in Brussels in 1514, disregarded the taboos of the time and dissected human corpses in the course of his studies. His discoveries revolutionised medical practice and formed the basis of modern anatomy.

This may have been a cultural golden age, but outside Brabant there was poverty and unrest. Dark clouds were looming on the horizon as the Reformation got under way.

Philip II, a ruthless ruler

When Charles V abdicated in 1555, he was succeeded by his son, Philip II, who proceeded to rule the Low Countries ruthlessly from Spain. Charles V's way of preventing the forward march of the Reformation had been to have Calvinists beheaded or burned at the stake as heretics; Philip took even firmer action and sent in the Inquisition. When the religious struggle developed inexorably into a popular uprising against Spanish rule, the troops of the Duke of Alva set out for the Netherlands.

The ruthless duke established the "Council of Blood", intervening mercilessly and suppressing the revolt with great cruelty, executing

fund-raiser, he succeeded in breathing new life into the struggle for civil rights and freedom of religious practice throughout the Netherlands, and finally forced the Spanish to give way. In 1576 he entered Brussels at the head of a triumphal procession; and in 1579 he established the independence from Spain of seven Protestant provinces of the north (an area that corresponds approximately to modern Holland). But conflict continued.

North versus south

King Philip's desire to maintain absolute power led to repression and a series of military campaigns. Having previously sent the Duke of

some 12,000 citizens. In 1568, the two most prominent leaders of the revolt, Counts Egmont and Hoorn, were beheaded on Brussels' Grand-Place for demanding greater sovereignty for their country *(see page 89)*. After their deaths, a full-scale revolt ensued in the Low Countries that would last for 80 years.

Aristocratic leadership of the rebellion was assumed by Prince William I of Orange (William the Silent). A skilled negotiator and

Parma, Alexander Farnese, to the Low Countries at the head of a large army, Philip had been able to force the rebellious southern states to capitulate one by one; in 1585 Brussels, too, was retaken by Farnese. The Union of Arras was formed to join the provinces that accepted the Catholic king as their ruler – an area that became known as the Spanish Netherlands.

In 1598 Philip transferred his power over the Spanish Netherlands to his daughter Isabella and her husband, Archduke Albert of Austria. During their reign, the people of Brussels, which had remained capital of the Spanish Netherlands, enjoyed a more peaceful existence. The gallows and scaffold disappeared,

LEFT: the Brussels skyline has long been dominated by the soaring spire of the Town Hall.
ABOVE: *The Arrest of Count Egmont by the Duke of Alba on 9 September 1567* by Julius Hamel.

the economy boomed and a taste for courtly pomp and celebration prevailed once more. No other period in the capital's history witnessed as many processions and banquets as during the ensuing years. Peter Paul Rubens (1577–1640), the most famous baroque artist in Europe and court painter to the Spanish regents, captured the spirit of the era in his paintings.

Conflict continued in the second half of the 17th century. King Louis XIV of France's determination to conquer Europe led to a series of wars during which the Spanish Netherlands came under attack. In 1695 the French king sent an army to Brussels – the city was all but destroyed *(see page 22)*.

Austrian power

The peace treaties signed at the end of the later War of the Spanish Succession granted sovereignty over the Spanish Netherlands to Austria. Under Maria Theresa, Belgium experienced enormous economic prosperity. Trade and industry were subsidised and roads were built, linking important cities such as Brussels and Vienna. But while the Austrian government, Belgian industrialists and city merchants were turning huge profits, the common folk fared badly. Low wages, unemployment and social destitution were the lot of a large portion of the population, conditions that would eventually bring about revolts.

NO TEARS FOR NAPOLEON

When the French revolutionaries annexed Belgium in 1795, the hopes cherished by Brussels' citizens in these new rulers were unfulfilled. Reforms were introduced but they scarcely improved the misery of the masses. The Napoleonic Wars drained the city of its few remaining resources and only the wealthy benefited from the new regime. When in 1803 Napoleon visited the city for a reunion with Josephine, he attempted to ingratiate himself with the populace; the fountains gushed wine, and craftsmen were inundated with contracts. Nonetheless, few tears were shed in Brussels when Napoleon's empire came to a bloody end in 1815 at Waterloo.

But while the sun shone upon the rulers and the wealthy classes their interests developed in the direction of fine arts and crafts. The gold-and-blue Belgian porcelain graced the finest drawing-rooms of Europe. The fashion for lace also reached its peak during this period, and the industry entered one of its most productive periods. Brussels lace *(see page 94)* was worn by anyone in a position of power and wealth. Architecture flourished as well, and Brussels became known for its magnificent buildings and splendid squares. The Place Royale and the Forêt de Soignes both date from this period.

Maria Theresa died in 1780 and her son, Joseph II, who had been co-regent since 1765, succeeded her. However, his hasty reforms fanned the smouldering resistance to Austrian rule. Although Joseph's attempts to curb the influence of the Church of Rome left most citizens other than the Catholic clergy indifferent, he aroused unpopularity at every level with his range of judicial and administrative reforms. In particular, his plans for a centrally run German-speaking empire met with universal opposition.

Encouraged by the revolutionary turn of events in France, the people of Brabant revolted in 1789. They evicted the Austrians, and on 11 January 1790, one month before the death of Joseph II, the "United States of Belgium" was proclaimed.

French, with the aid of a Belgian legion, defeated the Austrian army near Jemappes. It seemed that Belgium was at last free of the Habsburg yoke. By June 1794 France had taken up occupation of both Belgium and the Netherlands. The two countries were combined and renamed the Batavian Republic. The French reformist administration succeeded in dismantling, piece by piece, the old absolutist system.

The fact that the economy was subsidised by the government helped Belgium develop into the most progressive industrialised state on the Continent. But French domination had its drawbacks. From 1797 Belgians were conscripted to serve in the campaigns of Napoleon.

Paradise postponed

This new state of affairs was not to last. The new Austrian emperor, Leopold II, sent troops into Belgium to pull it back into the empire. The fledgling country was quickly defeated, and after just one short year of freedom, Belgium once again found itself under Austrian rule. In 1792 the Austrian and Prussian war against revolutionary France broke out, and Belgium was drawn into the battle. On 6 November, the

The so-called Holy Alliance, formed by Austria, Britain, Prussia and Russia, defeated Napoleon once and for all near the Belgian village of Waterloo in 1815 *(see pages 26–7)*. The Batavian Republic was dissolved, but a large number of Belgians were soon to regret the departure of the French, in view of what was decided at the peace conference held in Vienna.

The Congress of Vienna established a new order in Europe. The unification of Belgium and the Netherlands would now be ruled over by the Dutch House of Orange. The patience of the Belgians was at an end, and 15 years later, the revolution of 1830 was to result in a free and independent Belgium at last. → *page 28*

LEFT: *The Lacemaker* by Vermeer (1665).
ABOVE: weaving brought prosperity, and Brussels tapestries were highly sought after (painting by Isaac Clacsz, *c.*1600).

The Battle of Waterloo

On 26 February 1815 Napoleon escaped from exile on the island of Elba, and on 20 March he entered Paris in triumph. An alliance was formed between Austria, Britain, Prussia and Russia to defeat him once and for all. In June of that year the decisive battle was fought at Waterloo, 18 km (11 miles) south of Brussels.

The battle plans

Napoleon's strategy was to defeat the Allies in detail – one at a time – before their scat-

tered forces had time to concentrate. In the opening play, he invaded Belgium, intending to deal first with the Prussian Marshal Blücher and Britain's Duke of Wellington before they could combine against him.

He made a good start, defeating the Prussians at Ligny, while a detached force struck Wellington's advance guard at Quatre Bras. French casualties were heavy, but Napoleon had prevented the juncture of his opponents and, as he believed, forced the Prussians into retreat towards the Meuse. He sent a strong force under Marshal Grouchy after them and moved north with the main body on Brussels.

Wellington had assembled his own disparate forces for a stand along the ridge of Mont St-Jean astride the road to Brussels. He could shelter his 72,000 troops from the strong French artillery behind the ridge, and to get at them the French would have to attack uphill. But Napoleon had the initiative, and with 76,000 men a slight advantage in numbers. His decision was to eschew manoeuvre and to attack frontally, trusting to superior French experience, firepower and courage to smash Wellington's line and drive him headlong from the field.

Napoleon and his troops rose early that Sunday. The breakfast table was laid before 5am. But, as fate would have it, bad rain impaired visibility, and the attack, planned for 9am, was delayed. The gun crews could hardly move the cannon on the muddy ground, even with teams of 15 men and 12 horses per gun. But, despite such unpromising conditions, Napoleon was sure that victory would be his: "Gentlemen, if you carry out my orders well, we shall sleep tonight in Brussels," he said.

Battle is joined

At 11.30am, from his command post south of La Belle Alliance inn, the emperor gave the signal to attack. The Allied troops were engulfed in the fire from 120 French cannon. Opposite, in his headquarters at Mont St-Jean, Wellington took shelter under an elm tree, from where he could direct his army.

In the valley between Mont St-Jean and La Belle Alliance lay the ancient manor-farm of Hougoumont to the west and the farmstead of La Haie-Sainte to the east; both were fortified and occupied by Allied troops. If the French wanted to storm Mont St-Jean they needed to take both strongholds first.

The attack on Hougoumont soon opened. At 5pm the French gave up the attempt. Piled in front of the perimeter wall was a gruesome heap of corpses – 3,000 French soldiers lost their lives here. Meanwhile, Napoleon had ordered an attack on Wellington's centre, although he was already aware that the Prussians, far from retreating, were approaching, and that there was no sign of Gouchy, who was meant to be in pursuit. He was forced to reposition troops to delay the Prussians while the assault on the centre went ahead.

The French infantry corps of Count Drouet d'Erlon advanced down into the valley in close-packed columns and started up the long, gentle slope on the far side. The Allied forces waited behind the embrasures of La Haie-Sainte or behind the ridge. To the amazement of the French, thousands of British and other Allied soldiers suddenly rose up from the crest of the hill and fired one devastating blast of musketry after another full in their faces. Flailed by this storm of lead, few of the French troops managed to reach the top of the hill.

When flesh and blood could stand no more they began to withdraw, sped on their way by a pursuing British cavalry brigade that slashed at their backs and unwisely charged on towards the French artillery, where they in turn were cut to pieces. By this time Marshal Ney had brought the French cavalry into action, charging Wellington's centre with thousands of men and horses. Most of the Anglo-Prussian troops were able to deploy into square formations, bristling with bayonets, which the milling horsemen were unable to break. Losses were heavy on both sides. "Hard pounding," Wellington observed calmly, "Let us see who will pound the longest."

At 6.30pm the French Tricolour was finally hoisted above La Haie-Sainte. Wellington's bleeding front at the heart of Mont St-Jean wavered. He had no more reserves. Hope for the arrival of Blücher or nightfall was the only comfort he could offer his generals when they demanded reinforcements and fresh ammunition.

With the Prussians breaking through on his right, Napoleon had only his loyal and veteran Old Guard left in reserve. It was time for a last roll of the dice that would settle the issue of the battle and of Europe's future. The emperor sent his personal guard up the hill, but they were slaughtered at close range by Wellington's artillery fire and musket vol-

leys. By 8.30pm, Blücher and his entire army had arrived. Wellington ordered a general advance by his own survivors. The French knew they faced defeat and the cry went up, "Run for your life!", as the Prussians and British careered down the hillside after them. The remnant of the Old Guard fought to the end to shield their emperor from capture and Napoleon was able to escape. In Wellington's words, the battle had been "the nearest run thing you ever saw in your life".

Victory and defeat

At 9.30pm, the victorious leaders Wellington and Blücher embraced each other in the

courtyard of La Belle Alliance. Four days later, Napoleon dictated his second document of abdication in Paris.

Casualties from all sides totalled 48,000 dead and wounded. The field of Waterloo after the battle was a compact scene of horror, in fields carpeted with dead and wounded men and horses, their gaily coloured uniforms and caparisons stained with blood and smeared with mud. People came from all around to view the sight. Some attempted to relieve the wounded of their suffering, others succeeded in relieving both dead and wounded of their valuables. The Napoleonic Wars were over. ❏

LEFT: *The Battle of Waterloo, 1815; "The Battle in Full Flood"* by W. Heath.

RIGHT: the English prepare for battle in a modern re-enactment of the Battle of Waterloo.

The Kingdom of Belgium

After more than two centuries of separation, the dream of a single country finally came true – albeit for only 15 years. Brussels and The Hague were nominated joint capitals, but the northern half of the united country, economically the stronger, set the tone. The constitution received no majority vote in the south.

King William I of Orange introduced Dutch as the official language in both halves of the country. Much to the annoyance of the citizens of Brussels – for many years a French-speaking city – he ruled that Dutch was to be spoken in the schools and courts, and by all official bodies. Unrest was also provoked by the king's

the yoke before which we tremble; away with the foreigner who laughs at our torment!" These words perfectly expressed the feelings of the majority of Belgians under Dutch rule. The finale of Act III heightened tensions in the theatre: "Bring your weapons! Bring your torches! Courage! We shall fight now for the victory of our cause!" And during Act IV, as the cry went up, "No more tyranny! No more slavery! Power henceforth to the citizens!", the audience rose from their seats and stormed into the streets where a workers' demonstration was taking place. Together the insurgents stormed the Palais de Justice. The revolution had begun.

interference in the training of priests and the curriculum. Catholics and liberals alike felt themselves badly treated.

France's second revolution, which broke out in July of 1830, was the signal for Belgians to rise up against the House of Orange. The call for revolt went up on the evening of 25 August 1830, during a performance of Auber's opera *Masaniello (La Muette de Portici)* at Brussels' Théâtre de la Monnaie. The subject of the opera, written in 1828, was the Naples rebellion of 1647. The audience became increasingly restless during the aria *Sacred love of Our Fatherland.* "Far better to die than to live a wretched life in slavery and shame! Away with

William sent troops into Brussels, but they were beaten back. On 25 September 1830 a provisional government was established which declared the independence of Belgium on 4 October of that year. A national congress was elected which then decided on a new constitution. Brussels became the new capital. The next thing the new country needed was a king. In their search for an appropriate sovereign, the leaders agreed upon the German Leopold of Saxe-Coburg-Gotha, an uncle of Queen Victoria.

In 1831, as Léopold I, he became first King of the Belgians, and 21 July, the day he pledged himself to the constitution, was proclaimed a day of national rejoicing and is now Belgium's national day. The next year he married Louise-Marie, daughter of King Louis-Philippe of France.

Post-revolution Brussels

The Belgians had their own country at last and rapidly became something of a wonder to the rest of Europe. Fired by the taste of freedom they went straight to the forefront of 19th-century Europe, when the application of science and engineering seemed to promise a vista of endless progress.

The Industrial Revolution began with the construction in 1835 of a railway line between

ishing arms industry. A wave of construction, in the grand style appropriate to a vibrant new nation, hit the capital, giving it a monumental look. Among the many fine edifices were the Galeries Royales St-Hubert shopping arcade.

Not everybody benefited from the boom; wages were low and working hours long. Female and child labour were commonplace. Social security, industrial safety standards and free Sundays were a long way off the political agenda. Brussels had the highest infant mortality of all European capitals. The working class lived in misery in damp, cramped apartments; their diet consisting largely of cabbage, potatoes and bread. Their wretched

Brussels and Mechelen, the first on the Continent, and the rail network became steadily denser as coal mining in the south and the development of the iron and steel industry around Liège raised Belgium to a position alongside the principal industrial nations. This process was supported by a flourishing textile industry centred around Ghent and Kortrijk, expansion of the port of Antwerp, and a flour-

LEFT: The 1830 uprising brought Belgium liberation and independence; British explorer Henry Morton Stanley "discovered" the Congo and "bought" the Africans in the name of Léopold I.
ABOVE: transporting coal through the mineshaft, 1873.

existence was exemplified by the Marolles. This was the district in the city centre where the poor and the oppressed had lived together for centuries. It was here, too, that the first workers' associations were formed.

Yet on other fronts Belgium and Brussels enjoyed a reputation for progressiveness. The country's freedom of speech and of the press were held up as examples. Brussels became an asylum for persecuted socialists from all over Europe. Karl Marx sought refuge here in 1845. In 1848, he and Friedrich Engels published *The Communist Manifesto*. This, however, stretched the liberal attitude of the city fathers too far, and Marx was expelled from the country.

His ideas, however, did not go unheeded by the citizens of Brussels. As in the rest of Europe, socialism was gaining support from the proletariat. The Belgian Workers' Party was established and 1886 was marked by strikes and protests. The century ended with bitter fighting, leading to the introduction in 1893 of universal male suffrage and the right to strike. In 1894, the socialists gained their first parliamentary seats.

Colonial power

On his death in 1865, Léopold I had bequeathed many social problems to his successor. With scant regard to these, Léopold II allocated a

Jules Anspach, the Senne river was covered over to create a series of grand boulevards. Léopold died in 1909.

This gargantuanism in its public face, was counterbalanced to a degree by the appearance of Art Nouveau in the private sphere, and the development of a constellation of great architects – foremost among them Victor Horta – working in this genre. Consequently, there is a distinctly personal feel to the fine houses that grace many of the city's communes.

The World Wars

On 3 August 1914, Germany demanded that Belgium allow its army passage through Bel-

large part of the income from his merciless exploitation of the Belgian colony of the Congo to the aggrandisement of Brussels. He constructed magnificent avenues and various fine buildings. The Palais des Colonies (today's Central Africa Museum) was built in the suburb of Tervuren; the Palais de Justice, whose way-over-the-top design renders even superlatives deficient, in 1883; and the great triumphal arch and museum complex of the Parc du Cinquantenaire to celebrate the 50th anniversary of Belgium's existence.

The city's old defensive walls were demolished to make way for the roads that now form the inner ring road, and, on the orders of Mayor

gian territory. When the government denied the request, the Germans marched across the border regardless. Great Britain, France and Russia all made calls for an immediate retreat of the German forces, but in the meantime the war had already begun. The Belgian army put up a spirited and intense resistance to the invasion, but by the end of 1914 almost the entire country was in German hands.

Even after the invaders were securely entrenched, fighting continued, as the civilian population countered the occupation with attacks designed to weaken the German position. These included destroying rail tracks, telephone lines and telegraph cables. Brussels' mayor, Adolphe Max, gained fame for his resistance to the occupiers. The German reaction was to seize and kill hostages at random, and to send women, teenagers and elderly men to work as forced labourers in Germany. As the war drew to a close, the fiercest battles were fought in the Ardennes and also on French soil, most notably at the Somme. By the time a ceasefire was declared on 11 November 1918, millions lay dead and years of fighting had turned the Flemish soil into a massive graveyard. Mines, weapons and skeletons are still uncovered in the area to this day.

King Albert I acquired a glorious reputation during World War I. He led the Belgian army

World War II

Nazi Germany attacked France, the Netherlands, Luxembourg and Belgium on 10 May 1940. The Belgian government fled to London where it operated in exile, while King Léopold III chose to become a self-styled prisoner at the Royal Palace in Laeken until June 1944, when the Nazis removed him to Germany.

The number of Belgian collaborators with the occupying forces is reckoned to have been considerable, and the king himself was unable to dispel suspicions that he had collaborated. Most collaborators came from the ranks of the fascist-monarchist movement, which still exists today. But many Belgians showed great

in its resistance to the foreign invaders, and vociferously encouraged the country's citizens to do likewise.

Society was very different after the war. The badly damaged economy was slow to recover. There was a brief recovery in the late 1920s, but Belgium did not escape the Great Depression of the 1930s. Unemployment rose rapidly and, as in other countries across the Continent, fascist groups profited from the general unrest.

LEFT: German field kitchen on the Grand-Place (World War I). **ABOVE:** young members of the Resistance fought as a "secret army" against the Germans (1944).

BELGIUM'S JEWISH POPULATION

From June 1942, Belgian Jews were required to wear the yellow star of David to mark them out from the rest of the population. When called upon to volunteer for the labour camps in the early summer of 1942, many actually did so, tragically believing this was their safest course of action – in this way, thousands unwittingly boarded trains only to perish in the Nazi death camps. Approximately 2,700 Jewish children from Belgium survived, however. Their escape was thanks to the relentless efforts of a unique underground network that hid the children under false names in convents, boarding schools and with private families.

courage in their commitment to the Resistance, protecting the persecuted and destroying transport and communication lines to hinder the occupying forces. Socialists, communists, liberals and Christians fought side by side as Belgians and anti-fascists. Many Belgian Jews, in addition to German and Austrian Jews who had fled to Belgium to escape persecution in their own countries, were murdered by the Nazis. But some – calculations suggest about half – were hidden by the non-Jewish population.

The liberation of Belgium started at the beginning of September 1944, and its success was swift. By 3 September Brussels had been

reached by Allied forces. When Germany surrendered on 8 May, Belgium was in ruins; the task of rebuilding the cities and the nation now lay ahead.

Renewal and reform

Belgium's economic recovery after the war was quite rapid. The harbour of Antwerp had been spared major damage during the conflict, and the country's energy reserves were adequate to supply all the necessary power. But reorganisation on the political level was very slow in coming. Post-war Belgium has been characterised by linguistic and territorial disputes.

In May 1945, Léopold III returned from exile in Germany, and the crisis between the king and his ministers turned into open conflict. In 1950, a referendum was held to determine what constitutional rights the monarch should be granted. Throughout Belgium 58 percent of the voters were in favour of allowing the king to return to the throne. But the results demonstrated a regional polarisation. In Flanders, 72 percent favoured the king's return; in Brussels it was only 48 percent, and in Wallonia it was just 42 percent.

Parliament voted to reinstate the king, and, on 22 July 1950, Léopold returned to Laeken Palace. There followed a wave of protest in Wallonia. The king abdicated in favour of his son, and in July 1951 Baudouin I was crowned.

In 1958 – the same year that the city's landmark Atomium was built – Brussels began its trajectory to European power when it became the seat of the European Economic Community, the forerunner of today's European Union. This growing influence was cemented on a politico-military level when Nato headquarters transferred from Paris to Brussels.

During the early 1960s the social climate was marked by strikes. Demonstrations were held to protest against the so-called "law of uniformity" regulating economic development, social progress and the reorganisation of state finances. Tensions developed not only between the language groups and different religions, but also within the parties and trade unions. Constitutional revisions of the 1970s and 1980s were designed to preserve the language, culture, lifestyle and spiritual beliefs of the different groups within the country. In 1980 measures were taken to expand the authority of the Flemish and Walloon regions, which were granted their own rights and institutions. In order to regulate the balance of power between the central organs of the state, the different communities and the regions, a committee of accordance and a disputes court were established.

Today, Belgium has a complex system of municipalities, provinces and regions as well as a centralised state. In 1995 this process reached a symbolic peak – or nadir, as some saw it – when the ancient and once powerful province of Brabant was divided along communal lines into Flemish Brabant and Walloon Brabant, with Brussels close to the line of division.

The development of the Brussels Capital Region is the latest outcome of the constitutional reform. The institutional reform has succeeded in bringing a temporary halt to the historic development towards the fragmentation of an entirely federal state. Many Belgians feel that this policy, known as the *compromis à la belge*, attempting to devolve power to every conceivable minority, has got out of hand.

In 1993, the monarchy changed hands when King Baudouin died. He was succeeded by his brother, Albert II, who has been a cautious, even lacklustre constitutional monarch, evidently fully aware of the many pitfalls, both seen and unseen, that lurk in front of a Belgian sovereign,

cial systems, with corruption prevalent at the highest levels. The criminal investigation system is open to abuse and rather passive, based as it is on witness statements rather than on systematic investigation and the gathering of hard evidence. In the 1980s, it was the Brabant supermarket killers, an attempt to destabilise the government by shadowy right-wing groups. In the 1990s, the pillars of Belgian society were shaken by a paedophile scandal. This provoked the 1996 "White March", which brought 300,000 people onto the streets of Brussels in protest at police incompetence and a malfunctioning justice system, and was the largest public protest ever seen in Belgium. A wave of

and determined to avoid all of them. But he has won respect for a kind of dogged determination to see it through.

Brussels today

Nowhere in the European Union do citizens have such little faith in a functioning democracy or in those who govern them. The country has a reputation for clan-like political and judi-

LEFT: the 1996 "White March" was the largest protest march ever seen in Belgium; many of the protestors were children. **ABOVE:** Princess Elizabeth, daughter of Prince Philippe and Princess Mathilde, is the youngest royal family member.

hysteria engulfed the government, with charges of involvement extending to the upper echelons of the police, judiciary and government.

Although Belgium has always been a divided country, it has managed to remain unified against the odds. Hitherto, the constitution and the royal family have acted as unifying forces, bolstered by the pivotal role of Brussels as the capital of Europe. For now, at least, the linguistic line holds.

Meanwhile, Brussels gets on with the job of renovating its architectural heritage – instead of the previously more common wanton destruction of it – and in general smartening itself up to justify its vaunted "capital of Europe" tag. ❑

Decisive Dates

***c*.600:** According to legend St Géry, builds a residence and chapel on an island in the Senne.

966: The first documented reference to Brussels, as *Bruocsella* (Village in the swamp).

979: Celebrated as the city's official foundation – Charles Duke of Lower Lorraine occupies a castle built on St-Géry island at Bruocsella.

1005: The counts of Louvain (Leuven), later Dukes of Brabant, inherit the settlement.

11th and 12th centuries: Brussels grows in prosperity, thanks to its position on the trade route between Bruges and Cologne.

***c*.1100:** Construction begins on the city's first defensive wall.

1225: Construction begins on the Gothic cathedral dedicated to St Michael and St Gudula.

1229: Duke Henry of Brabant grants Brussels its first town charter.

1302–6: Revolution by craftsmen and tradesmen against the aristocratic government fails, though the plebeians win some concessions.

1357: Construction of the city's second defensive wall; now dismantled, it followed the course of today's inner ring road, the *petite ceinture*.

1369: Margaret, daughter of the last Count of Flanders, marries Philip the Bold of Burgundy. Flanders passes to Burgundian rule.

1402: Construction of the Gothic Town Hall (Hôtel de Ville) in the Grand-Place begins.

1421: A popular uprising leads to a fairer system of government, with local powers divided between the patrician families and the emergent guilds of craftsmen and other workers.

1425: Pope Martin V founds the university at Leuven, which develops into a European centre of jurisprudence.

1430: The Duchy of Brabant, including Brussels, passes to the rule of Duke Philip the Good of Burgundy, who already controls Flanders. The Burgundian Empire begins a cultural golden age; by 1459 Brussels is the empire's capital. Textile industries are the economic mainstay.

1435: Rogier van der Weyden, important Netherlands painter, is appointed city artist.

1455: The magnificent Town Hall is completed.

1477: Mary of Burgundy grants permission to dig the Willebroek Canal, which gives Brussels access to the sea by way of the Scheldt. Mary, daughter and heiress of the last Duke of Burgundy, Charles the Bold, marries Maximilian I of Austria. The Low Countries come increasingly under the sway of the Habsburg dynasty.

1500: Charles V, grandson of Maximilian and later Habsburg emperor, is born in Ghent.

1514: Vesalius, who is considered the father of anatomy, is born in Brussels.

1521: Humanist Desiderius Erasmus lives in Anderlecht, then a village outside Brussels.

1522: Two Lutheran preachers are burned at the stake in Brussels; their martyrdom strengthens the forces of the Reformation in the city.

1526: Artist Pieter Brueghel the Elder settles in Brussels.

1531: Brussels becomes the capital of the Habsburg Low Countries.

1555: Charles V abdicates the throne in favour of his son, Philip II.

1566: Protestant iconoclasts ransack churches across the Low Countries. Catholic Spain sends the Duke of Alba to suppress the movement. As the representative of the Inquisition, he launches a reign of terror that leads thousands of Protestants to emigrate.

1568: Counts Egmont and Hoorn, who had tried to moderate the religious intolerance of Spanish rule, are beheaded in the Grand-Place.

1579: Under Prince William I of Orange, seven northern provinces of the Low Countries declare independence.

1585: The southern part of the Low Countries recognises Philip II as its sovereign.

1648: By the Treaty of Westphalia, Belgium remains under Spanish control.

1695: French army of Louis XIV bombards and destroys the Grand-Place.

1701–13: The War of the Spanish Succession turns Belgium into a battlefield. The 1715 Treaty of Utrecht ends the war and the present-day territory of Belgium passes under the authority of the Austrian Holy Roman Emperor Charles VI and his Habsburg successors.

1744: Duke Charles of Lorraine, governor of the Austrian Netherlands, beautifies Brussels with many neo-classical buildings.

1794: French revolutionaries annex Belgium, which remains under French control until the defeat of Napoleon Bonaparte.

1815: Wellington and Blücher defeat Emperor Napoleon at the Battle of Waterloo. Holland and Belgium form the Kingdom of the Netherlands under William I of Orange.

1830–1: Belgium, led by opera-goers in Brussels, revolts against the rule of the House of Orange, and the country achieves independence under King of the Belgians, Léopold I.

1834: Free University of Brussels founded.

1835: Inauguration of the first Continental railway, between Brussels and Mechelen.

1847: The Galeries Royales St-Hubert open.

1871: Construction of the *grands boulevards* through the marshy Lower City; the polluted Senne river is covered over.

1883: The colossal Palais de Justice built.

1885: Congo Free State acquired by Belgium.

1914–18: German troops invade Belgium and occupy Brussels during World War I.

1940–4: Nazi Germany invades Belgium during World War II. The Belgian government seeks exile in London. In 1944, the Nazis send King Léopold III to Germany; the Allies liberate Belgium, entering Brussels on 3 September.

1948: A customs union is agreed between Belgium, Netherlands and Luxembourg (Benelux).

1951: King Baudouin I ascends the throne after the abdication of Léopold III.

1957: Belgium joins the European Economic Community (now the European Union).

1958: The World Fair at Heysel Stadium in Brussels; its highlight is the Atomium.

1959: Brussels becomes headquarters of the European Commission.

1967: Brussels made headquarters of NATO.

1971 and 1980: Constitutional reform gives both Belgian linguistic groups (Flemish and French) more autonomy.

1977: Belgium divided into three regions: Flanders, Wallonia and the Brussels conurbation.

1989: In a further reorganisation of the Belgian state, Brussels becomes the Capital Region.

1993: King Baudouin I dies and is succeeded by his brother, Albert II.

1995: The provinces of Vlaams-Brabant

(Flemish Brabant) and Brabant-Wallon (Walloon Brabant) are created from the old province of Brabant, surrounding Brussels.

2001: A daughter, Elizabeth, is born to Crown Prince Philippe and Princess Mathilde.

2002: The Belgian franc is replaced by the euro.

2003: Belgium amends its 1993 war crimes law, which had seen actions brought in Belgian courts against President Bush, British Prime Minister Tony Blair and Israeli Prime Minister Ariel Sharon, and had led to threats to boycott Brussels as an international meeting-place.

2004: Ten new member states join the EU.

2005: Referendums in France and the Netherlands vote against the EU Constitution. ❏

LEFT: Leo Belgicus, a powerful symbol of the nation.
RIGHT: the Palais du Berlaymont, displaying the 25 flags of the EU member states.

THE UNBORING BRUXELLOIS

Brussels is a city cast in its residents' image: at once provincial and international, with bourgeois bonhomie undercut by a subversive, surreal and self-critical spirit

I f Brussels played that fatuous party game of naming 10 famous Belgians, from the artistic hall of fame it could summon up Breughel the Younger, or Jacques Brel, the song-writing and singing genius. However, it would also have to confess to the "Muscles from Brussels", martial arts supremo Jean-Claude van Damme, and Tintin, that comic-strip Belgian reporter in his baggy plus-fours. Contemporary Brussels is left in a celebrity vacuum. Most city celebrities are nondescript or pretend to be, a distinction lost on mere tourists. The city's modern heroes have tended to apologise, emigrate or feel lonely in the limelight.

Jacques Brel (1929–78) managed all three. As the country's greatest singer-songwriter, Brel drew on the traditions of the ballad and the music hall in powerful yet poetic lyrics that capture the spirit of the country: "This flat country of mine, with a sky so low that it engenders humility, with a sky so grey it has to be forgiven for it, with the north wind that comes to blow it apart". The themes of separatism and self-awareness, cultural identity and self-confidence form part of Brel's understanding of the city.

Big fish in a small pond

The residents share an ambivalence about Brussels which reveals much about themselves. While most citizens are puzzled as to whether they live in a provincial or cos-

LEFT: modelling one of the eccentric creations of Elvis Pompilio, Belgium's "Mad Hatter".
RIGHT: Meiboom festival revellers; Brussels loves a fancy-dress parade.

mopolitan capital, all share a judgemental, critical streak, proof that Belgians are far from boring. Hat maker Elvis Pompilio finds Brussels "at once a convivial big city and a small village", but blessed with as much surrealism and savoir-faire as his own weird *couture* creations. By contrast, intellectual Juan d'Oultrement pulls no punches, describing the city as: "a small provincial backwater suddenly catapulted centre-stage as capital of Europe; it is a complex place weighed down by disappointed hopes and unrealisable dreams. Brussels needs to unlock its creative potential…" The individualistic Benoit Van Innis, an inspired cartoonist for the Flemish press, praises Brussels as appealing to his anarchic side: "It is an enigmatic, seductive city whose absurdity is accentuated by the charm of its ugliness."

The tourist board has turned its back on over-selling sunny scenes in city brochures in favour of sophisticated yet sombre presentations, with blue-tinted black-and-white photos. This intelligent approach is reaping rewards in the form of cultured tourists prepared to make the city more than just a coffee and chocolate stop on a European tour. Beer and bonhomie are here in abundance, but Brussels is essentially a discreet city which requires an inquisitive nature to tease out its charms.

number of pensioners in Europe. In another corner may be a faintly disreputable couple of Bruxellois businessmen enjoying a beer in an easy-going environment. In the same bar-brasserie, a group of self-consciously creative Flemish musicians and designers share a light lunch of moules marinières. The classless, convivial atmosphere matches the *joie de vivre* of the city at its best. As natural bon vivants, the Bruxellois emanate Burgundian warmth rather than French chic. Brussels is a city of mussels and mayonnaise, beer and chocolate, and the citizens are determined to have their cake and eat it. As a result, Belgian *joie de vivre* always comes in large portions, a fact appreciated by

Cultural crossover

As befits the crossroads of Europe, Brussels exudes Latin verve and Teutonic sobriety; speaks French and Dutch; and drinks beer and wine. Although there is no cachet in being Bruxellois, the citizens are noted for their solid Flemish virtues and French savoir-faire. In a city of slow-burning pleasures, the Bruxellois treat life as a bourgeois rehearsal for the perfect dinner.

Most Brussels bars boast a broad cast of characters and lowlife scenes straight out of a bitter-sweet Jacques Brel song. In one wood-panelled corner sit grizzled, avuncular habitués with walrus moustaches, a reminder that Belgium equals Germany in having the highest

the Flemish master of merry-making, Pieter Brueghel. His paintings capture the celebratory spirit of jolly, rosy-cheeked characters, revealing the people as they see themselves in the mirror: pragmatic and pleasure-loving rather than in care-worn, contradictory or bureaucratic mode.

Bourgeois and bon vivants

However, on the streets, conformist bourgeois Brussels types are much in evidence. When shopping on Avenue Louise, a stylish mother is invariably clad in Strelli, the Belgian Armani, while her husband sports an olive-green Austrian loden coat, the uniform of the old-style bourgeoisie. If Francophone, the family might have smart, preppy children and live in a leafy suburb such as Uccle, but have a holiday villa at the fashionable but rather dull Flemish seaside resort Knokke-Heist's upscale Het Zoute suburb (which they'll call Le Zoute). High-profile cultural pursuits in the capital include classical concerts and *vernissages*, art openings in the elegant Sablon district. Given the political polarisation of society, the stereotypical Bruxellois family draws comfort from the reassuring certainties of bourgeois life: a detached house; good food; large family gatherings; and a civilised lifestyle sanctioned by the security blanket of Roman Catholicism.

However, any caricature of a certain type of old-fashioned provincialism fails to take account of the smug self-sufficiency of bourgeois society, partly redeemed by surrealist flights of fancy. Scratch a Bruxellois and you find a surrealist, whether a hobbyist planning to open a penguin museum, or a dreamer recalling Delvaux's ethereal nudes draped over moonlit train stations.

Anarchic streak

Brussels is not known as an outpost of revolutionary chic. Yet given the prickly individuality of local citizens, the clash between conformity and subversion is a popular city pastime. The

The quintessential burgher of Brussels is noted for his salt-of-the-earth qualities, and is a good-natured soul, as well as being dignified, undemonstrative and unostentatious. The popular Fête Nationale celebrations provide the city with a rare display of national unity and patriotic pageantry, ending in fireworks outside the royal palace. As wholesome fun, the holiday attracts the frites-munching masses who are unabashed at the heavy-handedness of the military parade and the awesome displays of deadly hardware.

LEFT: designer shopping on Boulevard Waterloo.
ABOVE: card players in the Marolles.

painter Magritte, who played at being irredeemably bourgeois, joined the Communist Party three times. In contemporary Brussels, the heads of establishment galleries and theatres can be surprisingly iconoclastic. Gérard Mortier, the well-respected former director of the Monnaie opera house, is refreshingly irreverent and un-politically correct. After dismissing Brussels as "the ugliest city in the world", the Flemish arts supremo explained his anti-elitist attitude towards opera management: "I always try to dismantle the cultural bastions that employ me – a palace putsch is the only way to clear the decks". Refusing to rest on one's artistic laurels is an admirable city trait, particularly valued on

The Great Divide

The complex linguistic and cultural divide between the city's French- and Dutch-speaking communities colours life for all Brussels residents. Linguistic affiliation underscores every political decision, even underwriting such personal matters as the choice of schooling, sports clubs, hospitals and cultural associations. Every institution has its linguistic shadow, doubling the amount of bureaucracy and the scope for confusion. Everything is calibrated linguistically, down to the last cultural centre.

It is ironic that in the capital of Europe, the symbol of an "ever closer union" should be creating ever more distance between its two main communities. However, in politically correct mode, Bruxellois tend to downplay the linguistic divide, or to put an upbeat, pluralistic spin on multicultural Brussels, talking up the summer ethnic festivals and the convivial mixed-community bars.

Since the 1970s, Francophone Bruxellois have watched their historical dominance of national affairs eroded by the economic and cultural resurgence of Flanders. In response to such power shifts, the Belgian government made a series of constitutional reforms granting greater autonomy to the regions, notably to the two rival communities.

In 1989 Brussels was promoted to regional status and given very tightly drawn boundaries to avoid racial clashes with the Flemish and Francophone communities. In 1993 the city was accorded the same status as the larger regions of Flemish-speaking Flanders and French-speaking Wallonia. Now officially called Brussels Capital Region, greater Brussels is perched at the southern extreme of the Flemish region, forming a buffer zone between thriving Flanders to the north and depressed Wallonia to the south.

Today, in certain *communes* (boroughs) of Brussels, speaking the rival language is tantamount to making a political statement about citizenship and belonging. In 1995, a political decree stated that official information and business in Flemish-run outlying districts of Brussels would henceforth be conducted solely in Flemish. To the more intransigent Flemish-speakers, this was the only way of asserting their racial identity, and of fighting back against the invasion of "their" charming, leafy suburbs by better-paid Eurocrats whose very presence diluted the Flemish purity of the area. To French-speakers, this was considered a linguistic putsch. Residents without the slightest smattering of Flemish were forced to deal with the complexities of Belgian bureaucracy in an entirely alien language. Since the officials' refusal to speak French was purely a policy decision, foreigners experienced the Kafka-esque situation of failing to communicate in Flemish when both parties could understand each other perfectly well in French.

Conversely, there are also classic examples of *compromis à la belge*, suitably complicated Belgian compromises. Amongst Brussels' neighbouring boroughs, the controversial *communes à facilités* stand out – boroughs such as Kraainem, Wemmel and Rode-St-Genese – where education is available in either Dutch or French. Faced with the changed balance of power, younger French-speaking Bruxellois have made an effort to learn Flemish, but in language learning, they are generally outshone by the Flemish.

LEFT: cultural disputes take to the streets.

the Flemish cultural scene. So too, is Mortier's desire that art should come to the people, and overcome Belgian factionalism; the icing on the cake is to succeed in the face of Kafka-esque bureaucracy, within limited budgets.

From iconoclasm to subversion is a small step in Brussels. In the surreal world of art, Magritte was outwardly conventional to the point of eccentricity. As if setting out for a day at the office, he donned his coat, hat and brolly, kissed his wife goodbye, and briefly walked around the block before returning home, hanging up his "office" clothes and climbing upstairs to his studio to begin work. Despite becoming a legend in his own life-

criminal offence to wear loose swimming trunks. In public baths, bureaucratic doggedness is immortalised in a sign reminiscent of the spirit of Magritte: "Maillot classique: ceci n'est pas un maillot classique" – illustrations of legal and illegal types of trunks are clearly displayed.

Royalists and republicans

Surrealism, subversion and sheer eccentricity abound in Brussels. Even the worthy, self-effacing Belgian royal family has a surreal side. King Léopold III abdicated in favour of his son, Baudouin, after being denounced as a wartime collaborator. Baudouin himself abdicated for a day rather than sign a law legalising abortion;

ABOVE: "This is not a cow" – Magritte's spirit lives on.

time, Magritte behaved like a slightly surreal version of a bourgeois Bruxellois. Belgian philosopher Jean Ladrière explains this streak of surrealism as a healthy reaction against an overdose of reality: "People are so pragmatic, so rooted in a reality as palpable as the city's sombre skies, that they desperately seek solace in the world of the imagination".

Everyone loves Magritte's flat denials, his famous conceit of a pipe that is not a pipe, but such paradoxes are part and parcel of city life. One popular pastime is bending or breaking the law, which is not difficult in a city where it's a

the country became a republic for the day, the law was passed, and the king was duly invited to reclaim his throne. Baudouin, the unifying, pragmatic idealist, received slavish coverage by the French-speaking press until his death in 1993. However, in 1999, it emerged that Baudouin's brother, the staunchly Catholic King Albert II, allegedly had an illegitimate daughter, one Delphine Boel, a London-based sculptor. While more republican Flemings were amused to learn that their king apparently had catholic tastes, royalist French-speakers claimed to be shocked. Behind the furore was the familiar Francophone-Flemish divide *(see left)*. The Francophones, who consider the respected royal family to be the best weapon against the Flemish forces of separatism, accused the Flemish of fabricating the story to further their cause, thereby damaging the Belgian state. But the ensuing scandal at least helped revive Brussels' dull reputation abroad.

Brussels has enough linguistic and cultural flashpoints to trigger a crisis of its own. In the capital, there is a feeling that *compromis à la belge*, the process of devolving power to every conceivable minority at every conceivable level, has come to an end. There is a hardening of positions on both sides. Overijse, a wealthy Flemish suburb, studded with well-heeled Eurocrats, is typical of the fault lines. The Flemings

feel trapped within this linguistic corridor linking the French-speaking blocs of Brussels and Wallonia. A common cry is: "We are becoming strangers in our own land, forced out by wealthy Eurocrats who can't even speak our language." Here, and in other outlying districts of Brussels, Flemish-speakers increasingly see themselves as dispossessed in their own land.

After Brussels was promoted to regional status in 1989, the city was granted its own parliament, governed according to a uniquely Belgian formula: two Flemish ministers, two Francophones, and one "linguistically asexual" minister-president. However, *The Bulletin*, Brussels' respected English-language magazine,

described the ensuing linguistic disputes in the city's controversial mixed-community boroughs as "a problem that makes the Balkans look like a Sunday-school picnic".

In some ways, Brussels lags behind the prosperous Flemish provinces, and lacks the surface gloss of Antwerp, its self-assured rival. Where Brussels is insecure, complex, and riven by different factions, Antwerp is a shiny, sleek entrepreneurial city pleased with its party spirit and newly regained wealth. And to add insult to injury from a Brussels' perspective, Flanders also claims Brussels as its federal capital city. As if to underline the Bruxellois' insecurity, local tourist brochures ask visitors not to make jokes at Brussels' expense. This is rather unfair given that the natives are known for their self-mockery. Indeed, the tourist board considers that the city welcome leaves something to be desired because the locals are too self-denigrating, too unwilling to promote the city's heritage.

Conservation and conservatism

The Bruxellois are not noted for treasuring their architectural heritage, but there has been a decided culture shift in recent years, partly due to the worthy struggle of urban heritage bodies, and partly due to the increasing awareness of the citizens themselves. The city has passed its first test, with the results revealing the renovation of landmark buildings, the ongoing gentrification of inner-city quarters and even cleaner streets. If Brussels still lags behind many capital cities in its urban and environmental concern, enlightened bodies now exist to challenge the notion of Belgium as an urban-planning disaster. ARAU, an organisation of committed architects and concerned individuals, was once a lone voice in fighting for Brussels' heritage, but now the cause is increasingly popular and effective.

By contrast, the Bruxellois are happier with their garden heritage and are proud to live in Europe's greenest capital city. Apart from a profusion of romantic English gardens and classical French parks, Brussels is ringed by rambling woods, lakes and open parkland. For a privileged elite, the cosy garden suburbs, pockets of manicured pastoral bliss, embody the Brussels bourgeois ideal. Based on the English model, the garden suburb is a concept dear to Belgian hearts: seclusion, space, safety and harmony, and all a short drive from the city centre.

Heritage aside, the Brussels-born journalist India Knight felt emboldened enough by her Belgian passport to deliver coruscating condemnations of city society: "Brussels is an oddly beautiful little town populated by a disproportionate number of the kind of bourgeois women – all blonde highlights, Cartier rings, and designer labels – that make you think perhaps class war has a point." Certainly, the political ethos is conformist and culturally conservative, but this social cocooning and indifference reflect a deeper disaffection with a system that has been described as rotten to the core. The *Sunday Times* journalist goes on to call her former homeland "officially the most racist

Multicultural Brussels

Outside the bourgeois districts of the city, Brussels reveals its true ethnic diversity. Welcome to Cuban music clubs, halal butchers, all-male Turkish coffee shops, Spanish tapas bars, Thai take aways, and shops selling Turkish ceramics, African prints and Berber tribal rugs.

Brussels is a multiracial society in that myriad races work side by side here. With a 30 per cent non-Belgian population, Brussels has a higher proportion of immigrants than most other European capitals, but real integration is rare. The ethnic mix may be diverse and dynamic enough to rival any capital city, but exotic restaurants and music festivals are no substitute

country in Europe, with paedophile scandals of outsize proportions, and never-caught mass-murderers, not forgetting the extraordinary corruption at the highest political levels". But against this accurate if overstated view must be set the reawakening of civil consciousness in the aftermath of the 1990s paedophile scandals. A very un-Belgian fury crossed communities, classes and language barriers and led to the transformation of the criminal justice system.

***

LEFT: a park-bench lunch – Bruxellois are proud of their garden city and make full use of its green spaces.
ABOVE: beyond the bourgeois districts, Brussels' true ethnic diversity is seen in the school playground.

for real social integration. The immigrant underclass, who have flocked to the city from Turkey, Morocco, Poland, the Congo and Rwanda, generally face social exclusion, and are consigned to menial jobs and homes in disadvantaged districts. These immigrants are in an entirely different category from the diplomats, Eurocrats, Nato personnel, international business executives and white-collar workers who come from prosperous European countries, or are sent on secondment from the US.

Given Belgium's colonial past, many immigrants come from the Congo, a country 80 times the size of Belgium, yet lacking a high profile in Brussels, despite the number of street names that evoke the former colonies. However, Tervuren's Central Africa Museum, built by the imperialistic Léopold II in 1897, redresses the balance somewhat, with displays of ivory carvings, dancers' masks, cult objects and sculpted doors. Elsewhere, African Brussels can be tasted as well as felt, with restaurants serving the cuisine of the Ivory Coast, Senegal, Burundi, Chad and Angola. Many African immigrants have congregated in the Matongé district off Chaussée d'Ixelles.

As for European immigrants, although the Italians represent Belgium's biggest foreign community, the immigrants mostly settled in the southern industrial heartland to work in the

mining industry. In Brussels itself, Italians are no more representative of the city than, say, English- or Spanish-speakers. However, given the universal popularity of pizza and pasta, the Italians exert a disproportionate influence on the city cuisine. As for Portuguese- and Spanish-speakers, the arty, mixed St-Gilles district is a popular choice, with poorer families confined to the dilapidated Gare du Midi area. At the other end of the scale, the influx of moneyed yet homesick Eurocrats to the so-called European district has spawned a number of foreign restaurants, notably Italian, Spanish and Greek haunts, not to mention a sprinkling of fake Irish pubs and American bars.

The growing number of Asian restaurants represents a response to the influx of Vietnamese, Chinese and Thais in recent years.

Worlds apart

With the notable exception of young, single or open-minded European and American residents, the vast majority of privileged foreigners prefer to live in the attractive outlying suburbs of Brussels, and commute into the centre. Although most inner-city boroughs boast pockets or sizeable stretches of gentrification, the un-chic districts of Molenbeek, Anderlecht, St-Josse and Schaerbeek are home to the majority of immigrants. Partly as a belated gesture of acceptance towards many immigrants' Muslim faith and traditions, the city decided to put its Islamic collection on permanent display in the prestigious Cinquantenaire Museum.

As in any major city, there is a dark underside of ethnic ghettos and gangs, but this is outweighed by the cosy world of family-run Spanish snack bars and African rappers chatting on street corners. For a subtler taste of ethnic Brussels, the city abounds in exotic bars and the baroque gastronomic fantasies that pass for bohemian ethnic restaurants.

Celebrating ethnicity

Street parties, ethnic fairs and music festivals represent some of the only occasions when "multicultural Brussels" can truly claim to exist. Increasingly, the city also stages multicultural street festivals or ethnic arts festivals in offbeat venues. Brussels is belatedly beginning to seek out its Turkish, Andalusian and African musicians, who had hitherto been confined to playing within their own communities. Whereas in the recent past, such initiatives smacked of tokenism, today they feel more part of the tapestry of city life. Much of the credit is due to the explosion of world music that is Couleur Café, the festival of live music from Africa and the Caribbean held at the end of June *(see page 75)*. Staged over several nights, the sultry atmosphere of the festival succeeds in uniting the Flemish, French-speaking and immigrant communities in a shared love of Latin and World music. Can multiculturalism be far behind? ❏

LEFT: Couleur Café festival live performance.

Façadisme

Bruxellisation is an architectural expression referring to the city's wilful demolition of treasured buildings and heritage sites. In the 1960s, a period of political laissez-faire led to the razing of quarters and architectural landmarks, including such masterpieces as Horta's Maison du Peuple in 1965. The worst heritage crimes took place in the northern district around the World Trade Centre, Brussels' misguided attempt to ape Manhattan, and in the European district, the site of the European institutions. During the black years of bruxellisation (1960–90), when the city seemed to give developers carte blanche, many sites simply disappeared, and uninspired office blocks were often erected in their place. Effective urban heritage laws belatedly came into effect in 1993, and made the demolition of significant buildings illegal. However, it was too late for large parts of the city.

Towards the end of the 1980s, citizens were so disheartened by the disastrous examples of new buildings in the city that there was little enthusiasm for contemporary architecture. Instead, architects raided the toy-box of Flemish vernacular and came up with fake gabled hotels, erected between the Grand-Place and the Gare Centrale, amongst other prominent sites. Façadisme, the art of gutting and remodelling the building while leaving the facade intact, was the alternative but more enduring legacy. This was the solution the city found to satisfy speculators whilst appeasing the heritage police.

The technique is visible in countless buildings in the historic centre: behind an authentic baroque or *belle époque* facade stands a functional, sheer-glass interior. Place des Martyrs, the grandest neo-classical square in Brussels, is a more successful version of the technique. Set just off the soulless shopping street of Rue Neuve, the square was a long-abandoned eyesore until its belated rescue. Behind the cool classical frontage, a theatre, cultural centre, offices and accommodation occupy the remodelled interiors.

RIGHT: the former market hall of St-Géry.

One of the first impressions of Brussels is of a city centre suffering from neglect: dilapidated buildings lie just a stone's throw from major monuments. The dismal northern district has had its heart and communities torn asunder, with under-occupied skyscrapers now planted in the middle of windswept spaces. The European quarter, canal district and royal district are deserted after office hours. The eerie emptiness of areas that should be animated is accentuated by the preference of bourgeois Bruxellois to live in the leafy suburbs. But this, in itself, is connected with bruxellisation, which drove many despairing residents out of town.

There has been a creative backlash after so much desecration. The newly restored royal district has installed bars and public spaces to attract visitors to the area. Throughout the city, enlightened planners have risked architecturally exciting projects, notably the conversion of abandoned industrial buildings into cultural centres. In the pipeline is the conversion of the impressive canal-side Tour et Taxis warehouses into a museum and cultural centre. Successful projects include the restructuring of former factories, warehouses and covered markets, with St-Géry and the Halles de Schaerbeek two of the best-known conversions. ❑

THE GREENEST CAPITAL IN EUROPE

Apart from a profusion of romantic gardens and formal parks, Brussels is ringed by rambling woods, lakes and open parkland

ABOVE: Take a break. The French-style Parc de Bruxelles in the Upper City has been cleverly laid out to represent Masonic symbols and combines shady paths with open avenues dotted with statues *(see page 128)*.

Brussels has an extent and quality of greenery that would grace a city many times larger. It is surrounded by parks, forests and lakes, all a short drive or tram ride from the centre. To the east lie the wide open spaces of Tervuren and the Parc de Woluwe; to the north, beyond the city limits, is the National Botanical Garden at Meise; in the southern reaches are Les Etangs d'Ixelles, the Bois de la Cambre and the adjacent Forêt de Soignes *(see below)*. Although it merges with garden suburbs, the west is the least well served with public parks.

Forest walks

Pride of place among the city's line-up of green spaces goes to the Forêt de Soignes, which you can compare more usefully to Belgium's tangled Ardennes forests than to any mere city park. Once the hunting ground of the Dukes of Brabant, this is a favourite place for weekend walks. Although the forest retains only a third of its 19th-century area, at 4,380 hectares (17 sq. miles) this green sea of tranquillity is big enough that even on its busiest days you can lose yourself in its silent depths. Its wilderness character has, sadly but inevitably, been tamed, and access to it simplified by the addition of walking and horse-riding paths *(see page 184)*.

ABOVE: Colonial splendour. Tervuren Park, with its manicured lawns and boating lakes, is a favourite day-trip destination. While here you can visit the Central Africa Museum *(see page 181)*, Belgium's monument to its former colony in the Congo.

ESCAPE IN THE CITY

If wandering through the urban jungle – even one as civilised as Brussels – begins to pall, escape is never far away. From the elegant Parc de Bruxelles, in the heart of the city, in whichever direction you care to go, it isn't long before you bump into something green. Near by, between Place Louise and Porte de Namur, a path leads to the Jardin d'Egmont, the ornamental garden of the Palais d'Egmont – which in turn is a stone's throw from the lovely Petit Sablon square. To the east lie Parc Léopold and Parc du Cinquantenaire, both popular with Eurocrats. The latter was laid out in 1880 to celebrate 50 years of Belgian independence. Most of the parkland in the Domaine Royal de Laeken area to the north belongs to the royal family and is off-limits to ordinary mortals, but the big Parc de Laeken with its Royal Greenhouses and oriental pavilions are open to the public.

Parc Josaphat in unfashionable Schaerbeek is one of the more interesting city parks, with a sculpture collection, an area set aside for sporting activities, and free summer concerts.

RIGHT: Calm refuge. Place du Petit Sablon's ornamental garden in the "Sablon village" quarter is surrounded by 48 neo-Gothic columns topped by bronze statues representing Brussels' medieval guilds *(see page 135)*.

BELOW: Autumnal display. The Forêt de Soignes is at its most stunning in the autumn when it is carpeted in reds, browns and golds *(see left)*.

ABOVE: Exotic flora. Just north of Brussels in the village of Meise is the Domaine de Bouchot, where you will find a sumptuous 12th-century castle and the National Botanical Garden *(see page 193)*.

ABOVE: The magnificent Royal Greenhouses in Laeken open their doors in late April and early May when the exotic flowers are in full bloom *(see page 167)*.

CAPITAL OF EUROPE

How many people work in the European Commission? About a third of them. (This is a Belgian joke)

By a convenient quirk of history, Brussels became the capital of Europe. As such, the city is charged with enshrining the European dream (as well as ensuring the protection of the Iberian lynx, French camembert, Belgian chocolate and the great British crisp). The Brussels bureaucrats are the archetypal European bogeymen, residents of a city famous for its faceless image. Behind the mask is a surreal world, more Magritte than Kafka, in which doubting Eurocrats and diplomats are inevitably beguiled. Bland bureaucracy is transformed into an expatriate playground of garden suburbs and gourmet dining experiences.

Brussels remains an anomaly, a French-speaking island in a Flemish-speaking region. Unsurprisingly, a third of the city's population is foreign, mainly European. Apart from being the capital of the European Union, Brussels is the headquarters of Nato and home to over 50 inter-governmental agencies, as well as countless trade associations and many international companies. The Brussels region is prosperous, and in terms of GDP per head, is the third wealthiest in the European Union.

Eurocrats and fat cats

As a capital transformed by institutional wealth, Brussels is a city of corporate lawyers and thrusting lobbyists, Europhiles and Eurosceptics, international agencies and multinationals. The Commission's role as European chief competition watchdog means that lawyers and

LEFT: celebration to mark the expansion of the EU to 25 states in 2004. RIGHT: Eurocrat outside Parliament.

lobbyists come to study or manipulate the Brussels political machine.

For business and bureaucracy, the lure of this city is great. With such a prestigious international role, numerous foreign companies have chosen to base their European operations here, from IBM and ICI to Bayer and Mitsubishi – Brussels has more office space per head than any other European capital. Sweeteners such as tax breaks and prime property locations ensure that Brussels finds favour with the multinationals. In particular, the capital prides itself on offering a multilingual, cosmopolitan, highly skilled labour force and excellent living conditions for foreign inhabitants.

Visually, the European district is uninspiring: Quartier Léopold, the most fashionable quarter in the 1850s, has disappeared under a dispiriting urban wasteland. As journalist Neil Buckley says, "Visitors to Brussels often expect to see an elegant European Union quarter, Europe's equivalent of Washington, DC. They find instead a soulless administrative district where drab office blocks have replaced the 19th-century town houses, dotted with building sites and criss-crossed by six-lane highways."

The Council of Ministers (metro Schuman) is a sprawling, low-slung building which opened in 1995. Nicknamed the "Kremlin", this peach-coloured fortress is already too small,

The Commission is a curious constitutional hybrid, part executive body, part policy innovator and proposer of laws. As the European Union's civil service, it is a powerful employer, with more than 15,000 permanent staff, including a vast number of translators and interpreters. The Commission is only reluctantly practising what it preaches: publicly, it advocates flexible labour forces while privately protecting its own civil servants. These *fonctionnaires* enjoy generous perks and jobs for life. However, the concept of performance-related pay was raised in 1998, much to the horror of the personnel unions and to the delight of the Belgian public. EU civil servants are paid three times as much

designed for 12 EU members rather than 25. Facing it is Berlaymont, the seat of the European Commission, the executive body. Near by is the European Parliament, Espace Léopold (metro Maalbeek), a glittering blue-green affair resembling a covered city. The lavish public buildings are a sign of European success or excess, depending on one's point of view. Only Eurocrats are allowed access to the Residence Palace, a fabulous Art Deco apartment block that was saved from destruction. In 2004, an architectural competition was announced for proposals to remodel the palace's interior to be the headquarters of the European Council and the EU Council of Ministers.

as their counterparts in the Belgian ministries. As well as avoiding punitive Belgian taxes, they can claim an expatriation bonus, child benefit and school subsidies.

Political farce

After the star-shaped 1960s eyesore Berlaymont was found to be contaminated by asbestos in 1991, the 3,000 Commission staff who occupied it were evacuated to sites all over the city. During the move, over £140 million (US$230 million) of property mysteriously vanished, from cars to computers and carpets. The Eurocrats were outraged at the implication that their flats were furnished with purloined public property. As a French official retorted, "Have you seen the colour of the textiles? And everything is numbered, even the bland Euro-carpets." After ridding itself of asbestos and being, in effect, rebuilt, Berlaymont reopened in 2002. Ironically, the Commission itself has been slow to implement legislation protecting European workers from exposure to asbestos.

The European Parliament, the latest symbol of European unity, is set in Espace Léopold, the heart of the Euro-district. It is dubbed Caprice des Dieux, the folly of the gods, after the French cheese whose shape it echoes. The Parliament is paralleled by an equally grandiose European assembly in Strasbourg. The existence of two follies aims to assuage Gallic pride, and to prevent the French city from being sidelined by Brussels. Given the duplication of parliaments, on average, MEPs spend only two days a week in Brussels. However, as a talking shop and temple to self-aggrandisement, the Parliament has few equals.

Upon completion, this glass-and-steel behemoth became the biggest building project in Europe. Opened by King Albert II in 1998, it cost US$1.66 billion, and has vast annual running costs. The 682-member body (due to rise to 732 on the accession of Bulgaria and Romania) oversees the European Central Bank.

Rampant bureaucracy

Eurosceptics wishing to find fault with Brussels need look no further than this folly: during sessions, there are often more multilingual interpreters than delegates needing translation. Likewise, the hemicycle, the huge debating chamber, holds 1,000 delegates but is used for only two weeks a year. The press delights in reporting stories of rampant bureaucracy within these walls. One such revelation featured the fitting irony that the capital of bureaucracy lacked its own office supplies: it was only when all fax machines in the Commission ran out of paper that civil servants admitted that supplies were kept in Strasbourg.

For model members of the modern Euro-state, there is little need to visit the outside world. Apart from restaurants and sports facilities, there are 15 conference chambers and

countless briefing rooms and offices with bedrooms and bathrooms, as well as meditation rooms and a printing plant. Although the main corridors are as wide as motorways, a Dutch MEP was forbidden from riding his bicycle through the building. More seriously, the Parliament overruled the city by creating a vast underground car park which causes daily gridlock and the near asphyxiation of local residents.

After just two months, the giant glass monolith required repairs: Belgian birds, attracted to the luxuriant palm trees growing in the atrium, failed to notice the glass ceiling as they hurtled into the corridors of power. This is an apposite image for the Belgian attitude to the European

institutions: an exotic honey-pot from which most native residents feel excluded. Belgian citizens often sense that the "capital of Europe" has little to do with their lives. There are great disparities in wealth between the corps of diplomats and Eurocrats and the average Bruxellois.

For the privileged Eurocrats, the comfort and convenience of life in Brussels transforms Europhobes into Europhiles. In time, both prim British civil servants at the Commission and critical Canadian translators at Nato are accused of "going native" by their compatriots at home. "Going native" in Brussels tends to mean embracing pro-European views and gourmet cuisine in equal measure. ❏

LEFT: Meeting of the Convention on the future of Europe. **RIGHT:** a show of solidarity.

BRUSSELS ON A PLATE

Despite the pre-eminence of French cuisine,
Belgians claim that foodies can eat well
more often in Brussels than in Paris

Belgians are both gourmet and gourmand. When Pierre Wynants, Belgium's most celebrated chef, comes out to greet diners in Comme Chez Soi, his questions are as down-to-earth as his cuisine is out of this world: *"C'était suffisant?"* (Did you get enough to eat?). Not for him the pretentious posturing of his Parisian counterparts. Even for one of Europe's *maîtres-cuisiniers*, quantity is a prime concern, coming just after quality on the Belgian scale of gastronomic virtues.

Moreover, although this three-star Michelin establishment is in a scruffy area near the Gare du Midi, Wynants is endearingly uninterested in moving or expanding. Nor, unlike his French or British peers, does he wish to commercialise his name, go into catering, executive chef-dom, or create his own brand of Belgian television dinners. Instead, as a true Bruxellois, this paunchy, modest master-chef shuns publicity and offers second helpings of everything.

For the same reason, the fashion for nouvelle cuisine failed to make a mark on old-style Belgian stomachs. While the temples of gastronomy are not cheap, the mark-up is essentially on wine. At the other end of the scale, a bistrot-style appearance is no guarantee that prices will be lower than in an overtly formal restaurant. Compared with the French, the Bruxellois favour unpretentious settings and less formal service but are prepared to pay for a special

occasion, on the understanding that the cost covers top-quality ingredients and not the frills. Not that the city lacks a sense of culinary spectacle: when a restaurant decides to do dramatic, it can surpass the French in Art Nouveau splendour, producing surrealist fantasies in the dining room and seductive flavours on the plate. But the Bruxellois' heart is really in robust cooking, perfectly fresh ingredients, man-sized portions, and more than a pinch of panache. Leave rarefied service, rich sauces and culinary refinement to the Parisian stars; leave television chefs, celebrity diners and marketing hype to the Londoners; and let Brussels concentrate on the cooking.

LEFT: A La Mort Subite, a traditional no-frills tavern with an astonishing array of beers. **RIGHT:** Pierre Wynants, virtuoso chef, and his team in the kitchen of Comme Chez Soi, Brussels' best restaurant.

Culinary claims to fame

Internationally, Brussels boasts the highest number of Michelin-rated restaurants per head of population. As the world's best producers of beer, chocolate, mussels and chips, the citizens clearly place comfort eating before calorie-counting. The Bruxellois also claim to have invented the french fry, despite the fact that the credit has gone to their more gastronomically famous neighbours. And as the world's largest producers of white asparagus, sprouts and endive, the Bruxellois can belatedly claim some interest in healthy eating. Local tastes embrace silky truffle chocolates, steaks with creamy sauces, tomatoes stuffed with Ostend shrimps, smooth Ardennes pâté and steamy bowls of mussels cooked in white wine and leeks. Burgundian feasts also feature guinea fowl in raspberry beer, rabbit casserole, meaty hotpots, beer-enriched beef stews known as *carbonades*, and a chicken or fish stew known as *waterzooi*. Vegetarians must content themselves with irresistible patisserie and fruity beers, or subsist on chips, cheese croquettes and chocolate.

Culinary quarters

Despite the profusion of city eateries, there is no bona fide restaurant district in Brussels. First-time visitors risk equating the Ilot Sacré area behind the Grand-Place with fine dining, but it is

MUSSELS IN BRUSSELS

Moules-frites is the classic national dish. But true Brussels mussels must come from the North Sea waters off Zeeland, and no self-respecting Bruxellois would dream of eating mussels outside their mid-July to mid-February season. The mussels are served in large-lidded black enamel pots, with a bowl provided for empty shells. Mussel-eating etiquette requires the use of the mussel shell as a pincer to pick out mussels from their carapace, with any closed shells being discarded. The most popular ways of eating mussels include *moules au vin blanc à la crème* (with dry white wine and cream), *moules marinières* (with celery and shallots), *moules provençales* (with tomatoes and garlic) and *à l'escargot* (grilled with garlic butter). However, mussels can also be cooked with parsley, onions, watercress, leeks, spinach, fennel, or even with ginger and mixed spice.

Mussels are best eaten in the Ste-Catherine seafood quarter or in well-known places close to the Grand-Place, including **Chez Léon** and **In't Spinnekopke**. Opposite Chez Léon is **Aux Armes de Bruxelles** *(all three listed on page 116)*, a classic place for mussels. Here, the clarion call for "*un complet*" brings mussels, chips and a draught lager to your table in an instant. You can try any of the classic mussel recipes (mentioned above), or if you're feeling adventurous, raw mussels with lemon and mustard sauce.

essentially a quaint tourist trap. The colourful Ste-Catherine quarter is the closest Brussels comes to a reliable restaurant district, but it is solely for seafood. As for ethnic restaurants, with notable exceptions, these are scattered throughout the city, with basic Turkish or Portuguese fare confined to poorer immigrant districts. The European quarter around Rond-Point Schuman contains a number of middle-range but often charmless French and Italian restaurants, while the Matongé district around the Chaussée d'Ixelles has more than its fair share of African restaurants.

Each *commune* (borough) has a range of good restaurants, along with its own *traiteurs* (delicatessens) and pastry shops. Fortunately, however, a number of the best restaurants are within walking distance of the Grand-Place, or a short metro ride away.

If atmosphere is as important as food, then there are old-fashioned gourmet restaurants close to such touristy areas as the Grand-Place, the Bourse and the Grand Sablon. For people-watching and upmarket dining, the elegant Place du Grand Sablon is an obvious choice. A variant on this theme is provided by the stylish Châtelain quarter, a less conservative version of the Sablon. By contrast, the mixed St-Géry district is home to some of the city's younger, hipper brasseries.

This hugger-mugger historic area behind the Grand-Place represents the first port of call for most hungry first-time visitors to Brussels. Centred on the Petite Rue des Bouchers, and known as the Ilot Sacré, this hotchpotch of genuine and fake gabled houses is home to an equally mixed array of restaurants. What is on offer in these cute alleys is local colour and concentrated "essence of restaurants". Residents tend to dismiss the quaint quarter as a tourist trap, confirmed by the shenanigans of waiters touting their wares in front of a slab of seafood or freshly-slaughtered fluffy bunnies. Certainly, the mediocre quality of most of the restaurants does not merit the hassle or high prices. But it is all part of the Brussels experience to be willingly seduced by red awnings and inviting outdoor

tables, before finally being fleeced by waiters with a nice line in Euro backchat.

Local advice is to avoid all ostentatious displays of seafood and to steer clear of *couleur locale*. Yet, on the right occasion, the visual feast and the sheer concentration of restaurants is irresistible, and lemming-like, you succumb to the first charmer who promises seafood on a sunny terrace. Even without the greatest meal of your life, the spectacle will probably exude Burgundian jollity and excessive bustle; and if not, brusque service is also part of the Brussels experience. Aux Armes de Bruxelles and Chez Léon are reliable Ilot Sacré options *(see page 116)*.

Temples of gastronomy

For those on a lavish budget, nothing surpasses Belgian gourmet cuisine. This is not common-denominator Eurocrat fare or fake internationalism but inspired *cuisine française*, albeit with a nod to Belgian sensibilities and individual creativity. Although the language and style of Brussels' gastronomy is undeniably French, the Belgians often do it better. The settings are generally dignified and old-fashioned, possibly Art Nouveau or *belle époque*, with service respectful rather than servile, and generous portions. Apart from the aforementioned Comme Chez Soi, other temples of gastronomy worth blowing your budget on include

LEFT: mussels are traditionally served in big black enamel pots. **RIGHT:** preparing for the evening rush in the Ilot Sacré.

L'Alban Chambon in the Métropole Hotel *(see page 116)* and La Maison du Cygne on the Grand-Place *(see page 97).*

Fishy fare

Place Ste-Catherine is the most characteristic seafood quarter, set by the old quayside, which, although largely covered over, retains a certain charm. Lovers of seafood will eat well at many of these reliable restaurants, enjoying such dishes as oysters, greyish-pink shrimps from the Belgian coast, or filet of sole in white wine. In summer, the square is transformed by café terraces, creating a truly Continental feel.

Branchée Brussels

Despite Brussels' staid image, the city abounds in *branché* (modish) restaurants and funky, Flemish-influenced places, as well as doing a nice line in seductive spots designed for a discreet Euro-romance. Although a number of the hippest brasseries are clustered around the fashionable St-Géry quarter, others are situated in the chic Châtelain area, not far from Avenue Louise, or in the bohemian Chaussée d'Ixelles district. Unlike many capital cities, Brussels is welcoming yet provincial enough for such stylish places not to remain the preserve of the hip singles scene. As for romantic restaurants, these are dotted throughout the city, but tend to be of the charming and quaint variety in the historic lower city. However, on a summer's evening, it is worth seeking out a romantic restaurant on the outskirts of Brussels, a surprisingly bucolic experience, often centred on a leafy villa in one of the smarter villages, such as Uccle.

Ethnic eating

The capital's range of ethnic restaurants reflects the demands of the Eurocrats' expense-account mentality as well as the presence of long-established foreign communities. For visiting foodies, this results in a happy combination of fancy, prestigious French cuisine and satisfying culinary surprises in Italian, African, Moroccan and Thai restaurants. The African and Italian communities are amongst the most prominent to put their stamp on the city cuisine. By comparison with the staid French restaurants in Brussels, the city's best Moroccan, Lebanese and Thai restaurants tend to offer a complete adventure into an exotic land rather than a mere meal. Given the symbiotic link between Belgium and France, French cuisine is naturally the predominant influence. A number of the foremost city restaurants are French, with gourmet restaurants tending to serve classic French cuisine with a twist, leaving more fashionable places to focus on French regional cuisine.

Belgian brasseries

Estaminets are homely taverns that specialise in food as well as drink, with the emphasis on Trappist ales, hearty Flemish stews and *moules-frites*. Many of these big, buzzing brasseries serve filling hot meals from noon until closing time. Such taverns are typical places for a boisterous late-night meal after the cinema or a bar crawl. Classic examples of an old-style tavern include Falstaff *(see page 104)* and De Ultieme Hallucinatie *(see page 127).*

Given the choice of Parisian-style brasseries and citadels of haute cuisine, it is hardly surprising that Brussels is where many French gastronomes choose to spend their weekends. ❏

● *A full listing of places to eat and drink appears at the end of each area chapter.*

LEFT: appetising displays along Rue des Bouchers draw in the hungry tourists, but Place Ste-Catherine is the best place for fish.

Chocolate City

Chocolate was once reserved for the upper echelons of Aztec society, when fruit of the cacao tree was mixed with spices, whisked into a froth and drunk ceremonially. The cacao, or cocoa, bean made its transition from South America to the shores of Spain with the return of Cortez in 1520. It rapidly spread a sweet path throughout Europe, allowing Belgians their first taste of the bean for which they would acquire a passion. Anne of Austria, the daughter of Philip of Spain, supposedly popularised cocoa in France and Flanders, but chocolate remained a luxury product until the 19th century.

In 1815, Kaspar van Houten, an Amsterdammer, successfully discovered the secret of separating cocoa butter and solids, and modern chocolate manufacturing began. The Belgian chocolate industry took off in the 1870s, spurred by the gain of the Congo in 1885, with its burgeoning and highly profitable cocoa plantations. By 1900, Belgium was a major exporter, with manufacturing standards strictly controlled.

All Brussels-based chocolatiers stand firm on the principle of not adulterating chocolate with vegetable fats. Unlike British and American chocolate-makers, the Belgians believe that there is no substitute for cocoa butter. Fortunately for die-hard fans, recent EU directives support the Belgian definition of chocolate: any concoctions made from vegetable fats are simply not "real" chocolate. Given their freshness, Brussels handmade chocolates must be eaten within two weeks. The jargon of Belgian chocolates means that superior handmade ones are known as pralines and are always sold in beautifully packaged boxes, known as *ballotins*.

Neuhaus and Godiva, the two best-established traditional chocolatiers, enjoy a friendly rivalry, with connoisseurs ready to spend as much on a particular selection of chocolates as one would on a meal. Godiva, cosily set on the Grand-Place, proudly dis-

plays its royal warrant, while Neuhaus, set in the neighbouring galleries *(see page 112)*, boasts artfully dressed windows bedecked with ribbons, as well as a centrepiece of nuts "enrobed in chocolate", as they say in Brussels. Although cocoa butter, cream, sugar and possibly liqueurs find their way into Brussels truffles, the quality of the ingredients prevents the nausea of over-indulgence produced by inferior brands.

Pierre Marcolini, the *haute couture* king of chocolates, seeks to combine the best of French and Belgian traditions, creating more inspired chocolates than are made in France, but smaller, less sugary concoctions than

are generally made in Belgium. What sets Marcolini apart from other chocolatiers is the originality of his flavours and soft centres, as well as the delicacy of the dark chocolate. His range embraces classic flavours, as well as satisfying those in search of gingerbread or jasmine-scented chocolates.

Wittamer, the city's top patisserie *(see page 134)*, also makes cream-filled pralines on the same square, including the prized white chocolate. In supermarkets, Côte d'Or may be the mass-market leader, but Léonidas is clearly the best of the more industrially produced chocolates, with commercial outlets all over the world. ❑

RIGHT: the cachet of Belgian chocolate comes from its smooth, velvety quality and rich subtlety.

CAFÉS AND BARS

**From the traditional to the trendy, there's
somewhere to quench your thirst and
soak up the atmosphere around every corner**

In Brussels, there is a bar for every mood, a café for every occasion. Like the earthy citizens themselves, Brussels cafés avoid the worst of Parisian pretentiousness, Amsterdammer kitsch and London transitoriness. These are tried and trusted places which spell home to all but the most demanding customers.

Given the vagaries of the weather and the charms of the cafés, it is easy to misspend a day on a bar crawl with only the slightest nod to museum culture beyond the stained-glass windows. Cosy, wood-panelled dens induce a feeling of warmth and intimacy on the bleakest Brussels day. Vaulted brick cellars offer secret lovers' alcoves, while the heated outdoor terraces provide a pleasing illusion of summer. In this comforting, faintly soporific universe, even coffee comes complete with a spicy *speculoos* biscuit or a miniature chocolate. As the day wears on, the latest tavern on the trail is always the best, confirmed by the strength of the last beer in an ever-stranger glass.

The cafés are also a pretext for game-playing: in the course of a day, visitors can drift between different moods and personas. You can share a croissant, coffee and the Dow Jones Index with young Brussels professionals in any branch of Le Pain Quotidien. In the late morning, try downing heady Trappist beer in the populist Marolles district, probably beside a jovial junk-dealer with a walrus moustache. Or, on the chic Sablon square, sip wine and nibble on delicate pastries with the designer-clad "ladies who lunch". While away the afternoon playing chess with Flemish intellectuals in the St-Géry quarter. Alternatively, let your alter ego soak up the melancholic mood of the cafés by the Bourse. As night falls, drift into a transatlantic accent and order a dry martini at an authentic American-style cocktail bar around Avenue Louise. Saunter into the glittering ballroom of a cruise liner, in reality a piano bar just beyond the portals of Brussels' grander hotels. Or venture to Ixelles and join Brussels' movers and groovers in über-trendy Café Belga in the Flagey building, a 1930s radio station turned arts venue.

After dinner, catch up with the Eurocrats in a Latin American cocktail bar or fake Irish pub; or slip into a surrealist café to mingle with an arty crowd. Call it a surreal nightcap or a slice of life, it is simply Brussels at its best.

Traditional tastes

Many of the typical snug cafés and bars are in and around the Grand-Place. Residents tend to have a favourite Grand-Place café: people-watchers are attached to the rambling Le Roy d'Espagne. Its main rival is La Chaloupe d'Or, which offers a cosy interior. In the Lower City, A La Mort Subite is a city institution, with a staggering range of beers. Au Bon Vieux Temps, near the Bourse, is one of the oldest city cafés. A gentle stroll towards the upper city takes in the elegant Place du Grand Sablon, which is lined with wine bars and sidewalk cafés. Le Grain du Sable is the one to see and be seen in.

match their mood. *Stamcafés*, neighbourhood bars in working-class districts, are increasingly popular with bourgeois Bruxellois. Manned by paunchy waiters or hatchet-faced waitresses, these corners of old Brussels are known for their cool beer and heated chat.

Alternatively, visitors can gain "street cred" with the arty crowd by visiting retro bars awash with Art Deco artefacts. At the more populist end of the scale, the Marolles is dotted with unpretentious *stamcafés* and brasseries where the staple fare is Jupiler beer, slabs of buttered bread and plain soups, or fresh mussels. Completing the picture is an ageing accordionist, who churns out a sequence of folksy favourites.

Retro chic

Homesick company executives, diplomatic or military staff often seek out predictable expat security blankets. Brussels abounds in custom-made bars for such significant minorities as the American, British, Dutch, Irish and Italian communities. For locals and foreigners alike, there are also funky Flemish bars, fake Irish pubs, Latin hotspots, blatantly erotic dives, and genuine French brasseries. In typical Brussels fashion, many residents are fans of both staid and streetwise styles, and choose a café to

The St-Géry quarter near Place Ste-Catherine has become a focal point for younger residents looking for a relaxed drink. On summer evenings and at weekends, all café tables are taken around the former covered market. In the same fashionable area are bars with background jazz such as L'Archiduc. The bar/bistrot rated the best by beer connoisseurs is Chez Moeder Lambic in lively St-Gilles, a favoured district for struggling artists and bourgeois students. The African quarter of Matongé in neighbouring Ixelles is full of noisy bars and restaurants and really comes to life at night.   ❏

LEFT: café in the lively Matongé district.
ABOVE: La Mort Subite, a beer and a bar.

● *Recommended bars and cafés are listed at the end of each area chapter.*

BELGIAN BEERS AND BREWERIES

The best Belgian beers are treated as reverentially as the finest wines – justly so. From a cloudy wheat beer to a fruity brew, the variety is remarkable

The Belgians have always been great beer-drinkers. A frothy lambic beer can still conjure up images of a Breughelian banquet, while a Trappist ale evokes the jollier side of monastic life. Until 1900 each Belgian village had its own brewery, with 3,000 in Wallonia alone. Today, the number of breweries has fallen to 111, but there are still over 450 different beers to choose from, many still produced by the small breweries. Belgian beer enthusiasts can choose the likes of Mort Subite (Sudden Death) or Verboden Vrucht (Forbidden Fruit), while Ghent's Stropken (literally "Noose") is a tangy brew named after a humiliating event in 1453 when Philip the Good commanded the city burghers to parade with nooses around their necks.

Belgian beers encompass light *bières blanches* and potent Trappist ales, including the renowned Chimay. The tangy flavour of a blanche comes from such spicy additions as orange peel and coriander. More of an acquired taste are the cherry-flavoured Kriek and sparkling raspberry-flavoured Framboise – the rosé of beers. Lambic beer has no yeast added, and ferments spontaneously. Stella Artois, created in Leuven in 1926, is the most popular Belgian beer. Gueuze, a Brussels beer made by combining five or six lambics, is a cider-like concoction known as the champagne of beers by connoisseurs.

Peter Crombecq, an expert on the national tipple, explains why the Belgians never seem drunk and disorderly: "We do it gradually: we get drunk around the clock and sober up around the clock."

ABOVE: Hoegaarden is considered by many to be the best of the white beers *(bières blanches)*, while Leffe is Belgium's original abbey beer, whose origins can be traced back to 1152,

LEFT: Sudden death. The refreshing Kriek beer is made by adding cherries or cherry juice to lambic during final fermentation.

BELOW: Bottles up. There is a strict protocol about serving beer in the correct glass. The choice of glass affects the amount of froth and taste of the beer.

THE BREWING OF TRAPPIST BEERS

Trappist beers are made by monks and lay brothers who follow the ancient monastic brewing traditions. Only six Cistercian abbeys in the world have the right to term their beer Trappist, and all of these are in Belgium: Orval, Rochefort, Westmalle, Chimay, Achel and Westvleteren. Chimay, the "Burgundy of Belgium", is the best-known beer, produced according to a secret monastic recipe in Hainaut and matured in the bottle. At 7% proof, Chimay rouge is the least strong of the beers – even so, the monks claim to dilute it before serving it with their daily lunch.

Orval Abbey is home to 25 contemplative monks who have chosen to live in silence and solitude. Theirs is a fruitier brew than the strong Sint Sixtus Abdij beers from Westvleteren, near Ypres (Ieper).

As for Rochefort, it's first brewery was founded in 1595 near Namur, but the current brewery only dates from 1899. It produces a powerful, dark, chocolatey brew. Westmalle Abbey, in Antwerp province, was founded in 1791. The abbey has produced a rich, sweetish, malty beer since 1836. Achel's Sint-Benedictus resumed production in 1998 after a beer-free interval of more than 60 years.

RIGHT: Grimbergen, along with similar abbey beers (known as *abdijbier* in Flemish), are commercially produced using traditional Trappist beer-making methods.

ABOVE: Brussels brew. The Cantillon Brewery is the sole surviving independent lambic brewery. The beer can be brewed only between October and April.

FROM FLEMISH MASTERS
TO LES VINGT

Early Flemish painting is noted for its naturalism, vivacity and intensity; later Belgian art for the dynamism of "The Twenty" and wild fantasy of the Surrealists

As the Middle Ages gave way to modern times, Gothic art began its transition into the Renaissance. This marked the beginning of a glorious period in Flemish art. Jan van Eyck's *The Betrothal of the Arnolfini* (1434) opened a new chapter in art history. Through the details of the composition, the painter revealed the minutiae of the subjects' lives and times. A prosperous burgher and his bride are exchanging marriage vows, in a room that is the epitome of Gothic bourgeois taste. The painting marked the beginning of the tradition of bourgeois art, as the role of the artist became that of an eyewitness, recording the expression and possessions of a new class of bourgeois patrons.

Panel painting

Across the centuries, Brussels was always a forum of European trade. As trade flourished, the arts blossomed. It is therefore not surprising that panel painting was invented here. Before the advent of panel painting, the only pictures were murals or illustrations in books. The Limbourg brothers were the most famous illustrators of the period, painting the Book of Hours known as the *Très Riches Heures* for the Burgundian Duke of Berry. Burgundian Flanders, equally noted for its illuminated manuscripts and fine miniatures, provided a fertile ground for 15th-century artists.

LEFT: *The Betrothal of the Arnolfini* (1434) by Jan van Eyck initiated a new chapter in art history.
RIGHT: *The Fight between Carnival and Lent* (1559) detail, by Pieter Bruegel the Elder.

Whilst not as revolutionary as their Florentine counterparts, the van Eyck brothers (Jan and Hubert), who began as illustrators, used similarly realistic techniques, offering a mirror to reality, and developed the technique of painting pictures on wooden or canvas panels. In the opinion of Ernst Gombrich, the celebrated art historian, "Jan van Eyck pursued the methods of the brothers Limbourg, and brought them to such a pitch of perfection that he left the ideas of medieval art behind." Jan van Eyck is the artist credited with the invention of oil painting. Although this was not strictly a discovery, the use of oil as a medium for mixing pigments and for applying glazes proved a more malleable and longer lasting medium than egg-based tempera. Van Eyck also created the Ghent altarpiece, the polyptych of *The Adoration of the Holy Lamb* (1432), which is acclaimed as one of the wonders of Belgium. Panel painting spread rapidly across Flanders and artists were highly esteemed (and rewarded).

Flemish art

Flemish art transcended the emerging Dutch/Belgian borders of the 16th century, and it is impossible to divide such art by national characteristics. The genius of Flemish art was to move from stylised miniatures and the illusion

(1415–75) and Hans Memling (*c.*1433–94), and on the gamut of European art, from Germany to Spain. Unfortunately, relatively few of his works remain in Belgium.

Hans Memling was a mystical innovator in the Flemish school. His travels along the Main and Rhine rivers took him to Cologne. Completing his training under Rogier van der Weyden in Brussels, Memling settled in Bruges, where he personified the spirit of the wealthy merchant city. As the most popular Flemish painter under Charles the Bold, his work radiates lyricism and pastoral charm. Memling is generally considered the last representative of the school of Flemish Primitives.

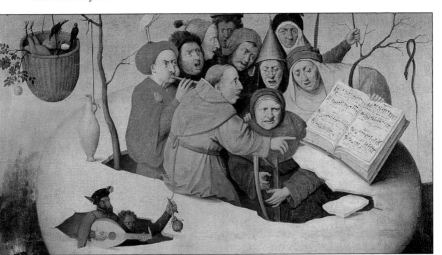

of reality to the conquest of reality in the works of the so-called Flemish Primitives. Clarity and realism, an acute sense of light, robustly naturalistic native backgrounds and a gift for portraiture are the hallmarks of Flemish art. The artists' patient powers of observation ensured an accurate portrayal of the texture of cloth, the warmth of flesh and the vivid surfaces of life.

If van Eyck was the precursor of Flemish art, Rogier van der Weyden (*c.*1400–64) continued in the same vein, with realism matched by religious intensity, apparent in his touching *tableaux vivants*. As the town painter of Brussels, van der Weyden exerted considerable influence on Hugo van der Goes (1440–82), Dirk Bouts

The first industrial painting

Gérard David's influence is much in evidence in the works of Joachim Patinier (*c.*1475–1524), a Belgium-born landscape specialist, respected by Albrecht Dürer and generally regarded as being the creator of the first industrial landscape painting, *River Landscape with Furnaces*.

Quentin Matsys (1466–1530) learnt the art of realistic portraiture from the works of Dirk Bouts. Matsys used religious subject matter and also painted scenes of commercial activity. In Antwerp, painting became progressively more stylised. Joos van Cleve (Joos van der Beke, *c.*1485–1541) stood between the Mannerists and the late Romance artists. Jan Mabuse (Jan

Gossaert, 1478–1533/6) was the founder of the new style; he journeyed to Italy with Philip of Burgundy, and became profoundly influenced by artists south of the Alps.

Master of fantasy

Although based in Holland, Hieronymus Bosch (c.1450–1516) had a distinctly Flemish style. He created a world of pictorial fantasy using realistic forms. Some consider him to be the greatest master of fantasy that ever lived. Bosch's world is a mixture of paradise and hell, dominated by sensory impressions, lust and love transformed into sin. Religion and faith are linked with alchemy, arcane erudition

sophical bent, paradoxically the master of vivid allegories and of minutely observed realism. As the first major Flemish landscape painter, he could depict a still winter landscape with as much skill as he did the dramatic fall of Icarus. These are genre paintings of a high order, human comedies with Flemish settings, inspired by the Brabant countryside. Despite his sophistication and lofty court connections, Bruegel's talent was for portraying peasant life, scenes of earthy enjoyment and merrymaking.

Pieter Bruegel, widely known as "Peasant Bruegel" (who spelt his name with or without an "h") was the father of two artist sons. Pieter Brueghel the Younger (1564–1638) became

and obscene jokes. His haunting representations of evil evoke the fearful demons that plagued medieval minds. In these macabre and grotesque paintings, it is tempting to see Bosch as a precursor of Belgian surrealism.

Pieter Bruegel the Elder (c.1525–69), who lived in Antwerp and Brussels, began his artistic career inspired by the style of Bosch. In Brussels, he founded a family dynasty of painters who were to become popular and famous. Bruegel was an all-round artist with a philo-

LEFT: the highly surreal *Concert in the Egg* by Hieronymus Bosch (c.1450–1516). **ABOVE:** the hellish vision of Pieter Brueghel the Younger (1564–1638).

known for his demonic scenes, partly influenced by the works of Hieronymus Bosch. Such violent images earned him the nickname "Hell Brueghel". By contrast, Pieter Bruegel's other son, Jan Brueghel the Elder (1568–1625), was known as "Velvet Brueghel" or "Flower Brueghel" because of his predilection for painting detailed pictures of flower arrangements, set against a background of richly-coloured velvet. He became court painter to the Spanish stadtholder and produced a number of works in collaboration with his friend Rubens. In turn, Velvet Brueghel's own son, Jan Brueghel the Younger (1601–78), became a landscape painter in Antwerp.

Rubens and his followers

Peter Paul Rubens (1577–1640) was born into a Flemish family in Germany but considered Antwerp his home city. Under Spanish rule, Rubens and an artistic elite presided over a short but sweet Flemish Renaissance in Antwerp. However, as a prolific painter, and the greatest baroque artist in northern Europe, Rubens carried out commissions for European courts. The vitality and virtuosity of his work was at one with the extravagant Flemish baroque churches. Fortunately, his works are well represented in his home city, and visible in ten different locations. Rubens' fame was such that the Flemish tapestry industry

prospered on making copies of his greatest works. His eclectic range of subjects encompassed mythologies and landscapes as well as dazzling portraits of princes and prelates.

As a court painter, Rubens confirmed the political orthodoxies and was a servant of warring monarchs. Yet as a self-confident citizen, he was inspired by Italian art, notably the works of Caravaggio. Rubens was equally at home with hierarchy, sensuality or mystery, with the trappings of success, tumbling figures, fleshy, buxom women, or saints and angels. His art is characterised by intense vitality, robust figures, rich details, bold effects and large-scale canvases. As the most skilled of artists, he had a

facility for making his paintings live, with brushstrokes that suggest billowing, palpitating bodily flesh.

Like Rubens, Antoon van Dyck (1599–1641), his pupil and assistant, was much in demand as a court painter. His talent for portraying courtly refinement and the dignity of the sitter led him to the English court of Charles I. There he spent the last nine years of his life, his name anglicised to Sir Anthony Vandyke. As well as painting numerous equestrian images of Charles I, he inspired the English tradition of landscape painting. Despite his gift for surfaces, whether silk or skin, van Dyck was more than a glorified society painter. His aim was to match Rubens and the Venetian artists he greatly admired. Certainly, he succeeded in conveying sensitivity and pathos as well as virtuosity. Although best known as a portraitist, van Dyck was also a landscape artist, an important religious painter from the Counter-Reformation period and a superb engraver.

Lucas Fayd'herbe (1617–97), another of Rubens' pupils, worked as a sculptor and architect in Brussels. He may have been responsible for one of the city's loveliest churches, the baroque Saint-Jean-Baptiste au Béguinage.

Scenes from everyday life

In spite of plunderings by the Spanish, Antwerp remained a conducive artistic environment. Joost de Momper (1564–1635) was a landscape painter, while Frans Hals (1581/5–1666), a Haarlem-based artist, became a realistic portraitist of the bourgeoisie. Jacob Jordaens (1593–1678), an Antwerp-based follower of Rubens, favoured naturalistic, earthy depictions of everyday life; these were created alongside mythological and Biblical scenes. Adriaen Brouwer (1605–38) also painted scenes from everyday life.

Brouwer, born in Flanders but apprenticed to Frans Hals in Haarlem, bridges the gap between Flemish and Dutch art. He returned to Flanders in 1631, and was detained as a suspected spy by the Spaniards in Antwerp, where he remained for the last years of his life.

The realistic pictures of David Teniers the Younger (1610–90) reveal the influence of Rubens and Brouwer. In 1651, Teniers became court painter in Brussels and in 1665 founded an academy of art in Antwerp.

After a long period of Flemish and Dutch artistic supremacy in northern Europe, many years were to elapse before their art was to regain its former glory.

The emperor's painter

The revival of Belgian painting was instigated by the French painter and political activist, Jacques-Louis David (1748–1825). He was a leading representative of the classical movement as well as being a Jacobin. As such, he liked to portray the civic virtues of republicanism in an antique setting, thereby spreading a revolutionary consciousness. After the 1789 Revolution, David became a member of

Following the emperor's defeat, David fled to Brussels; there he exerted a profound influence over the new generation of young artists, evident in the works of J.F. Navez, Gustave Wappers, N. de Kayser, Louis Gallait, Edouard Bièfve and L. Leys. He devoted the final years of his life to large paintings and portraits inspired by mythology and ancient literature, exemplified by his *Venus Disarming Mars* in the Brussels Museum of Ancient Art.

The modern period begins

At the beginning of the 19th century, two artists pointed the way towards radically new artistic horizons: Antoine Wiertz (1806–65),

the National Convention, and was briefly its president, as well as Superintendent of Fine Arts. Among the many fine portraits he painted in this period is a poignant drawing of Marie Antoinette on her way to the guillotine. When Robespierre was overthrown, David fell from favour and was twice imprisoned. However, Napoleon's rise to power revived his fortunes; he supported David and made him his "First Painter".

LEFT: detail of a self-portrait by Peter Paul Rubens, perhaps the most accomplished painter of the northern Renaissance. **ABOVE:** *Samson and Delilah*, c.1628–30, by Anthony van Dyck.

a Romanticist whose monumental canvases and lyrical sculptures depict cruelty and beauty (his former home and studio in Brussels now houses the Wiertz Museum dedicated to his work; *see page 158*) and Guillaume Vogels (1836–96), one of the co-founders of the artistic association known as "XX" (Les Vingt), a group of 20 progressive Belgian painters and sculptors who played a key role on the European art scene, staging important exhibitions and luring famous artists from all over the world.

But it is James Ensor (1860–1949), one of the founders of Les Vingt, who is regarded as marking the beginning of the modern period and a forerunner of the Surrealists. His original, expressive pictures defied classification and reinvigorated the art world. His early works of "bourgeois interiors" adopted Impressionist techniques and expressed a strange intimacy. In the 1880s his subject matter changed, and his use of carnival masks, skeletons and other strange scenes call to mind the bizarre and often gruesome imaginings of Bosch and Brueghel. His most famous painting, the huge *The Entry of Christ into Brussels* (which can be seen in the Museum of Ancient Art), expressed his anarchic tendencies. It shocked public and critics alike, and resulted in his expulsion from Les Vingt.

Other artists influenced by naturalism include Jan Stobbaerts (1839–1914), who rebelled against the doctrines of his established fellow-artists in Antwerp and moved to Brussels in 1885, and Léon Frédéric (1856–1940), the most popular Belgian painter during the 1920s, who painted mainly peasants and workers.

Félix Labisse (1905–82), whose visionary paintings are characterised by nude figures often in iridescent shades of blue, was influenced by Magritte, Ensor and Delvaux.

Gaston Bogaert (born 1918) first came to Brussels as an actor. He then became an advertising designer for the Belgian airline Sabena.

Other artists in Belgium around this time were influenced by naturalism. Constantin Meunier (1831–1905) was not even 15 when he was admitted by the Brussels Academy of Fine Arts, but did not begin devoting himself to the celebration of labour until he was 50 years old, when he became fascinated with the iron and steel industry and coal mines. He is famous for his powerful sculptures and paintings depicting the hardships of labour and the nobility of labourers. A prolific artist, his former house and studio in Brussels has been turned into a museum housing over 170 of his sculptures and 120 of his paintings.

His first exhibition of paintings, displayed in a Brussels gallery in 1965, places him as another member of the Brussels visionary school.

Contemporary art in Brussels does not consist only of the abstract, as the work of Pierre Alechinsky (born 1927), Marcel Broodthaers (1924–76) and John C.F. Delogne (born in Uccle in 1933) makes clear. And artistic contributions of another kind are supplied by the artists who have transformed the underground railway stations into a gallery of contemporary art *(see page 133)*. ❏

ABOVE: James Ensor's *The Entry of Christ into Brussels* (1888) shocked both critics and public.

Two Surrealists

The Surrealist movement, which began in the 1920s, awakened the subconscious in revolt against rationalism, and produced an explosion of striking and subversive images which reflected the avantgarde's wish to scandalise and unsettle. Yet shocking the bourgeoisie was secondary to the desire for a new perception of reality, one forged by distortion or dissociation of everyday images. The movement struck a chord in Belgium, a country familiar with Hieronymus Bosch and the murky fears of the medieval mind. In Delvaux's modern visions, the outpourings of his fevered imagination produced skeletons engaged in pedestrian activities, recalling the macabre subject matter of Pieter Brueghel the Younger.

René Magritte (1898–1967) was the master of Surrealism, a painter rivalled only by Dalí as the pre-eminent painter of the subconscious mind. Born into a petit-bourgeois background, Magritte is seen as a quintessentially Bruxellois artist. Although a legend in his lifetime, this enigmatic artist took pains to be conventional and self-effacing to the point of eccentricity. In his anonymous suburban house, he erected an easel in the dining room and painted subversive works in a business suit. It was a convincing act, both a self-confident statement of bourgeois intent and the subversive's best uniform, a protection against charges of self-aggrandisement or flagrant bohemianism.

Unlike many Surrealists, Magritte rejected collective myths and spontaneous dreamscapes. He realised that the more realistic the image was, the more it supplanted reality. Instead, he placed experience of the world above pictorial experimentation or the tyranny of symbolism. In a neutral, understated style, he "homed in on reality as it was while hoping that it would be sublime".

Magritte also played linguistic games. The celebrated statement "This is not a pipe" (*Ceci n'est pas une pipe*) plays with reality and illusion: a picture of the object

RIGHT: *Le Dormeur Téméraire* (the Reckless Sleeper) by René Magritte (1898–1967).

cannot be the object; it is merely a picture. As to the arbitrary nature of names, Magritte said this: "An object is not so attached to its name that another cannot be found for it that suits it better."

Dubbed "a dreamer with his eyes wide shut", Paul Delvaux (1897–1994) rejected the philosophical side of Surrealism in favour of "poetic shock and mystery". Bourgeois interiors meet sombre railway stations on Delvaux's canvases, and sleeping beauties are lit by gas lamps. According to critic Jacques Sojcher, "He made the world a museum protected by a female custodian, a vestal doomed to perpetual waiting."

Delvaux was born into a wealthy Walloon background and nurtured on the classics, art and architecture. He became a Surrealist in 1934 after seeing De Chirico's strange landscapes and falling for their "simplicity and grandeur". As an introduction to Delvaux's somnambulistic style, travellers can admire the mural of trams at the Bourse metro station in Brussels, while Bohemian beer-drinkers may prefer the shrine to Surrealism, La Fleur en Papier Doré, the Brussels café favoured by Magritte *(see page 137)*. In keeping with the café's carefree spirit, poets and chess players devised paradoxical titles to Magritte's paintings. ❏

CITY OF CULTURE

The Bruxellois are enthusiastic art-lovers and concert-goers, but the identity of a confident, cohesive, multilingual and multicultural society is still being forged

B eer, chocolate and the comic strip are not the country's sole contributions to European culture. Nor are Belgian jokes and boring bureaucracy the summation of Brussels' cultural contribution to civilisation. The unloved child of Belgium is, in fact, a vibrant city blessed with a musical soul, a dynamic arts scene, engaging museums, multicultural aspirations and some of the sassiest venues in Europe. What Australians term "the cultural cringe" takes the form of a lingering inferiority complex vis-à-vis Paris, Amsterdam, and even Antwerp, Brussels' chosen cultural reference points.

The authorities finally realised that the heritage of the capital of Europe could no longer be marketed on the back of the Manneken-Pis, a statue of a small boy peeing in the street. In recent years, Brussels has sought to shake off its provincial image and emerge from the shadow of Paris and Amsterdam. It is doing this by highlighting its contemporary creativity, drawing more on its melting-pot, culturally diverse character, at the same time gaining confidence in itself and becoming more convinced of its role as an important cultural centre.

Restoration and modernisation

At the forefront of this rebranding of Brussels as a city of culture, is the Palais des Beaux-Arts. Following a major restoration, the 'Palace of

LEFT: Bozar, the revamped and repackaged Palais des Beaux-Arts, Brussels' "Palace of Culture".
RIGHT: hundreds of acts take to open-air stages throughout the city for the annual Jazz Marathon.

Fine Arts' changed its traditional and rather staid name – which no longer did justice to the changing institution it represented – to the upbeat Bozar, more fitting for this prestigious arts institution which offers a very varied programme of theatre, dance, art, music and film. Flagey is another rising star in the cultural firmament. Brussels' former radio broadcast and recording studio has been transformed from a near ruin to a dynamic contemporary arts centre, injecting new life into the previously downbeat district of southern Ixelles.

As far as museum culture is concerned, middle-class Bruxellois vie with resident Eurocrats and foreign visitors in their eagerness to keep abreast of the latest exhibitions. This cultural one-upmanship is particularly marked in the new millennium, which has signalled the creation, restoration or reopening of a vast range of museums.

Cinema and theatre

The Bruxellois tend to be sophisticated cinemagoers, and, unlike most Continentals, are quite capable of watching a film in a foreign language if need be. The international nature of the city ensures a wider variety of foreign releases than in most capitals, with most films shown in their original version, accompanied by French and Flemish subtitles. Set in Heysel's Bruparck,

Kinepolis, the vast concrete bunker that passes for a multiplex cinema, draws huge crowds to its 25 screens of mostly American blockbusters (and one giant IMAX wraparound screen for a different kind of big-film event). However, in the city centre, several more charming cinemas survive, notably the Arenberg, an independent cinema in the Galerie de la Reine.

The Actor's Studio, around the corner, tends to focus on European and American art-house movies as well as the classics, while the neighbouring Cinema Museum focuses on both the classics and blockbusters, with regular worthy retrospectives. Near by, the novel Cinema Nova successfully bucks the commercial trend

with its film-linked events, often followed by discussions; on other occasions, DJs are invited to create their own musical soundtrack to selected films. Close to the European quarter, a young, popcorn-eating, pleasure-seeking crowd is drawn to the summer drive-in movies on the Cinquantenaire Esplanade, where those arriving in vintage or classic cars are accorded discounted tickets to see the latest releases.

Although plays are generally performed in French or Dutch, the cosmopolitan nature of the city means that some drama is staged in other languages, especially English. Such international awareness finds favour with foreign writers and directors, and attracts performers of the quality of the Nobel-prize-winning Dario Fo, who has staged an irreverent farce about Italian immigrants living in Belgium's industrial heartland. As in other artistic fields, the revamping of major venues and the creation of more offbeat performance spaces is popular with the public. In the pristine Galeries Royales St-Hubert off the Grand-Place, the once splendid *belle époque* Théâtre du Vaudeville has been restored and reopened.

Elsewhere, the intimate Théâtre de Poche, set in the wooded Bois de la Cambre, tackles contemporary drama and avant-garde work in French. More mainstream is the remodelled Théâtre Royal du Parc, or the Théâtre National de la Communauté Nationale Wallonie Bruxelles, which has moved from its monstrous bunker in the now redeveloped Centre Rogier, to much better, if equally modernistic, premises on nearby Boulevard Emile Jacqmain. These are the places to see a classic repertoire in French. For Flemish theatre (in Dutch primarily, but with a smattering of English pieces), there's the Koninklijke Vlaamse Schouwburg. Its graceful neo-classical venue on Laekensestraat (Rue de Laeken) is currently undergoing renovations, and performances are being staged in its new annexe around the corner on Quai aux Arduinkaai (Pierres de Tailles).

Circus and contemporary dance

Circus thrives in Brussels, partly because, like dance, it is a genre that transcends language. If Brussels is an international centre for circus skills, it is also thanks to the versatile artistes who cross the metaphorical trapeze into puppetry and music, drama and dance. Given the cultural divide in Brussels, foreign ballet companies often do better than their native rivals, since they are less subject to restrictions and political correctness. Maurice Béjart, for instance, brought much-needed verve and flair to the Brussels ballet world, and put the Théâtre Royal de la Monnaie at the forefront of contemporary dance. When he and his company left for Lausanne, Brussels slipped off the international ballet map and has yet fully to regain its place amongst the European elite.

Béjart's absence has been partly filled by younger Belgian and foreign companies. The Monnaie's resident dance troupe, Anne

Musical feast

However, in the cultural firmament of Brussels, music reigns supreme, with classical music and opera particularly prized. Cosmopolitan audiences in the capital expect prestigious events, and the most successful art forms tend to be music or dance. Of the city's many music venues, Horta's innovative Art Deco Palais des Beaux-Arts – since renamed "Bozar" *(see page 71)* – is one of the finest. The concert hall, home of the Belgian National Orchestra, has been renovated to reveal the architect's original design, and greatly improve the acoustics. Here, culture-vulture Bruxellois are satisfied by visits from international con-

Theresa de Keersmaeker's Group Rosas, has plenty of inventive and emotional modern moves. Anne Meg Stuart, an American with a Brussels-based dance company, is typical of foreign choreographers who thrive in the city. Wim Vandekeybus, a Belgian choreographer of explosive, dynamic dance forms, also runs a select international Brussels-based company in which the dancers rely on adrenaline and intensity as much as technique.

LEFT: master puppeteer at the Toone Theatre, Brussels' last surviving puppet theatre.
ABOVE: Brussels has many venues for classical and contemporary music.

ductors of the standing of Simon Rattle or composer-conductor Pierre Boulez.

A popular summer series of organ recitals takes place in historic churches such as Sts-Jean-et-Etienne aux Minimes or Notre-Dame de la Chapelle. Although the major venues place increasing emphasis on contemporary classical music, the guest list is eclectic enough to include musicians and singers as different in style and genre as Youssou N'Dour, Ricky Martin and Björk.

Café-théâtre is a Franco-Belgian genre, and rarely better than in La Samaritaine. The vaulted cellars of this atmospheric club provide an intimate setting for low-key jazz, *chanson* or speech-based shows. Set in the Marolles, a stone's throw from the chic Sablon, this cross-over club is equally comfortable with poetry, speech and music.

In May, the Nuits Botanique festival is a two-week long celebration of independent rock, pop, and world music as well as French *chanson*. Concerts are staged in the rooms and grounds of the Botanique French cultural centre, which hosts the festival jointly with the Cirque Royal.

L'Ancienne Belgique is an established venue where singers of the standing of Edith Piaf and Jacques Brel once performed. Following a recent revamp, it has lost none of its

cachet, and remains a venue for international bands from Morcheeba to The Darkness. Further afield, Forest National is the soulless stadium where mainstream rock and pop superstars tend to perform, from Madonna to Céline Dion. Even so, between Riverdance and The Rolling Stones there is space for those with closer Brussels connections, whether Béjart's ballet company or Johnny Hallyday, the Belgian-born crooner who made his name in France.

Belgium has produced a number of great jazz musicians, not least Django Reinhardt and Toots Thielemans, Belgium's legendary harmonica player (who wrote the theme music

to *Midnight Cowboy*). No surprise then, that Brussels is a great city for jazz aficionados. In the course of one weekend in May, the sounds of mellow jazz, Dixieland, blues and acid jazz echo around the clubs of the St-Boniface, Avenue Louise and St-Géry districts. For the rest of the year, live jazz can be heard in a number of venues: L'Archiduc, L'Arts-O-Bases, Studio Athanor, Sounds Jazz Club and Théâtre Marni to name but a few.

Separate but equal

Brussels is fond of presenting itself as a cultural crossroads, where two major communities come together to forge a creative cross-over – or not, as the case may be. "Bi-community" is the current buzzword to describe joint initiatives in which both Flemish and French speakers have equal weight. But *les conflits communautaires*, cultural divisions, are more common, with promising projects often hijacked by factions. Even so, the creative friction between the French and Flemish-speaking communities can produce novel artistic hybrids, often in the fields of circus or the comic strip.

Certain avowedly monocultural venues daringly invite performers from the other community. In theory, the eclectic L'Ancienne Belgique is a Flemish theatre, but French singers and musicians are also welcome. Yet much more common is the separate-but-equal approach, which applies to all aspects of Brussels cultural life, with equal funding allocated to both language communities regardless of need.

In Brussels itself, every cultural association, club or television station has to choose its linguistic community. In the arts world, there tend to be French- or Flemish-run cultural centres or theatres, and never the twain shall meet. In general, such centres are far keener to invite foreign companies than to welcome their fellow citizens on the other side of the language divide. As a final absurd touch, each community boasts its own cultural showcase, but, as if to negate one another, they stage the rival Flanders Festival and Festival of Wallonia at the same time, with clashing events held in Brussels.   ❏

LEFT: singer-songwriter Jacques Brel (1929–78), performing in 1959.

Festive Fun

In March, Brussels promises film fans a fortnight of madness in the form of the **International Fantasy Film Festival**. For music-lovers, the city gets into its stride with **Ars Musica**, a festival of contemporary classical music. The week is a frenetic affair, with opportunities to attend rehearsals, masterclasses, musical talks and concerts.

The prestigious **KunstenFESTIVALdes-Arts** in May focuses on the performing arts, notably ballet, contemporary dance, theatre and opera, at various locations. Also in May, the **Nuits Botanique** festival is a celebration of independent rock, pop, world music and *chansons*. In the same month, the week-long **Baroque Spring Festival** a musical feast of chamber music, takes place on the Sablon in churches and clubs. The last weekend of the month is a treat for jazz-lovers, with the **Brussels Jazz Marathon** bringing mellow jazz, Dixieland, blues and acid jazz to Le Travers, the city's main jazz club, and to the cool clubs of the St-Boniface, Avenue Louise and St-Géry districts, culminating in a series of concerts on the Grand-Place. The biennial **Zinneke Festival** celebrates Brussels' ethnicity and promotes racial tolerance. The highlight of this May festival is the "artistic parade" – its theme for 2006 is "the future".

Couleur Café is the big summer festival. Staged in late June, this three-day event is a multicultural jamboree held in a former bonded warehouse. World music, acid jazz and Cuban dancing make a heady combination, with tropical cocktails, handcrafts and ethnic dishes sold from stalls. For summer visitors and locals left behind after the summer exodus, the city stages a series of **open-air concerts** in July and August, including lunchtime concerts in historic churches.

Summer is the time when several of the best folkloric festivals are staged. In early July, the renaissance pageant known as the **Ommegang** comes to town. A procession of

costumed cavaliers, Burgundian lords and ladies wends its way from the Sablon to the Grand-Place for a mock battle and firework display *(see page 87)*. Equally authentic is the **Meiboom** in early August, a recreation of a medieval ceremony recalling the successful defence of the city against Leuven in 1213. Amidst much pomp, a felled tree is carried through the streets of the old town and "planted" in Rue des Sables. Another of the more engaging traditional events is the mid-August **Carpet of Flowers**. Every other year the Grand-Place is "carpeted" by 700,000 begonias and turned into an impressive patchwork *(see page 87)*.

The September return of the Eurocrats and bourgeois Bruxellois signals the launch of the autumn season. **Europalia**, a celebration of the diversity of European culture, focuses on a different country every autumn, and involves prestigious events and exhibitions around town. **Sablon Nights**, at the end of November, is a curiously elitist event that draws a moneyed crowd to three evenings of antique-hunting and chic café-crawling. Horse-drawn carriages take revellers from antique shop to art gallery in search of pricey baubles. The season ends on the Grand-Place, with the **Christmas Market** displaying festive handcrafts from around the world. ❑

RIGHT: "Puppeteer and His Marionette", participants in a body-painting contest during the Fantastic Film Festival

PLACES

A detailed guide to the city with the principal sites
clearly cross-referenced by number to the maps

The best way to explore Brussels – or its centre at least – is on foot and at a leisurely pace. The obvious starting point is the Grand-Place, one of the loveliest city squares in Europe, graced by baroque, Gothic and Flemish Renaissance architecture. North of the square, the glass-vaulted Galeries Royales St-Hubert shelter sophisticated shops. At night you can wander through the neon-lit lanes of the Ilot Sacré – the so-called "Stomach of Brussels" – crammed with restaurants vying for tourist custom. West of the Grand-Place the streets around Place Ste-Catherine and Place St-Géry are lined with shabby but elegant town houses, trendy bars and boutiques, and plenty more good restaurants.

The prestigious Upper City, traditional home of the Francophile upper classes, can also be explored on foot with the odd tram or metro ride between destinations. The long Rue Royale acts as a dividing line between the two districts, leading from the magnificent Place Royale in front of the Royal Fine Arts Museums, past the municipal park and parliament buildings on to the botanical gardens and into the district of St-Josse beyond. At the opposite end of this long artery, the Rue de la Régence ends with the city's most imposing building, the monumental Palais de Justice.

At the foot of the Palais de Justice nestles the old working-class Marolles district, where you will find newly restored buildings, chic shops and restaurants alongside earthy cafés and battered side streets. The area west of the Marolles, across the Boulevard de Waterloo, forms one of the city's most diverse districts, offering a gentrified bohemian atmosphere with designer shopping in the glittering galleries around busy Place Louise, and quirky boutiques and African eateries, interspersed with Art Nouveau town houses around Ixelles and St-Gilles.

Those with more than a few days to spare will want to venture further afield. Within easy reach of Brussels lie Tervuren Park and the Central Africa Museum, the Waterloo battlefield and the lovely towns of Leuven and Lier. In Flanders, the medieval cities of Ghent or Bruges, and Antwerp, Belgium's second biggest city, are all worth an excursion. ❑

PRECEDING PAGES: the magnificent Royal Greenhouses; the Grand-Place Carpet of Flowers, 2004, inspired by art nouveau. **LEFT:** the elaborately decorated Hôtel de Ville on the Grand-Place is one of the finest examples of Gothic architecture in the country.

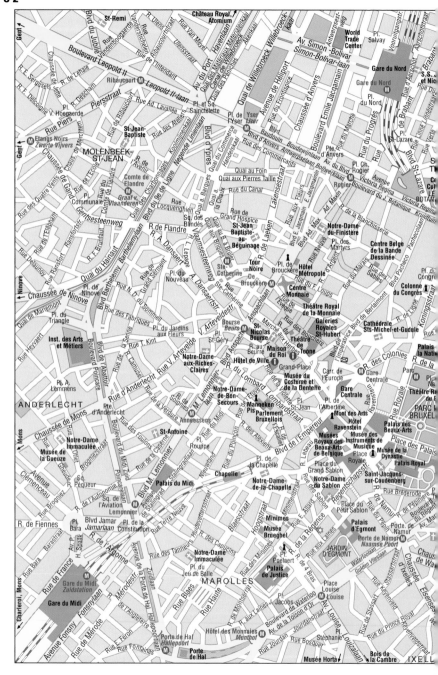

Château Royal

0   500 m
0   500 yds

Château Royal, Atomium
Rue de Palais
Paleizenstraat
Rue Rogier
Rue Royale Ste Marie
Haachtsesteenweg
Chaussée de Haecht
Chaussée Romaine
Antwerpen
Av. de l'Atomium
Avenue du Forum
PARC DU FORUM
Avenue du Forum
Avenue Mutsaard
Av. de Bologne
Pl. de la Reine
Konings straat
nstraat
Ste-Marie
Parc des Expositions
Avenue de Madrid
Avenue de la Croix-Rouge
Av. de Meysse
Avenue de Meysse
Rue de Wand
Av. des Pagodes
Ultieme Ilucinatie
Avenue Impératrice Charlotte
Trade Mart
Pl. du Centenaire
PARC D'OSSEGHEM
Madridlaan
Avenue des Croix du Feu
SSE-ODE
R. du Moulin
Stade du Roi Baudouin
Heysel
Bd de l'Atomium
Avenue de la Paille
Pavillon Chinois
Av. Jules Van Praet
ST-JOOST-
Avenue du Marathon
Bruparck
Atomium
Statue J. de Bologne
Tour Japonaise
nique ttuin Av. Galilée Quetelet
Planetarium
Pl. L. Steens
Gros-Tilleul
Avenue de Bouchout
Abeelenlaan
Villa Belvédère
Serres Royales
des cades
Houba Brugmann
HEYSEL
Avenue des Tagètes
Av. des Tagètes
Pl. St-Lambert
Monument Léopold I
Avenue du Parc Royal
sée Jouet
TEN-NODE
Avenue Houba de Strooper
Rue du Heysel
Rue Reper Vreven
Sacré Coeur et St-Lambert
Av. des Ebéniers
PARC DE LAEKEN
I. de iberte
Av. Rommelaere
Rue Stevens-Delannoy
Av. J. Sobieski, Sobieskilaan
Avenue de Trembles
Chapelle Ste-Anne
Château Royal
Chaussée de Louvain
Avenue Jean Baptiste Depaire
Hôpital Brugmann Brugmann Hospital
Houba de Strooperlaan
Rue du Cloître
Drève Ste-Anne
Koninklijk Parklaan
Chaussée de Louvain
Pl. Madou Madou
Rue Gustave Gilson
Rue de Laubespin
Av. J. Sobieski
Avenue des Robiniers
École des Cadets
R. de Pave
Rue Rasson
Avenue Eugène Plasky
Leuven
de Congrès oix de Fer
Chaussée de Louvain
R. Willems
R. du Cardinal
R. des Gravelines
R. des Éburons
R. des Confédérés
Rue de Beffroi
Eedgenotenstraat
Rue du Noyer
Pl. de Jamblinne de Meux
Rue de Linthout
Regentlaan Kunstlaan
R. Joseph II
Pl. des Deux Églises
Rue de Spa
Rue Stevin
Sq. Marie-Louise
Av. Palmerston
Square Ambiorix
Sq. Marguerite
R. des Patriotes
Franklinstr.
Av. J. Palmerston
R. Ch. Martel
Rue Véronèse
Arts-Loi Kunst-Wet
Rue de la Loi
Jozef II Straat
Bd Charlemagne
Rue Archimède
Stevinstr.
Rue Franklin
Rue Corrège
Kortenberglaan
École Royale Militaire
Noyerlaan
Noordstraat
straat
Bd du Régent
R. Guimard
Rue de l'Industrie
Wetenschapsstraat
Aarlenstraat
Maelbeek
Wetstraat
Rue J. de Lalaing
Schuman
Schuman
Rd-Pt R. Schuman
Berlaymont
Avenue de Cortenbergh
Av. de la Renaissance
Grand Mosquée de Bruxelles
Renaissancelaan
Hobbemastraat
Ridderstraat
Av. de l'Yser
St-Joseph
Rue Belliard
Chaussée d'Etterbeek
Consilium (Conseil Européen)
Froissartstr.
Avenue de la Joyeuse Entrée
Blijde Inkomstlaan
PARC DU CINQUANTENAIRE
Musée Royal de l'Armée et de l'Histoire Militaire
Arc de Cinquantenaire
Mérode
ais des émies
R. Montoyer Montoyerstraat
St-Sacrement
Belliardstraat
Av. d'Auderghem
Av. J. F. Kennedy
J. F. Kennedylaan
Autoworld
Musée du Cinquantenaire
Av. de la Chevalerie
Av. des Gaulois
Trône Troon
Sq. de Meeûs
Rue de Science
Rue d'Arlon
Ertebeekseweg
Quartier Léopold
PARC LÉOPOLD
Parlement Européen
Avenue des Nerviers
Nervierslaan
Rue de la Chasse
Pl. de Trône Londres
Rue R. Caroly
Rue Wiertz
Rue de Trèves
Hoornstraat
Pl. v. Meyel
St-Pietersteenweg
Pl. St-Pierre
Musée Camille Lemonnier
Musée Wiertz
Musée des Sciences Naturelles
Rue Froissart
Rue du Cornet
Pl. Jourdan
Rue Général Leman
Ste-Gertrude
Rue Col. V. Gala
Rue Louis Hap
face
ersesteenweg
St-Sacrement
Chaussée de Wavre
Wavre Vlaudicstr.
Waverseteenweg
Graystraat
Chaussée de Wavre
Waverstesteenweg
R. Louis Hap
Oudergemselaan
Rue Baron Lambert
Av. de la Chasse
Chaussée St-Pierre
R. Louis Hap
Rue du Conseil
Rue Goffart
Troonstraat
Rue du Sceptre
Rue de l'Orient
Rue Gray
Notre-Dame Immaculée
Rue du Brochet
Waverseteenweg
Tervuren

Brussels

0   200 m
0   200 yds

THE GRAND-PLACE

"The grandest stage set in the world," as Jean Cocteau called it, is at the core of Brussels life, representing both civic and commercial traditions

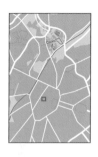

As civic pride burgeoned in medieval Flemish towns made rich by weaving and trade, the prosperous burghers and guilds built town halls, guild houses, cloth halls and Gothic mansions. These major public buildings were clustered around the main square, the *grote markt*, the finest of which is undoubtedly that of Brussels – which is now more commonly known by its French name: Grand-Place. The architectural pinnacle of any sightseeing tour of Brussels, and ideally seen for the first time at night, the capital's main square provides a sumptuous setting for the spectacle of city life. It is lined by gabled guild houses in Flemish Renaissance style, a tribute to the baroque ideals of balance and harmony. The guilds of haberdashers, tailors, artists, bakers, butchers, archers, coopers, cabinetmakers, tallow makers, brewers and boatmen rivalled one another by producing exuberant status symbols, adorned with gilded facades, scrolled gables and fanciful statuary.

The Grand-Place began as a medieval market square, but with the completion of Brussels' Town Hall in 1444, it became the civic heart of the city. This heart was torn out by a French artillery bombardment in 1695, with Brussels a casualty of dynastic battles between France and Spain. Cannon placed in front of the city walls bombarded the Grand-Place and its surroundings. Four thousand buildings in the city were burned to the ground and most of the original guild houses on the Grand-Place were destroyed. The bombardment was an act of vengeance on the part of Louis XIV of France, who ordered the storming of Brussels in response to the Belgian attack on his army. Only the Gothic Town Hall and a few guild houses survived more or less

Map on page 86

LEFT: the Grand-Place ranks among Europe's finest squares. **BELOW:** every two years, the Carpet of Flowers provides a spectacular floor show.

TIP

The main tourist
information office is on
the ground floor of the
Hôtel de Ville (Mon–
Sat 9am–6pm; Sun
9am–6pm summer,
10am–2pm winter;
closed on Sun
1 Jan–Easter;
tel: 02-513 89 40).

BELOW: the daily
flower market.

intact, but the citizens of Brussels
refused to admit defeat. In a wave
of civic pride, the guilds swiftly
banded together and rebuilt the
square, making it even more magnificent than before. The harmony
of the baroque facades is down to
the solidarity shown by the guilds
and the fact that the work was
completed within five years.

From the balcony of the Town
Hall, dignitaries have been honoured and ruling dukes have looked
down upon festivities; peace has
been proclaimed and pardons pronounced. Now guided tours visit the
sombre interior, with its 16th-
century Council Chamber and array
of Flemish tapestries and portraits.
Across the square, the mansion
called the Maison du Roi houses the
Musée de la Ville. Inside, among
many other items, is a display of historical city maps and the bizarre
wardrobe of the city's kitsch bronze
talisman, Manneken-Pis.

Pageantry and flowers

The **Grand-Place ❶** is still the
city's forum, particularly in good
weather, when the pavement terraces of cafés such as Le Roy d'Espagne and La Chaloupe d'Or are
open and the square is the place to
see and be seen. A small-scale
Flower Market (Mar–Oct Tues–
Sun 8am–6pm) is a colourful event
adding a sweet fragrance to the air.
It's a quiet affair, as stallholders sit
and wait patiently for customers.
Their buckets and pots are always
full of magnificent blooms. The large
umbrellas, in traditional red and
green, do not merely provide protection from sun and rain: when they are
tipped at a right angle to the pavement it is a sign that business is bad.

The year ends with a European
Union **Christmas Market**, set up
for three weeks in December in the
Grand-Place with traditional Christmas arts and crafts from EU member
nations for sale, along with hot food

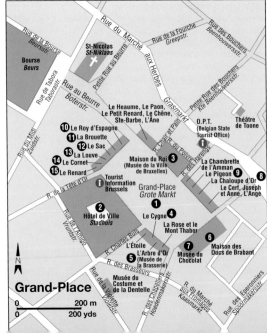

and drinks. In summer, street artists make a living from the tourists and in the evenings there is a *son-et-lumière* show.

For two days in the first week of July the Grand-Place is transformed into a dazzling scene from Renaissance times. The **Ommegang** – from the Dutch for "walk-around" – is a grand pageant which commemorates the entry into Brussels of the Habsburg Emperor Karel (Charles) V and his court in 1549 to present the Order of the Golden Fleece to the Belgian nobility. Two thousand people dressed in period costume – nobles, guildsmen, soldiers, peasants, standard bearers and jesters – process from the Place du Grand Sablon to the Grand-Place, and parade before the king, the royal family and city dignitaries. Some re-enactors, resplendent in red-black-and-yellow uniforms, parade on giant stilts, while others perform elaborate displays of flag-waving and horsemanship.

After dark the ancient cobbled square becomes filled with coloured lights, dancing, music and fireworks. The event is hugely popular. To get a rare seat on the Grand-Place for the finale, you need to book through the tourist office about six months ahead (and even then you'll need to be lucky). At heart, the Ommegang is a festival that traditionally provided the cream of Brussels society with the chance to lord it over the peasants. But for today's descendants of the original aristocrats, notables and guildsfolk, it is simply a parade of sumptuous costumes.

Another major event is the **Tapis des Fleurs**. Every two years in August (2006, 2008), on the weekend closest to the 15th of the month, the historic cobblestones of the Grand-Place are covered with an elaborate floral carpet made out of some 2 million begonias, occupying 1,860 sq. metres (20,000 sq. ft), spread out by the city's gardeners and florists. The begonias, chosen for their hardiness, are grown in Ghent, the world's largest producer. The composition of the floral carpet, which incorporates city emblems and motifs, can best be viewed from the balconies of the Hôtel de Ville or from the upper windows of the Grand-Place cafés.

Map on page 86

Christmas comes to the Grand-Place in the form of a giant fairylit tree and nativity scene, part of the three-week EU Christmas fair.

BELOW: the Ommegang.

Elaborately sculpted fountains stand in the Town Hall courtyard.

BELOW: waiting for custom outside the Hôtel de Ville.

Gothic masterpiece

With its soaring bell tower, the **Hôtel de Ville ②** (Town Hall; guided tours in English Apr–Sept, Tues and Wed 3.15pm, Sun 10.45am and 12.15pm; Oct–Mar, Tues and Wed 3.15pm; tel: 02-279 43 65; admission charge), on the long southern face of the square, is one of the finest Gothic buildings still standing. Along with that of Bruges, it represents one of the most beautiful examples of town-hall architecture in a country famous for its municipal buildings (the town halls of Leuven and Ghent were completed later and have Renaissance features). Air pollution took its toll, but after a major clean-up the once black and grimy facades and all 297 statues are gleaming once more.

Construction began at the start of the 15th century, a period of economic prosperity. Through its flourishing weaving industry, Brussels had gained wealth and status; the new town hall was to be a symbol worthy of this newly acquired importance. Its south wing, ascribed to master builder Jacob van Thiemen, was completed in 1404. The north wing was added in 1444 by an unknown craftsman. The central tower, which is 96 metres (307 ft) high, was designed by Jan van Ruysbroek. The lower rectangular section is not quite in the middle of the facade, and according to a spurious local legend, the builder threw himself from the top of the tower when he realised his "mistake". The openwork spire bears a massive gilt **Statue of the Archangel Michael**, one of the city's two patron saints. The bronze original survived the fire of 1695, but was replaced by a copy during the most recent restoration. If you climb the 400 steps to the top of the tower you will be rewarded by a spectacular view of the Grand-Place and the city beyond.

Between 1708 and 1717, Cornelis van Nerven rebuilt the section of the Town Hall between Rue de l'Amigo and Rue de la Tête d'Or in Louis XIV style. After its reconstruction, the building was used by the Brabant Estates until the annexation of Belgium by Revolutionary France in 1795.

The Town Hall **facade** is decorated with countless statues, including some fine examples of 14th- and 15th-century Brussels sculpture. Entering the courtyard, you notice two fountains. The one on the left, by Jan de Kinder (1714), represents the River Meuse, and the one on the right, by Pierre-Denis Plumiers (1715), symbolises the Scheldt. Inside, the **Grand Staircase** is decorated with busts of all Brussels' mayors since 1830, and the walls are hung with paintings from 1893 by Count Jacques Lalaing known collectively as *The Glorification of Municipal Power*. The ceiling fresco is entitled *Castle Keep, Defended by All Powers of the Town against Plague, Famine and War*.

Ceremonial rooms

In times past, citizens learned about local by-laws through formal procla-

mations from the Town Hall balcony. Another mural, entitled *To the Town and the World*, depicts an official reading a new regulation. The main Council Chamber, the **Gothic Hall**, retains its original fittings from the days when it was used for official ceremonies. Here the Dukes of Brabant took their oath of allegiance, swearing to uphold and defend the city's rights and privileges. The last such dedication took place on 21 September 1815. In the presence of the council of the States General, William I took the oath as King of the Netherlands. Originally the chamber was decorated with paintings by Rogier van der Weyden; these were destroyed during the 1695 bombardment.

Built in neo-classical style, the chamber was redesigned in the Gothic idiom in 1868. Tapestries adorning the walls depict the city's principal crafts and the guilds that practised them. These were created between 1875 and 1881 in Mechelen, at the workshops of Bracquenié. Former municipal council presidents are represented as gilt bronze statues in front of the columns. The windows illustrate the coats of arms of noble Brussels families.

The Town Hall wedding chamber has been completely restored. A large mural by Cardon depicts, in the middle, the City of Brussels presiding over marriage. On the left stands the Law and on the right, Justice. The coats of arms of the old guilds can be seen on the ceiling, recalling the fact that the heads of the nine corporations formed in 1421 from the assembly of craftsmen's guilds met here in council, with the representatives of the municipal authorities to decide – among other things – the affairs of the town. At the far end of the chamber a row of wooden statues represents famous citizens of the 14th, 15th and 16th centuries, among them the artist Rogier van der Weyden and Ludwig van Bodeghem, architect of the "Bread House" *(see page 90)*. The statues were carved by the Goyers brothers in Leuven. Guided tours take in offices of the mayor and councillors not normally open to the public, and the Brussels Tapestries from the 16th to 18th centuries.

Map on page 86

In 1998, the Grand-Place was added to UNESCO's list of World Cultural Heritage sites.

LEFT: every statue tells a story.

Rebels with Good Cause

In 1568, Count Egmont and Count Hoorn, leaders of the revolt against the Catholic policies pursued by Philip II in the Spanish Netherlands, were held in the Maison du Roi before their execution on the Grand-Place. Egmont had notably distinguished himself in Charles V's military campaigns before becoming dissatisfied with Spanish rule. Although his pleas for religious tolerance for the Protestants were to no avail, he remained loyal to the crown, refusing to side with Prince William I of Orange and suppressing Calvinist uprisings. But in 1567 Philip II dispatched the Duke of Alva to the Low Countries with 10,000 troops to crush his religious opponents once and for all. Backed by the Inquisition, the Duke set up the "Council of Disorders" (which became known as the Council of Blood). Egmont and Hoorn were both charged with high treason and beheaded on the Grand-Place; they were two of around 12,000 citizens who received death sentences.

In memory of the rebellion, statues of the two folk heroes were erected in front of the Maison du Roi; today they stand in the peaceful garden of the Place du Petit Sablon *(see page 135)*. The Maison du Roi itself bears a commemorative plaque to Egmont and Hoorn.

TIP

For a stay of several
days, it is worth getting
a Brussels Card from
the tourist office. The
pass, valid for three
days, offers discounts
on museum and
attraction admission
charges, and allows
free travel on public
transport.

BELOW: (from left to
right) the Maison du
Roi, guild houses
and the Maison des
Ducs de Brabant.

The Maison du Roi

Across the square from the Town Hall
stands the grand **Maison du Roi** ❸
(King's House), which has a long and
chequered history. At the end of the
12th century an earlier incarnation of
the building was the headquarters of
the bakers of Brussels and was
known as the Broodhuis ("Bread
House"). The bakers used it less and
less frequently and eventually abandoned it. In the 15th century a new
building was erected on the site
which became known as 't Hertogen-
huis (The Duke's House), since the
Duke of Brabant set up the high court
here. In about 1512 the building had
to be demolished because its clay
foundations gave way. The most distinguished architects of the day,
Antoon Keldermans, Ludwig van
Bodeghem and Heinrich van Prede,
were called in for the reconstruction.
The third building was again rechris-
tened under King Philip II, who had
the royal assizes installed here. Its
new designation, Pretorium Regium,
led to its current name, since it was
here that legal verdicts were pronounced in the name of the King of
Spain. In 1568, the counts of Egmont
and Hoorn, leaders of the opposition
to Philip II's vicious anti-Protestant
policies in the Spanish Low Countries, were held in the King's House
before their execution on the Grand-
Place *(see page 89)*.

Archduchess Isabella had the
Maison du Roi rebuilt in stone during the 17th century, dedicating it to
the Virgin Mary, whose statue can
still be seen today. During the 1695
attack on the city the building was
almost destroyed. Not until 1768 did
the authorities decide on its reconstruction, ignoring the original style.

After changing hands several
times, the Maison du Roi was
bought in 1860 by the municipal
authorities. They demolished and
rebuilt it as a neo-Gothic pastiche of
the original plans under the supervi-
sion of architect Victor Jamar, who
used old etchings in his search for
authenticity. A stone tablet in the
entrance hall records that the project
took from 1873 to 1896, longer than
the original building had done. The
facade is of Belgian limestone and
blue stone, the spire of oak covered

with slates. Like the Town Hall, the Maison du Roi has been cleaned of its surface grime and restored to its former glory – together they exemplify the shiny new public face of the city. The weather vane bears a loaf of bread and a crown, reflecting the building's two names – the Bread House and the King's House.

City of Brussels Museum

In 1887, Brussels transformed the Maison du Roi into the **Musée de la Ville de Bruxelles** (City of Brussels Museum; Tues–Sun 10am–5pm; admission charge), which traces the city's development from a Dark Ages village to the capital of Europe. The first and second floors spotlight the city's urban development and provide a historic over-view of life in the capital. There are fascinating glimpses of a Venice-like town clustered along the Senne river, which was paved over in the 19th century. Among the museum's most important exhibits, apart from collections illustrating aspects of the city's development and a selection of local decorative arts – tapestries, porcelain

and pottery – is a series of 26 paintings donated by an Englishman, John Waterloo Wilson. These include the *Allegory of the United Provinces* by N. Verkolie, *Still Life with Food* by Willem Glaesz Heda and *Portrait of a Clergyman*, attributed to Josse van Clece.

Two 16th-century Brussels works of art enrich the museum's collection: *The Wedding Procession*, which is attributed to Pieter Brueghel the Elder, and is a light-hearted take on peasant life, and *The Legend of Notre-Dame du Sablon*, which is probably the work of Barend van Orley. Don't miss the huge 15th-century **Saluces Altarpiece**, with its extraordinarily detailed niche carvings, and *The Marriage Proposal*, an 18th-century tapestry depicting the story of Clovis.

The museum also contains the original sculptures from the Town Hall facade, renovated in 1840. The second floor has a more kitsch display of the 750-plus costumes of Manneken-Pis, including army uniforms, football strips and a skintight Elvis suit.

Map on page 86

In 1873, the Rue des Brasseurs behind the Hôtel de Ville was the scene of a crime of passion. French poet Verlaine, somewhat the worse for drink, shot his lover and fellow poet, Rimbaud, who had threatened to leave him – an assault that cost him two years in prison.

BELOW: *The Wedding Procession* by Pieter Brueghel the Elder hangs in the City of Brussels Museum.

TIP

Brussels is officially bilingual, and the names of sites and streets are in both French and Dutch. However, as French-speakers are in the majority, this is the language most foreign visitors will attempt if they want to communicate with the locals. For this reason, most Brussels names in this book are given in French. In those places outside of the city in Flanders, where Dutch is the official language, place names are given in Dutch.

BELOW: monument to rebel folk hero Everard 't Serclaes.

Brussels hero

Just left of the Hôtel de Ville stands **L'Etoile** (The Star), one of the smallest buildings in the Grand-Place. During the 14th century it served as the chief justice's office. In 1852 it was demolished in a street-widening project, and rebuilt above an arcade in 1897. Under the arcade is a recumbent bronze statue of folk hero **Everard 't Serclaes**, who, in 1356, freed the city briefly from the tyrannical Counts of Flanders before being executed. The sculpture has been polished to a shine by passers-by who stroke its limbs to absorb some of the good luck he supposedly endows.

Butchers and brewers

Following the 1695 bombardment of the square, the prosperous craftsmen of Brussels commissioned the best architects of the day, most notably Guillaume de Bruyn and Antoine Pasteron, to rebuild the guild houses which had been destroyed. The guild houses, whose main function was the glorification of the guilds they represented, were built in Italo-Flemish baroque style. In the 17th century, most architects were primarily stonemasons, carpenters, painters or sculptors, and their original profession naturally influenced the style of building they favoured.

On the south side of the square, to the left of the Town Hall, is **Le Cygne ❹** (The Swan). Rebuilt in 1698, this house was the headquarters of the butchers' guild from 1720. Above the door is a carved swan with outstretched wings, and the three statues above the second floor symbolise Abundance, Agriculture and Slaughter. It was here that Friedrich Engels and Karl Marx founded the Workers' Association and planned *The Communist Manifesto*, following which the authorities requested Marx to leave the country. The house later became headquarters of the Belgian Workers' Party and finally of the Belgian Socialist Party. Today, it is occupied by the **Maison du Cygne**, an exclusive restaurant (*see page 97*).

The adjacent **L'Arbre d'Or ❺** (The Golden Tree) is owned by the

Map on page 86

brewers' guild, who took it over from the weavers. Before the introduction of piped water in the 19th century, most of the population drank beer – men, women and children alike. Not surprisingly, the brewers' guild was one of the richest. Three bas-reliefs between the storeys depict different aspects of the art of brewing: the vintage, the transport of beer and the hop harvest. Today, the building's cellars contain the small **Musée de la Brasserie** (Museum of Brewing; Apr–Nov daily 10am–5pm; Dec–Mar Sat–Sun noon–5pm; admission charge), displaying an old brewery with a collection of tools and implements. A glass of Belgian beer from the bar is included in the ticket price.

The next guild house, **La Rose** (The Rose), was owned during the 15th century by the Van der Rosen family. It has an unadorned facade typical of the burghers' houses from the end of the 17th century.

Grand ducal facade

The southeast side of the Grand-Place is occupied by a row of houses designed in 1698 by the architect Guillaume de Bruyn and unified by a single facade. Known collectively as the **Maison des Ducs de Brabant** ❻ (House of the Dukes of Brabant), the seven houses have such diverse individual names as **La Fortune** (Wealth), **Le Moulin à Vent** (The Windmill), **Le Pot d'Etain** (The Pewter Jug), **La Colline** (The Hill) and **La Bourse** (The Stock Exchange). Just as the King's House was never the residence of a monarch, no dukes ever lived in the House of the Dukes of Brabant. It got its name from the busts of 19 dukes that decorate the capitals of the Ionic columns along the facade.

One of Brussels' most convivial restaurants, **'t Kelderke**, occupies the cellar below No. 14 (see page 97). The small **Musée du Chocolat** ❼ (Cocoa and Chocolate Museum; Tues–Sun (Jul–Aug daily) 10am–4.30pm; admission charge) at No. 13 outlines the the origins of chocolate, the culture of cocoa and the processes of making Belgium's famous handmade chocolates. And of course there is the opportunity to sample and buy chocolate.

Le Cygne (The Swan), former home of the butchers' guild, is now a celebrated restaurant.

BELOW: gabled facades of the guild houses.

Brussels Lace

Brussels lace is world-famous. Developed during the 15th century and initially sewn onto the shirt collars and cuffs of the nobility, it soon became widespread. At one point, entire gowns were made of the precious fabric, which was particularly sought after at the royal courts in Paris and London. Queen Elizabeth I of England reputedly owned 3,000 lace dresses, and it is said that Empress Eugénie of France owned a lace gown which 600 women had toiled over for 10 months using a total of 90,000 bobbins.

By the second half of the 16th century, women throughout Belgium were engaged in the craft, and lace was exported to prosperous families all over Europe. At the end of the century there was scarcely a young girl, even in the most rural areas, who was not employed by lace merchants. During the 17th century, 22,000 women and girls worked as lacemakers; during the 19th century, the total reached 50,000. Brussels alone, the capital of lace production, employed some 10,000 women.

For fineness of thread and beauty of motif, Brussels lace was unsurpassed. The capital's churches and museums are full of examples of the delicate work produced. There is a particularly fine specimen at the Cinquantenaire Museum *(see page 160)*, a bedspread which Albert I and his wife Isabella received on the occasion of Albert's elevation to Duke of Brabant. Other masterpieces include the Virgin Mary's veil, on display in Notre-Dame du Sablon, and, in the Costume and Lace Museum *(see page 100)*, a lace bedspread decorated with an imperial eagle, which belonged to Emperor Charles V.

Production of large covers and entire robes was made possible when the technique of lacemaking moved away from the use of a single continuous thread towards knotting. Until then, only small pieces could be produced, the size determined by the length of thread wound on the bobbin. Joining individual motifs to produce a single large piece revolutionised the industry, allowing the creation of large-scale items with highly imaginative patterns within a relatively short time.

No lacemaker ever became rich or famous. The reward for their arduous work was determined by the lace merchants, and few were generous; the lacemakers often had to work in poorly lit, damp cellars where the thread would be less likely to break.

Brussels lace remained a symbol of luxury until well into the 18th century. Inevitably, fashions changed, and by the end of the 19th century the art of lacemaking in Belgium had fallen into decline. Today, few women possess the requisite skills. Two schools, in Mons and Binche, continue to train people in the art, but too few want to learn the intricacies of lacemaking to satisfy the increasing demand for handmade lace. Much of that now on sale in Brussels is made in China, and is cheaper but inferior in quality.

One of the largest lace merchants in Brussels is Manufacture Belge de Dentelles at 6–8 Galerie de la Reine, where a wide variety of antique and modern lace is on sale. No. 26 Grand-Place also houses a lace shop. ❑

LEFT: formerly the artist's guild, 26 Grand-Place now houses a lace shop.

The northeast side

Along the northeast side of the square, opposite the Town Hall, stand three 17th-century private houses, less elaborate than the other houses surrounding the square. The first, **Le Cerf** (The Stag), is named after the emblem on the shield mounted above the door. Today it houses a private club of the same name. The next two houses, **Joseph** and **Anna**, share a common facade and now house a confectioner's shop where you can buy traditional home-made chocolates. Next door stands **L'Ange** (The Angel). The lower section of its facade is decorated with Ionic columns, the upper section with Corinthian columns.

La Taupe (The Mole) and **La Chaloupe d'Or** ❽ or La Maison des Tailleurs (The Golden Rowboat or House of Tailors) – now one of the best bars on the Grand-Place – once belonged to the guild of tailors. They were also rebuilt to architect Guillaume de Bruyn's designs with a shared facade, Ionic columns below and Corinthian columns above. The door is guarded by a bust of St Barbara, patron saint of tailors, and above the gable is a statue – somewhat underdressed – of St Boniface, a native of Brussels.

Next door at No. 26, **Le Pigeon** ❾ (The Pigeon), formerly the artists' guild, now houses a lace shop. It has a classical facade with Doric columns at street level, Ionic columns on the first floor and Corinthian on the second. Victor Hugo lived here in 1852, after being exiled by Napoleon III. Radical penmanship, aimed squarely at his exiler, earned Hugo an invitation from the city fathers to leave town, who were afraid the aggrieved French emperor might send an army after him.

The last house before the Maison du Roi is **La Chambrette de l'Amman** (The Little Room of the Amman – a city magistrate of the Duke of Brabant), also known as The Brabant Arms because of the multiple coats of arms that decorate the classical facade.

The houses on the other side of the Maison du Roi – **Le Heaume** (Helmet), **Le Paon** (Peacock), **Le Petit Renard** (Little Fox), **Le**

TIP

Getting around by Brussels' metro is quick and efficient, but you won't see much (if you exclude the works of modern art that grace many metro stations). Brussels is not such a big city, so unless you're really pushed for time, you'd do better to go by tram or by bus, in that order – and, in the central zone around the Grand-Place, on foot.

BELOW: La Chaloupe d'Or on the Grand-Place is a Brussels institution.

Chêne (Oak Tree), **Ste-Barbe** (St Barbara) and **L'Ane** (Donkey) – have no specific classical elements. They all house restaurants.

Grandest of guild houses

The most impressive row of guild houses lines the western side of the square. The first house after the Rue au Beurre is the **Roy d'Espagne** ❿ (King of Spain). This particularly fine building was originally commissioned by the bakers' guild, one of the wealthiest corporations in the city, as its headquarters. Named after the bust of King Carlos II of Spain, flanked by Moorish and Indian prisoners, on the second storey, the building is still also known as the Bakers' Hall. Completed in 1697 in classical style, it is thought to have been designed by the sculptor Jean Cosyn. A bust of Bishop Aubert, patron of bakers, decorates the doorway. This is the most famous and atmospheric of the Grand-Place bars.

Medallions depicting the Roman emperors Marcus Aurelius, Nerva, Decius and Trajan adorn the first-floor wall. On the balustrade above the bust of Carlos II stand six statues representing the elements needed to make bread: energy, grain, wind, fire, water and prudence.

The next guild house, the classical-style **La Brouette** ⓫ (The Wheelbarrow), served as the meeting-place of the city's tallow makers. The Corinthian columns on the third floor are roofed in by a gable, under which stands a statue of St Gilles, patron saint of tallow makers.

Le Sac ⓬ (The Sack) was the carpenters' and coopers' guild house. The lower section, which is classical in style, escaped destruction in 1695, and was restored by a master craftsman named Antoon Pastorana. Above the main entrance is the likeness of a man carrying a sack into which a second person is putting his head.

The next house, **La Louve** ⓭ (The She-Wolf), was also only partly destroyed in the French bombardment. It was rebuilt in Italo-Flemish style and acquired by the guild of archers. Decorative elements on the first-floor facade allude to the art of archery, and the balcony is decorated with cranks and quivers. In front of

TIP

There is invariably something happening on the Grand-Place, but in the absence of any planned event, people-watching from one of the open-air cafés is as good a spectacle as any.

BELOW:
street artists are a Grand-Place fixture.

each column on the second floor is a statue, above which an inscription has been added. The house owes its name to the carved relief of the she-wolf with Romulus and Remus, the twin founders of Rome. The female statue on the far left is holding an open book; accompanied by an eagle, she represents Truth. The inscription reads "The pillar of the kingdom". The next figure is False-hood; she is accompanied by a fox and carries a mask; her inscription reads "The nation's pitfalls". Then comes Peace, carrying a bundle and surrounded by doves, with the inscription "The salvation of man-kind". The statue on the extreme right is Discord; since her inscription pronounces her to be "The ruin of the republic", she has wolves at her feet and carries a torch. Dominating all is a golden phoenix with out-spread wings, bearing the inscription: "Charred, I returned more glorious through the efforts of the Guild of Sebastian".

Le Cornet ⓮ (The Horn), bought by the the river boatmen's guild in 1434, is one of the most original houses on the square. It was destroyed in 1695 and rebuilt in Italo-Flemish style again by Pastorana, who designed the gable in the form of a ship stern and decorated the upper part of the facade with nautical symbols. Beneath the gallery is a row of fish-like sea-gods and above the central window is the horn that gives the building its name.

The last house before Rue de la Tête d'Or, **Le Renard** ⓯ (The Fox), was rebuilt by the haberdashers' guild in 1699. The various bas-reliefs on the facade represent the haberdash-ers' trade and include a stone mer-chant, a dyer's shop, a fabric shop and children preparing hides.

Five statues decorate the first-floor facade: the central figure personifying Justice is blindfolded, and bears a sword in one hand and scales in the other. The remaining statues symbolise Europe, Asia, Africa and America. At the second-floor level are four caryatids which double as supporting pillars. A statue of St Nicholas, patron saint of haberdashers, stands on the crest of the gable. ❏

Map on page 86

Neuhaus sells unbeatable pralines at extravagant prices and has branches all over town, including one at 27 Grand-Place.

RESTAURANTS & CAFÉS

Restaurants

La Maison du Cygne
2 Rue Charles Buls.
Tel: 02-511 82 44.
Open: L & D Mon–Fri;
D only Sat. €€€€
In a sumptuous 17th-century guild house on the Grand-Place, this *chic et cher* restaurant affords good views over the square from window tables. The menu hon-ours Franco-Belgian haute cuisine, and rich items like foie gras and truffles. All the panelled dining rooms have their own charm, but the most appealing is probably the romantic first-floor room.

't Kelderke
15 Grand-Place.
Tel: 02-513 73 44.
Open: L & D daily. €€
This bustling traditional restaurant, which stays open late, is great for plain, hearty Belgian fare such as mussels, Flem-ish stews, black pudding, herring and sole meu-nière. All these and more are served up in copious amounts by friendly wait-ers in a convivial vaulted cellar below the square.

Cafés and bars

The Grand-Place boasts a number of fine cafés which, inevitably given the prime location, are not exactly cheap and are often overrun with tourists. But they are still worth a visit, and there's no better place to sit out-doors in fine weather. The elegant old bakers' guild house on the west side of the square is now a traditional *estaminet* (inn), **Le Roy d'Espagne** *(No. 1)*, with galleried nooks and crannies over-looking the picturesque bustle below. Its only seri-ous rival, on the north side and hemmed in by lace and chocolate shops, is **La Chaloupe d'Or** *(No. 24–25).* For-merly the tailors' guild house, it has an elegant gabled facade, a cosy, burnished interior and relaxed service.

● ● ● ● ● ● ● ● ● ● ● ●
Price includes dinner and half a bottle of house wine.
€ under €30, €€ €30–45, €€€ €45–60, €€€€ €60 +

THE LOWER CITY

A walk through part of the old city centre
takes in everything from the Comic Strip
Museum to the cathedral – and some of
the best seafood restaurants in town

Map
on page
100

Encircling the medieval heart of Brussels around the Grand-Place and the old port, this part of town was the original – and at the time, marshy – settlement of Brussels, with the present Stock Exchange set close to the site of the first feudal castle. As the pivot of the Old Town, the picturesque Grand-Place signifies the glorification of civic spirit and the guilds. As for the port, unlike most capital cities, Brussels has buried its river underground. Although paved over, the river is still reflected in the city's gabled quaysides and quaint seafood restaurants. At heart, this part of Brussels can still feel like a backwater, with its sleepy squares, quiet gardens, underrated art museums and old-fashioned cafés.

The historic core of the "Flemish Old City" occupies the area around the Grand-Place known as the Ilot Sacré (Holy Isle), the liveliest part of town, well known for its restaurants. The recent renovation of historic buildings adds to its charm. Close to the Grand-Place is Rue du Marché aux Herbes, a narrow street lined with small shops and grand mansions that have survived the rigours of more than three centuries, and are now protected by a preservation order. The street was once the link between the city port and the ducal castle on lofty Place Royale. The national tourist office, the Belgian Tourist Information Centre, is at No. 63 (the city's tourist office, Brussels International Tourism, is in the Hôtel de Ville on the Grand-Place).

Beyond the Grand-Place

The **Grand-Place ❶**, with its café terraces and inspired architecture, makes a welcoming introduction to the city *(see previous chapter)*. Since most sites people want to visit are within a compact area, it's best to explore the Lower City on foot,

LEFT: Le Cirio, a landmark *fin de siècle* café.
BELOW: mural by Schuiten on the Rue Marché au Charbon.

TIP

The Poechenellekelder tavern opposite Manneken-Pis is worth a visit for its "olde worlde" charm and its collection of theatre marionettes.

starting from here. Exit the Grand-Place on Rue Charles Buls, noting on your left as you pass under the arch a recumbent bronze sculpture of **Everard 't Serclaes** (see page 92). Next to the statue is an Art Nouveau monument to **Charles Buls**, artist, man of letters and Mayor of Brussels from 1881 to 1899, who initiated the restoration of the Grand-Place and other areas of the city (a statue of him also sits, with his dog, on a bench on Place de l'Agora, at the top end of Rue du Marché aux Herbes – pictured on page 108). At the point where Rue Charles Buls runs into

Rue de l'Etuve, turn left to 4–6 Rue de la Violette, to the **Musée du Costume et de la Dentelle 2** (Costume and Lace Museum; Thur–Fri and Mon–Tues 10am–12.30pm and 1.30–5pm, Sat–Sun 2–5pm; admission charge), in two combined, gabled 18th-century houses. Lace was once a vitally important industry in Brussels (see page 94), with 10,000 lacemakers working here in the 19th century, and the museum reflects this with an array of antique lace creations (along with pieces from other Belgian lacemaking centres) and high-society dresses from the 16th to

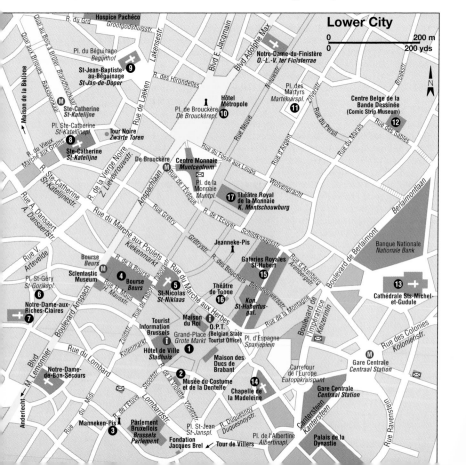

Lower City

0   200 m
0   200 yds

19th centuries. The ground floor hosts temporary costume exhibitions. Most lace pieces, including veils, religious vestments and reliquary coverings, are on view in cupboards and display cases upstairs.

Jacques Brel

If you're an admirer of the great Belgian singer-songwriter Jacques Brel (1929–78), you'll find it worthwhile to continue up Rue de la Violette, and across Place St-Jean to Place de la Vieille Halle aux Blés, a neat little square whose old Flemish houses have been refurbished. The **Fondation Brel** (Tues–Sat 11am–6pm) at No. 11, run by Brel's daughter, is a museum and information resource on Brel's life and career. Then, you can perhaps make a short detour on Rue de Villers to see the 12th-century **Tour de Villers**, a remnant of the original city walls.

Celebrity statue

Southwest of the Town Hall, on Rue de l'Etuve, stands the celebrated (and disappointingly small) **Manneken-Pis ❸**, the spirit of Brussels incar-nated in a bronze fountain in the shape of a naked boy peeing. The sculptor's inspiration is unknown but subject to inventive speculation. The best-known theory maintains that during the battle of Ransbeke in 1142, Godfried of Lorraine's son was hung in his cradle from an oak tree to give the soldiers courage. At some stage in the battle, he escaped his cradle unaided and was discovered urinating against the tree. The conclusion drawn from this action is that even as a child, he demonstrated his unswerving courage.

Another story tells of a Brussels nobleman's son who, at the age of five, cheekily left a procession in order to relieve himself. One variant has it that a wicked witch put a spell on the child because he dared to urinate against the wall of her house. She turned him to stone, thus condemning him to urinate forever.

The statue escaped damage during the city bombardment in 1695, but it was later stolen on a number of occasions. In 1745 it was captured by the British and two years later by the French, but was always recovered.

Map on page 100

The Manneken-Pis, in one of his many guises, performs dutifully for tourists.

BELOW: serving a thirsty crowd outside the Poechenellekelder.

The Fashion Trail

Belgian fashion has finally emerged from the backwoods. Until recently, Brussels had a respectable history of producing refined leatherwear, rather matronly womenswear, and prim children's clothes. Bruxellois with any fashion sense saved up for French, Italian or other foreign designs. However, Flemish fashion supremacy and superior marketing skills have brought more colour and creativity to the streets of Brussels. The results, pioneered by Antwerp-trained designers, but influenced by the increasingly multicultural nature of Brussels, display plenty of flair and a refreshing self-confidence.

While Avenue Louise is the place for mainstream fashion and foreign designer boutiques, and the Rue Neuve district focuses on cheaper clothes, the city centre welcomes both radical Flemish chic and more conservative French fashion goods. There remains a place for certain Brussels stalwarts – boutiques often housed in the appealingly traditional city galleries. The most charming, Galerie de la Reine, is home to Delvaux (No. 31), purveyor of hats, handbags and luggage to the Belgian court since 1883. As the main rival to Hermès, Delvaux has also provided elegant hand-made bags to countless generations of well-heeled local matrons and Eurocrats' wives. Yet a startling comparison between old and new Brussels lies just a few streets away. Elvis Pompilio (29 Rue des Pierres) is an outrageous hat-maker with an international reputation for quirky fun, from frothy, feathery couture concoctions to Basque berets (*see page 37*).

A stone's throw from the Bourse is Rue Antoine Dansaert, the style mecca for those in search of cutting-edge Flemish design. Set in the fashionable St-Géry area, the street is dotted with School of Antwerp boutiques, linked to designers who trained in Belgium's most prestigious fashion college. Olivier Strelli (No. 44) is an established Belgian designer who embraces a classic yet contemporary look.

Further along the street, Stijl (No. 74) is a sparsely modernist showcase to Flemish fashion featuring both menswear and womenswear. Here, Dries van Noten, Belgium's most famous designer, favours natural fabrics and classic design infused with a mildly ethnic look, inspired by a different country every season.

Olivier Theyskens, the young star of the Belgian fashion firmament, is the only *haute couture* designer, and numbers Madonna amongst his clientele. Couture prices are justified by well-cut, chic and feminine clothes. The popular Ann Demeulemeester chooses close-fitting fabrics, often in pure wool. By contrast, Dirk Bikkembergs is obsessed with detail, new techno fabrics, and a faintly bondage look. Martin Margiela, one of the most radical designers, sews blank labels into his clothes as an anti-design statement. Other home-grown talents making waves on the international fashion scene include Raf Simons, Véronique Branquinho and Xavier Delcour.

Before leaving Rue Dansaert, most fashion victims retreat to equally stylish Flemish eateries or bars, beginning with Bonsoir Clara or L'Archiduc (*see pages 116–17*). ❏

LEFT: Kaat Tilley, known for her floaty fairy-tale dresses, has a shop in Galerie du Roi.

As compensation for the French theft, Louis XV, who was in Brussels at the time, presented the statue with a costume of precious gold brocade. The king had the culprits arrested and honoured the Manneken-Pis with the title of Knight of St Louis.

In 1817, a newly released convict stole the statue, which was later recast to create the bronze replica. The Manneken-Pis was returned to its original site on the 6 December 1818, where it can still be seen today. On holidays, the statue is dressed in extravagant costumes. On 6 April, he sports an American GI's uniform to recall the anniversary of the United States' involvement in World War I. On 3 September, he is dressed as a Welsh Guard to celebrate their liberation of Brussels in 1944. On 15 September, the boy becomes a British Royal Air Force pilot, in remembrance of the Battle of Britain during World War II. In all, the statue possesses around 750 costumes, among them an Elvis costume, and they are stored in the Musée de la Ville de Bruxelles on the Grand-Place.

God and Mammon

Leaving Manneken-Pis, the Rue des Grands Carmes leads to Rue du Marché au Charbon, known for its Latin American bars and restaurants, and the church of **Notre-Dame-de-Bon-Secours** (Our Lady of Succour), built in 1664 by Jean Cortvriendt in a baroque Flemish Renaissance style. It contains a statue of the Holy Virgin that is reputed to have miraculous powers.

From here, head north on Rue du Marché au Charbon and Rue du Midi to the **Bourse ❹** (Stock Exchange) in Rue Henri Maus, the centre of Brussels' financial life. The first Brussels stock exchange was established in 1801. Once the city councillors became aware of the importance of such an institution, they decided to erect a grand building on the former site of a convent, which had been demolished to make way for the new boulevard that cut across the city from north to south. Léon Suys, one of the capital's most distinguished architects, supervised construction of this imposing temple of Mammon, between 1871 and

Map on page 100

TIP

A good place to keep the kids entertained on a rainy afternoon is the Scientastic Museum (Bourse metro, open 2–5.30pm on weekends and school holidays). Try your hand at any of the 80 amusing hands-on exhibits: make your voice sound like a duck, fly like a bird or sit cross-legged like a fakir.

BELOW: statues on the ornate stock exchange facade.

In 1985, Belgian feminists demanded a female version of the Manneken-Pis, to create an equilibrium in the world of urinating statuary. A new statue was commissioned; Jeanneke-Pis now squats in Impasse de la Fidelité, off Rue des Bouchers.

BELOW:
Dandoy, for the best biscuits in Brussels.

1873. The inspiration of this vast rectangular structure may have been neo-classical, but the lavish ornamentation is a far cry from neo-classical simplicity. At the main entrance, a colonnade of six Corinthian columns supports a triangular tympanum decorated with a garland of fruits and flowers, above which sits a figure representing Belgium. Statues by Rodin adorn the top.

The Bourse is not open to visitors, except over one weekend in September during La Journée du Patrimoine (Monument Day), when certain buildings open their doors to the public. Call the tourist office for more information *(see page 231)*.

Around the Bourse are several landmark cafés. **Le Falstaff** (25 Rue Henri Maus) is a glorious example of Belgian Art Nouveau and was once the haunt of intellectuals and artists, while **Le Cirio** (18 Rue de la Bourse) is a *fin de siècle* temple (formerly an Italian deli); large, dark and fraying at the edges *(see page 117)*.

Before leaving the area, take a peek inside the little **Eglise St-Nicolas** ❺ (St Nicholas church).

Dedicated to the patron saint of shopkeepers, this quaint early Gothic church on the corner of Rue au Beurre has a colourful history, dating back to the foundation of the city. The gloomy interior is panelled with wood and decorated with notable paintings – the *Virgin with Sleeping Child* is attributed to Rubens. A copper shrine in front of the pulpit recalls the Martyrs of Gorcum, put to death in Brielle (near Rotterdam) in 1572 after suffering horrific torture at the hands of the Gueux (Protestant Dutch "Sea Beggars"). Worth a closer look is the sinuous shape of the facade, which follows the line of the paved-over Senne river.

Just around the corner, at 31 Rue au Beurre, is the old-fashioned *biscuiterie* **Dandoy**, a true Brussels institution. Among other mouthwatering sweet treats, Dandoy specialises in *speculoos* – traditional spicy biscuits made with cinnamon, ginger, brown sugar and almonds, and baked in wooden moulds – and *pain à la grecque* – spicy caramelised pastries.

Brussels' birthplace

The Stock Exchange borders **Boulevard Anspach**, one of the city's busiest thoroughfares. These boulevards, designed in Parisian Haussmann style, were fashionable in the mid-19th century, a time of Belgian prosperity and self-confidence. Then, the bourgeoisie congregated in the cafés and eclectic palaces designed in Flemish Renaissance style. Today, the uninspiring boulevard is lined with cinemas and shops.

Cross over the boulevard to the short Rue Jules van Praet, which leads to **Place St-Géry** ❻, a chic and animated focal point of what is still something of down-at-heel quarter. The red-brick building in the middle of the square, the restored 1881 Flemish Renaissance

Marché St-Géry, was once a covered meat market in what was the heart of the city in the Middle Ages, and is now the centrepiece of a revived district. An original attempt during the early 1990s to re-establish it as Les Halles St-Géry, a home for bijoux boutiques and cafés, failed to take off. As a cultural centre it now hosts diverse exhibitions and has a cool café inside. Outside, trendy cafés and restaurants line the surrounding square and neighbouring streets, creating a scene that buzzes with life at weekends well into the wee small hours. This restored and now fashionable quarter, part of a socially complex urban renewal project, is more Flemish than French in character.

Place St-Géry occupies one of a cluster of former islands in the Senne river, which once flowed through the heart of the city. It was here, in 977, that Charles Duke of Lorraine built a fortress around which Brussels grew. Paintings in the Musée de la Ville de Bruxelles *(see page 91)* depict a changing, Venetian-style scene on these islands, with houses stacked up along their shores, lapped by water. In the 19th century, the river was deemed a health hazard following several outbreaks of cholera, and the decision was made to channel it underground. It was bricked over to make way for the *grands boulevards*.

Behind the Halles is the Lion St-Géry restaurant, and an entrance to a cobbled courtyard dating from 1811 where bricked-up arches indicate what became of the Senne. An open segment of tunnel allows you a glimpse of the subterranean river, in a pool of water that has goldfish swimming in it and coins thrown in for good luck.

Place St-Géry to Place Ste-Catherine

Leave the square on Rue de la Grande Ile, which outlines the shore of one of the long-lost islands in the Senne, and turn right into Rue des Riches Claires where you'll find the 17th-century church and convent of **Notre-Dame aux-Riches-Claires** ❼. This fine baroque church is the work of Luc Fayd'herbe (1617–97), a pupil of Rubens, and a renowned sculptor

Map on page 100

TIP

Those with a sweet tooth should visit the old-fashioned *biscuiterie* Dandoy at 31 Rue au Beurre (opposite the Hotel Amigo, just off the Grand-Place). The prettily packaged *speculoos* biscuits are a nice gift or souvenir. Or throw caution to the wind and sink your teeth into one of their cream-laden waffles dispensed from an outside window.

BELOW: the converted St-Géry market hall is the social hub of a vibrant district.

This bronze statue at the northern end of the old canal strip is dedicated to the messenger pigeons used by the Belgian military in World War I.

famous for his huge statues that adorn church pillars. The ornate gables represent a typical Brussels interpretation of the Italian Renaissance style.

Follow the curving Rue St-Christophe north to its junction with Rue des Chartreux, and cross over to tree-lined Rue du Vieux Marché aux Grains – where you can pick up artisanal cheeses at Crèmerie de Linkebeek or have a snack at the traditional Brussels restaurant Le Paon Royal next door. Then cross **Rue Antoine Dansaert** – the epicentre of hip and happening Brussels, lined with designer boutiques, trendy restaurants and bars – to Place Ste-Catherine.

The old port and fish market

The area referred to as **Place Ste-Catherine ❽** is a quaint bohemian corner of the old town, centred around the Eglise Ste-Catherine and the cobbled strip between Quai aux Briques (brick quay) and Quai au Bois à Brûler (firewood quay). From the 16th century until the mid-19th century, Brussels was connected to Antwerp and the North Sea by means

of a canal, once busy with river traffic carrying shipments of bricks, beer, wood, salt, grain and fish to and from the capital. The quays, lined with warehouses, thronged with dockers loading and unloading their cargoes. With the spread of the railways and the constant threat of flooding, the canal was finally closed in 1853. The basin was filled in and covered over to form a square (in fact, more of a rectangle), which became the site for the city fish market until 1955. Two rectangular pools are a faint echo of the busy commercial harbour that once connected Brussels with the sea.

Today, this breezy, endearing quarter – part gentrified, part shabby – is home to some of the best seafood restaurants in Brussels. Each one has its own covered terrace on the cobbles. This is a good place for lunch, but it's more atmospheric in the evening when the restaurants and terraces are all lit up. An increasing number of trendy bars and galleries are popping up in the area – a knock-on effect from the neighbouring St-Géry quarter – but the square retains its quayside atmosphere, particularly

during the weekly fish market, and many of the traditional cafés, shops and restaurants in the surrounding streets survive. But for how long is anyone's guess.

Home of the Black Virgin

Looming over the quays is the **Eglise Ste-Catherine** (Mon–Sat 8.30am–5.30pm, Sun 1–5.30pm), an eclectic blend of Romanesque, Gothic and Renaissance elements designed by Joseph Poelaert of Palais de Justice fame *(see page 136)*. The original 17th-century church was destroyed in 1850; all that remains is the baroque tower. The interior contains a painting of the saint and a famous sculpture called the Black Madonna dating from the 14th century; originally made of limestone, it has blackened with time. The church has survived numerous proposals to demolish it on the grounds of its questionable aesthetic merit.

Behind the church stands the **Tour Noire** (Black Tower), a rare piece of the original medieval city wall that was restored in 1888–9 and is now, controversially, engulfed by a hotel.

Nearby, Flemish Renaissance gabled houses line the surviving quaysides of Quai aux Briques and Quai au Bois à Brûler. Rue Ste-Catherine and Rue de Flandre display similar facades. On the latter, at no. 46, stands the flamboyant **Maison de la Bellone**, among the grandest baroque patrician residences in Brussels. It dates from the early 18th century and was designed by Jean Cosyn, one of the principal architects and sculptors of the Grand-Place. Encrusted with classical motifs, the facade and court-yard are among the loveliest in the city. It is now home to a French-speaking cultural centre (the Maison du Spectacle, Tues–Fri 10am–6pm; free) which houses a theatre, exhibition centre and offices of various cultural organisations. Performances are in French, but non-French-speakers can appreciate classical recitals and contemporary dance staged in this exquisite space.

The large fountain between the quays at the top end of the fish market square depicts St Michael slaying the devil and is known as the **Anspach Monument**. It was erected

Beyond Brussels' tourist traps and the simpler brasseries, it is usually best to reserve a table to avoid disap-pointment.

BELOW: the boutiques on Rue Dansaert showcase Belgium's top designers.

BELOW: statue of Charles Buls, former mayor of Brussels, Place de l'Agora (see page 111).

in memory of Jules Anspach, mayor of Brussels between 1863 and 1879 and the prime mover behind the construction of the city centre's grand avenues. Beside the Anspach Fountain, the Square des Blindés is dedicated to Belgium's armoured forces (although it also has a monument to the heroic carrier pigeons of World War I, *pictured on page 106*).

Rococo masterpiece

Turn right into Rue du Grand Hospice then Rue du Béguinage, which leads to the restored **Eglise St-Jean-Baptiste-au-Béguinage ❾** (Tues–Sat 10am–5pm, Sun 10am–8pm), one of the city's loveliest churches. Set in a former convent, the exuberant basilica is dedicated to St John the Baptist. Originally a Gothic basilica, it was rebuilt in the 17th century and now radiates Belgian rococo style, with onion domes, turrets and rich ornamentation. An 18th-century high altar as well as paintings from the Rubens school adorn the interior. In accordance with Low Countries tradition, a *béguinage* was a community of lay nuns, pious women who

never took the vows of chastity, poverty and obedience. In its heyday, the Beguine community in Brussels was home to 1,200 lay nuns, but was dissolved in the 19th century.

Behind the church, the short Rue de l'Infirmerie leads to a tree-lined square which fronts the huge neo-classical **Grand Hospice Pacheco**. It was built in the 1820s on the site of the former infirmary of the Beguine convent, to provide shelter for the poor and destitute. Despite the austerity of the building (which is closed to the public), it makes for a peaceful and harmonious spot.

Belle époque grandeur

Rue des Hirondelles leads east from the church of Saint-Jean-Baptiste to spacious **Place de Brouckère**, named after Charles de Brouckère, one of the founding fathers of the 1831 Belgian constitution. The square is seen at its best at night, when neon signs and street lamps bathe it in a flood of light, and locals fill the surrounding cinemas, bars and cafés. Its highlight is the grand **Hôtel Métropole ❿**; the glittering

The Ninth Art

La bande dessinée, the comic strip, is a cult in Belgium. Known as the Ninth Art, it is celebrated in comic shops, museums, metro stations and on city walls. Since Hergé created Tintin in 1929, the mainstream Belgian media have elevated comic books to high art. Tintin's success was phenomenal. He and his band of followers – Snowy, Captain Haddock, the Thompson Twins and the absent-minded Professor Calculus – became household names across the globe, and their adventures have been translated into no fewer than 50 languages. The baton has been passed to Brussels-based François Schuiten, the country's major comic-strip artist.

French Renaissance foyer, mirrored halls and public suites dripping with chandeliers provide a *belle époque* refuge in one of the city's most hurried districts. Once here, don't miss the chance to stop for a drink at the sumptuous *fin de siècle* café.

Martyrs' monument

Two blocks beyond the hotel, on Rue Neuve, is the baroque church of **Notre-Dame-du-Finistère**, built in 1708 and worth visiting for its elaborately decorated interior.

Continue across **Rue Neuve**, a brash and bustling pedestrian street packed with shops, boutiques and the City 2 shopping mall, and you reach **Place des Martyrs ⓫**, a charming neo-classical square dedicated to the martyrs of Belgium's struggle for independence from the Netherlands. The square, which had fallen into a state of total disrepair, has undergone a major restoration of the typical Brussels *façadisation* variety *(see page 45)*, which meant ripping out interiors and replacing them with modern fittings while retaining and restoring the original facades.

The symmetrical layout was devised by the architect Claude Fisco in 1755. In the centre is a monument dedicated to the memory of the 450 "martyrs" who died fighting the Dutch during the 1830 revolution. The crypt, in which these war victims were laid to rest, was consecrated on 4 October 1830. The white marble statue that rises above it is by Willem Geefs and symbolises the newly founded Belgian state.

Comic virtues

Take the eastern exit from the square, Rue du Persil, at the end of which a quick left-right shuffle brings you to Rue des Sables. At No. 20 is the **Centre Belge de la Bande Dessinée ⓬** (Comic Strip Museum; Tues–Sun 10am–6pm; admission charge). The building is a stunning example of Art Nouveau architecture by the famous Belgian architect Victor Horta (1861–1947) *(see pages 147–8)*. Known as Magazins Waucquez, the warehouse and shop premises opened in 1906, run by a fabric merchant named Waucquez. Customers entered a fine portal and then mounted the

Map on page 100

For lots of Tintin paraphernalia, visit La Boutique de Tintin just off the Grand-Place (13 Rue de la Colline).

BELOW: the Comic Strip Museum is housed in a converted Art Nouveau building.

sweeping staircase to the sales floors which were lit as far as possible by natural light. Today, these same stairs serve as the launching pad for the red-and-white rocket which Tintin and Snowy used to reach "Destination Moon" long before Neil Armstrong and Buzz Aldrin managed the feat.

The exhibitions inside feature some of the best-known characters and their creators, among them Belgium's own Smurfs, Lucky Luke and, of course, Tintin, created by the late Georges Remi, the initials of whose name, reversed and pronounced in French give you *errjée*, or Hergé as he preferred. A separate exhibition explains how animated cartoons are made, and includes drawings at every stage of development. As a believer in "art for everyone, art in everything", Victor Horta would doubtless have approved of this popular comic vision.

To the cathedral

Back outside the Comic Museum, climb the stairway and turn right on Boulevard de Berlaimont to the **Cathédrale Sts-Michel-et-Gudule**

The patron saint of Brussels is St Michael the Archangel, whose statue on the Hôtel de Ville spire spreads protective wings over the city. Yet residents have a special affection for St Gudula, joint patron of the cathedral, whose credentials suffered when the Vatican could find no record of her canonisation.

BELOW: Cathedral of St Michael and St Gudula.

❸ (Mon–Fri 8am–6pm, Sat–Sun 8.30am–6pm; admission charge), which rises majestically on the hillside between the Upper and Lower City, marking the boundary between the two. The monumental but over-restored Gothic cathedral stands on the site of a Carolingian baptistry, dedicated to the Archangel Michael. After the relics of St Gudula were placed here in 1047, the two saints came to be regarded as the joint patrons of the church. It is the city's principal place of worship, and for centuries has been the setting for grand state occasions.

Although work was begun on the present cathedral at the beginning of the 13th century, it was not completed until the end of the 15th. The building therefore exhibits a number of different architectural styles. Its recently completed restoration signalled the opening of the complete complex to the public for the first time, from the newly excavated Romanesque crypt to the choir.

The dimensions are impressive: the main body of the cathedral, 108 metres (345 ft) long by 50 metres (160 ft) wide, is flanked by twin 69-metre (220-ft) towers, which dominate the exterior. Inside, the triple-isled nave's clarity of form is equally impressive, characterised by 12 round columns and ribbed vaulting. The pillars are formed by statues of the Twelve Apostles. A typically Belgian baroque wooden pulpit, carved in 1699 by the Antwerp sculptor Hendrik Verbruggen, portrays the banishment of Adam and Eve from Paradise. Above them the Virgin Mary, with Jesus in her arms, crushes the head of the serpent at her feet.

Situated around the high altar are three monumental tombs: two are dedicated to Duke Johann of Brabant and his wife, Margaret of York, who died in 1312 and 1322 respectively. The third commemorates Archduke Ernst of Austria, Governor-General

THE LOWER CITY ◆ 111

of the Low Countries, who died in 1595. Behind the choir lies the **Chapel of St Mary Magdalene**, built in 1282 but remodelled in 1675 in baroque style. The alabaster altar originally stood in the Abbaye de la Cambre, which was destroyed in World War I by German forces.

To the right of the choir, the Gothic **Chapel of Our Lady of Redemption** dates from the mid-17th century. The windows in this chapel portray scenes from the life of the Virgin Mary, together with donors and their patron saints. The sketches for these windows are attributed to van Thulden, a pupil of Rubens.

Splendid stained glass

The stained glass within the cathedral is particularly fine. The west window offers a superb depiction of the Last Judgement from 1528. The remarkable windows in the north and south transepts, with their luminous blue backgrounds, were designed by Bernard van Orley (1490–1541). The first shows Habsburg emperor Charles V and his wife, Isabella of Portugal, before a shrine containing

the Holy Sacrament; also depicted are their patrons, Charlemagne and St Elizabeth. The window was commissioned by Charles V himself.

The second window portrays Louis II of Hungary and his wife, Mary of Hungary, kneeling in front of the Holy Trinity, accompanied by St Louis and Our Lady. The window was donated by Mary of Hungary, the sister of Charles V and Regent of the Netherlands.

Books, prints and crafts

Just past the Carrefour de l'Europe and Gare Centrale, turn right downhill on Rue de la Madeleine, where the small but handsome Gothic **Chapelle de la Madeleine** ⓮, from 1697, is worth visiting. Second-hand and antiquarian book enthusiasts might want to divert uphill a short way, to browse in the 1848 **Galerie Bortier**. Athough the gallery was designed by the same Jean-Pierre Cluysenaer who created the Galeries Royales St-Hubert *(see page 112)*, it's not as well known. Downhill, at **Place de l'Agora**, a sculpture of Charles Buls, Mayor of Brussels for

Map on page 100

The cathedral's 16th-century stained glass is superb.

BELOW: Chez Léon, a reliable bet for mussels and chips in the Ilôt Sacré.

The "Stomach of Brussels"

The pedestrianised area between the Grand-Place and the Stock Exchange is known as the Ilot Sacré, named after a campaign to preserve it in the 1950s. This "Holy Isle" is now dedicated to profane feasting. The focus is Petite Rue des Bouchers, named after the butchers' shops that were based here in medieval times. As part of a medieval patchwork, this street of stepped gables and decorated doorways connects with the city's elegant galleries. Lined by lively restaurants, the picturesque street is known as the "Stomach of Brussels". Vegetarians may turn pale at the array of unskinned rabbits and glassy-eyed fish, but to meat-eaters these are tantalising displays. A dinner here is worth sampling, if only to experience the cosmopolitan nature of Brussels. Belgians themselves are quite happy to join tourists in a quest for the genuine Bruxellois restaurants that remain. Even within this tiny district, there are sections dedicated to Chinese, Greek and Italian cuisines, but the main streets essentially offer home-grown fare, ranging from classic *moules-frites* (mussels and chips) at Chez Léon to filling Flemish dishes at Aux Armes de Bruxelles *(see page 116)*.

The great philosopher Erasmus (c.1469–1536) acted as adviser to the young emperor Charles V. Returning home to Rotterdam after a few months in Anderlecht, he looked back nostalgically on his visit: "Ah... if only Brabant were not so far away!"

BELOW: a tour of Anderlecht's Musée de la Gueuze ends with a beer-tasting.

nearly 20 years during the 19th century, sits alongside his little dog, by the fountain in this square which hosts a weekend **Arts and Crafts Market** (Sat–Sun and public holidays 10am–6pm). Adjacent Rue de Montagne has some fine old Flemish Renaissance gabled houses, most of them converted to shops, offices and restaurants.

Shopping in style

Continue downhill on Rue du Marché aux Herbes and you'll see to your right the entrance to the **Galeries Royales St-Hubert** ⑮. In 1830, the city, embracing its new role as capital of the Kingdom of Belgium, dedicated the exclusive shopping arcades to its new royal family. King Léopold I laid the foundation stone in 1846.

The glass-roofed galleries, lined with shops, comprise the Galerie du Roi (King's Gallery), Galerie de la Reine (Queen's Gallery) and Galerie des Princes (Princes' Gallery). The elegant classical facade is decorated with columns and a central motif that proclaims *Omnibus omnia* –

everything for everyone. In its day, the Galeries Royales St-Hubert formed the largest shopping arcade in Europe and immediately became the haunt of fashionable society. The exclusive yet old-fashioned shops remain – including **Ganterie Italienne** for gloves, **Delvaux** for handbags and leather goods, and the *chocolaterie* **Neuhaus** – as well as several appealing cafés, among them **De l'Ogenblik, Taverne du Passage** and **Mokafé**. Just off the galleries, in Rue Montagne aux Herbes Potagères, lurks the nicotine-stained **A La Mort Subite**, the most authentic and old-fashioned of Brussels' beer halls.

There are four entrances to the galleries: on Rue des Bouchers, Rue du Marché aux Herbes, Rue de l'Ecuyer and Rue des Dominicains. Rue des Bouchers crosses **Petite Rue des Bouchers**, which is closed to traffic, and is known as the "Stomach of Brussels", as it's lined with restaurants *(see box on page 111)*. Just off Rue des Bouchers, at the end of a cul-de-sac called Impasse de la Fidelité, squats the female counter-

Anderlecht, a place apart

Once a traditional village lying southwest of Brussels, Anderlecht was transformed in the 19th century by industrialisation; its boundaries spread until it became a suburb of the capital. Today it is a rather run-down *commune* straddling the industrial Charleroi Canal, but it has a number of attractions and is only a short metro ride from the city centre. Football fans will recognise the name from RSC Anderlecht, formerly one of Europe's premier football teams, and if you happen to be visiting on a match day you'll be joined by hordes of fans on their way to the stadium. Otherwise, most tourists come here to see the **Maison d'Erasme** (31 Rue du Chapitre; Tues–Sun 10am–5pm; admission charge), dedicated to the great Renaissance scholar, Erasmus *(c.1469–1536)*. You can see his study, alongside works by Bosch, Dürer, Holbein and others. Near by, the **Anderlecht Béguinage**, a convent founded in 1252, is now a religious museum (Tues–Sun 10am–noon and 2–5pm; admission charge). The **Musée de la Gueuze** (56 Rue Gheude; Mon–Fri 9am–5pm, Sat 10am–5pm; admission charge) in the Cantillon Brewery is the city's sole surviving brewery for gueuze and lambic beers, which ferment without yeast. Tours and tastings are available.

part to Manneken-Pis, from 1985. The bronze **Jeanneke-Pis** makes water with as much verve as her brother-sculpture but with little of the grace and (so far at least) none of the history.

Marionette theatre

In Impasse Schuddeveld, a narrow cul-de-sac leading off Petite Rue des Bouchers, is the **Théâtre de Toone** ⓰ (tel: 02-511 71 37), a famous traditional puppet theatre. It first came to public notice in 1830 under Toone I, who invented the "Woltje", the Little Walloon, both a variant on mocking Mr Punch and the epitome of the cheeky Brussels street urchin, who has become an irreplaceable member of the cast. Dressed in a checked jacket with his cap set at a jaunty angle, he acts as the narrator, playing all the roles in the irreverent tales.

The old house in Impasse Schuddeveld was acquired by the Toone family in the 1960s and turned into a puppet theatre with a little bar and restaurant. An antique pianola dominates the entrance; if you put a five-franc piece into the slot, it will tinkle out some old tunes. The wooden tables and benches together with a Gothic fireplace give the restaurant a cosy atmosphere. There is also a museum with an assortment of old puppets, posters and manuscripts relating to the theatre's history, which is open only during intermissions in performances.

Plays are performed in the upstairs theatre in the *bruxellois* (*brusseleir*) dialect which evolved in the Marolles district at the heart of the old city. It's a mixture of French and Flemish with some Spanish expressions adopted from soldiers of the Duke of Alba. The dialect is used for most performances in the Toone theatre's repertoire, but this shouldn't put you off; you don't need to understand the language to enjoy the unashamedly bawdy performances – though they are more for adults than children.

National opera house

It's a short stroll from Petite Rue des Bouchers to Place de la Monnaie, the focal point of which is the **Théâtre Royal de la Monnaie** ⓱. The Brussels opera house occupies the site of

You don't need to understand the local dialect to enjoy the puppet plays staged at the Toone theatre.

BELOW: Galeries Royales Saint-Hubert.

TIP

Looking rather out of place opposite the fine old opera house, the modern Centre Monnaie block houses shops, snack bars and one of Brussels' main post offices.

the former royal mint, which struck coins for the Duchy of Brabant. After the mint was demolished in 1531, a spacious square was laid out. Jean-Paul Bombarda, Governor-General of the Low Countries, had the first theatre – with seating for an audience of 1,200 – built in 1698 (the most recent renovation of the opera house coincided with its 300th anniversary).

Then the architect Damesne was commissioned to redesign and rebuild the theatre. He planned a neo-classical edifice, surrounded by a roofed-in arcade. A triangular tympanum surmounting eight Ionic columns was decorated with a bas-relief depicting the Harmony of Human Passions. The new building opened in 1819, but in 1855 fire destroyed extensive sections of it; restoration was completed by Joseph Poelaert within a year and the auditorium greatly extended. After its official opening by King Léopold I, the theatre was reserved exclusively for opera and ballet.

In August 1830, the Monnaie was literally the stage for the revolution against the Dutch that led to the country's independence. Auber's opera, *Masaniello*, based on the 1647 Neapolitan rebellion, was premiered on 25 August before a packed house. Its effect on the audience was electrifying. As the opera progressed they became increasingly agitated and when, in Act IV, the call to arms rang out, they streamed out of the auditorium with a patriotic fervour to ignite the fuse of revolution.

More recently, the handsome opera house was given a facelift in 1985. On the dance side, it has seen Maurice Béjart's Ballet du XXIème Siècle, and New York choreographer Mark Morris's dance troupe, come and go, and now hosts Anne Teresa de Keersmaeker's modern-dance group Rosas. Today, the opera house, which is the home of Belgium's Opéra National and the Orchestre Symphonique de la Monnaie, maintains a policy of promoting unknown singers rather than using well-known stars, and has a good reputation for its theatrical production. *(For information on how to obtain tickets, see page 219.)*

Satellite points

The southwestern edge of the city has one or two minor museums and lesser known attractions. At the Porte d'Anderlecht (where Rue d'Anderlecht meets Boulevard de l'Abattoir), is the **Musée des Egouts** (Sewer Museum; guided tours Wed 9am, 11am, 1pm and 3pm; open by appointment for groups of 10–20 on other days; admission charge). Here you will be led down into the bowels of the city to explore a small part of the vast 300-km (180-mile) labyrinth of sewers.

Further south, around the **Gare du Midi**, is a grim urban desert and an area best avoided, except if you can't help it because your train arrives at or departs from here (this is the Eurostar terminal), or you

BELOW: Théâtre Royal de la Monnaie.

choose to go for a meal at one of the inexpensive ethnic eateries or rough Belgian cafés off its east side.

Exotic market

You might make an exception for the colourful weekly **Marché du Midi** (Sun 6am–1.30pm at the Gare du Midi), the city's largest food market and ethnic Brussels at its best, where touts of bootleg Moroccan music cassettes rub shoulders with lugubrious sellers of oversize Belgian brassieres or Turkish harem slippers. The range of goods is overwhelming. You can buy clothes for every season and food of every kind, from live snails to chocolate gâteau. In between are fragrant bundles of fresh herbs, mounds of exotic fruits, nuts and spices, piles of pots and pans, pictures, leather goods and books. This is the place to buy olives, fresh cheese and charcuterie. The noise can be deafening: compact disc and cassette traders set their volume controls to maximum; cries in Flemish, French, Turkish and Arabic add to the babble of voices as greengrocers and iron-

mongers vie to draw attention to their wares. On neighbouring stalls under the railway arches, vendors of olives, pistachios and fresh herbs pass the time of day over a mint tea or hubble-bubble in this city souk. Be sure to explore the market's immediate vicinity. A constantly expanding network of stalls has spilled beyond the spacious square and surrounding side streets.

And then there's the **Foire du Midi**, the largest travelling funfair in Europe, which settles along the boulevards near the Gare du Midi from mid-July to mid-August. From the traditional hook-a-duck stall to a ride on the big wheel, there are attractions for all ages, and in the evenings those ethnic eateries and Belgian cafés put out long wooden tables to ensure that the festivities continue into the small hours.

Finally, west of the Gare du Midi, the **Musée de la Résistance** (14 Rue Van Lint; Mon–Tues and Thur–Fri 9am–4.30pm; free) covers the intrepid operations of the Belgian Resistance against the occupying German forces in World Wars I and II. ❑

Olive-sellers at the Sunday Midi market which starts at 6am.

BELOW: shopping at the Midi market, Brussels' largest and liveliest.

RESTAURANTS & CAFÉS

Restaurants

Aux Armes de Bruxelles
13 Rue des Bouchers.
Tel: 02-511 55 50.
Open: L & D Tues–Sun. €€
Family-run and a stickler
for service and fare, this
traditional Brussels
restaurant is among the
Ilot Sacré's most
respected. The dishes
range from mussels –
order un complet, and
mussels, fries and a beer
arrive at your table in an
instant – shrimp cro-
quettes and seafood to
Flemish hotpots, steaks
and crêpes tossed before
your eyes.

Belga Queen
32 Rue du Fossé aux Loups.
Tel: 02-217 21 87
Open: L & D daily. €€€
Glossy, cavernous
brasserie in a converted
bank with marble pillars,
skylights and plump din-
ing chairs. The menu
offers modern interpreta-
tions of Belgian classics,
though the food can be
hit and miss. A good
selection of beers and
great oyster bar.

Bonsoir Clara
22 Rue Antoine Dansaert.
Tel: 02-502 09 90. Open:
L & D Mon–Fri, D Sat. €€
This pioneering see-and-
be-seen eatery was the
first of its kind on the
city's hippest street and
is still going strong. A
modish clientele savours
the atmosphere amid a
funky decor of gaily

painted brick walls and
striking lighting. The
fusion cuisine is light,
appealing and aestheti-
cally presented. Booking
essential.

Chez Léon
18 Rue des Bouchers.
Tel: 02-511 04 26.
Open: L & D daily. €
A Brussels stalwart, in
business since 1893.
The menu is limited and
mussel-bound but none
the worse for that. Ser-
vice is brisk but friendly,
the prices reasonable
and the quality reliable.

Comme Chez Soi
23 Place Rouppe. Tel: 02-
512 29 21. Open: L & D
Tues–Sat. €€€€
Genial master-chef Pierre
Wynant's light, subtle
interpretations of classic
dishes have earned him
three Michelin stars.
The superb Art Nouveau
interior with its sumptu-
ous bar makes a suitably
elegant setting. An
unforgettable gastro-
nomic experience.
Reserve well ahead.

De l'Ogenblik
1 Galerie des Princes. Tel:
02-511 61 51. Open: L & D
Mon–Sat. €€–€€€
Correct cuisine bour-
geoise cooked with flair
and commitment and
served by engaging, pro-
fessional staff, is the
trademark of this superior
bistro, favoured by well-
heeled Bruxellois who
scorn the tourist traps in
the Ilot Sacré.

François
2 Quai aux Briques.
Tel: 02-511 60 89. Open:
L & D Tues–Sat. €€–€€€
Bright and breezy
seafood restaurant on
the corner of the Marché
aux Poissons. The
attached fishmonger's
display demonstrates a
proud family tradition of
quality. You can dine
alfresco on the square
in fine weather.

In 't Spinnekopke
1 Place du Jardin aux Fleurs.
Tel: 02-511 86 95. Open:
L & D Mon–Fri, D Sat. €–€€
One of Brussels' oldest
eateries, this traditional
estaminet proudly pro-
claims its affinity with the
best Belgian beers by
using them in its stews
and sauces. Specialities
include pot au feu, rabbit
in lambic, chicken water-
zooï, hearty carbonades
and, of course, mussels.

La Belle Maraîchère
11 Place Ste-Catherine.
Tel: 02-512 97 59.
Open: L & D Fri–Tues. €€
One of Brussels' best fish
restaurants, in a gabled
Flemish Renaissance
town house with a rustic,
wood-panelled main din-
ing room and a cooler
upstairs room. Zeeland
oysters, sole and crab are
recommended, and their
signature Flemish fish
stew is delicious.

La Kasbah
20 Rue Antoine Dansaert.
Tel: 02-502 40 26.
Open: L & D daily. €

Couscous, tagines,
mixed mezze and other
Middle Eastern dishes
with a modern twist are
served in an exotic
lantern-lit dining room.
The dresser laden with
sweet pastries is lovely
to look at and hard to
resist. There's a cosy
room in the basement for
afternoon mint tea.

La Manufacture
12–20 Rue Notre-Dame-
du-Sommeil. Tel: 02-502 25
25. Open: L & D Mon–Fri,
D Sat. €€
Set in a converted leather
factory, this designer
restaurant appeals to a
fashionable crowd, drawn
to the New World wines,
striking decor and modern
European food. Although
the cuisine is acceptable,
the atmosphere, sleek
diners and striking decor
are more impressive.

La Roue d'Or
26 Rue des Chapeliers.
Tel: 02-514 25 54.
Open: L & D daily. €
The brasserie decor at
this local favourite is an
Art Nouveau homage to
René Magritte. Service
and atmosphere are
friendly, and the rib-lining
Belgian specialities,
wholesome, authentic
and reasonably priced.

L'Achepot
1 Place Ste-Catherine.
Tel: 02-511 62 21.
Open: L & D Daily. €
Popular, informal restau-
rant specialising in fish
and offal dishes. A glass

or two of Belgian beer sends the generous helpings down nicely. There is an outdoor terrace for good weather.

L'Alban Chambon

Hôtel Métropole, 31 Place de Brouckère. Tel: 02-217 23 00. Open: L & D Mon–Fri. €€€
The formal *belle époque* setting, all marble, mirrors and chandeliers, provides a suitably grand framework for the inspired cuisine, a fresh, light take on classic French cooking. Extensive wine list.

Le Marmiton

43 Rue des Bouchers. Tel: 02-511 7910. Open: L & D daily. €€
This stands head and shoulders above the many mediocre Ilot Sacré establishments. The owner and sometime chef adds a touch of Portuguese to what is fundamentally a superior Belgian restaurant.

Le Paon Royal

6 Rue du Vieux Marché aux Grains. Tel: 02-513 08 68. Open: L Tues–Thur, L & D Fri. €–€€
A regular unsung hero, this timeless eatery is one of a dying breed of earthy Bruxellois eateries. Its ability to serve up tasty traditional dishes year in year out at reasonable prices appears effortless. A fine cast of Belgian beers plays a key supporting role. The leafy terrace is a relaxing lunchtime spot.

Le Scheltema

7 Rue des Dominicains. Tel: 02-512 20 84. Open: L & D Mon–Sat. €€

One of few restaurants in the Ilot Sacré tourist enclave to have maintained a standard of service, quality and price. The Belgian and French fare is more sophisticated than is the norm in this district.

Les Ateliers de la Grande Ile

33 Rue de la Grande Ile. Tel: 02-512 81 90. Open: D Tues–Sun. €–€€
High-spirited Russian restaurant, where blinis and chicken Kiev are washed down with large quantities of vodka. Musical entertainment comes courtesy of a Hungarian gypsy orchestra. Open until 2am.

Sea Grill

Radisson SAS Hotel, 47 Rue du Fossé aux Loups. Tel: 02-227 31 20. Open: L & D Mon–Sat. €€€€
This stellar hotel restaurant is about as near to perfection as seafood gets – harbour towns and fish-market gems notwithstanding – in a land that is no slouch when it comes to this type of cuisine. Quality, taste and invention are all brought together to great effect on the plate. Of course, such quality comes at a price.

Taverne du Passage

30 Galerie de la Reine. Tel: 02-512 37 32. Open: L & D daily. €–€€
A popular brasserie in the Galeries Royales St-Hubert that's very old-Brussels in atmosphere. This is the perfect place to try shrimp croquettes or a *steak au poivre*

flambé à la crème, but those in the know come here to eat the best steak tartare in town. There's an outdoor terrace in the gallery.

Vincent

8–10 Rue des Dominicains. Tel: 02-511 23 03. Open: L & D daily. €
This spacious but atmospheric restaurant, established in 1905, is strikingly decorated with larger-than-life images of coastal fishermen. Access is through the kitchens where *moules*, seafood, steaks and other traditional fare are cooked up with gusto. You can dine on the pavement terrace when the weather is fine. Great value for money.

Cafés and bars

The tiny **Toone Theatre bar** (*Impasse Schuddeveld, off Petite Rue des Bouchers*) is an engaging prelude to the authentic Brussels puppet show next door. Close by, **A La Mort Subite** (*7 Rue Montagne aux Herbes Potagères*) is renowned for its range of beers, nicotine-stained walls, period mirrors, and attitudinal waiters. On either side of the Bourse (Stock Exchange) are rival establishments **Le Cirio** (*18 Rue de la Bourse*), designed in opulent, if faded, *fin de siècle* style, and long-established **Falstaff** (*19–25 Rue Henri-Maus*), a much-vaunted Art Nouveau café

and brasserie. If you happen to be on or near Place de Brouckère, a visit to the *belle époque* **Café Métropole** (in the Hôtel Métropole), former haunt of Sarah Bernhardt, merits the price of a coffee or an aperitif. Between the Grand-Place and the Sablon is **La Fleur en Papier Doré** (*55 Rue des Alexiens*), a snug 17th-century *estaminet* with a bohemian air, formerly a Surrealist haunt popular with Magritte. Set in a semi-gentrified street in the heart of the hip St-Géry quarter (with plenty of bars to choose from), **Taverne Greenwich** (*7 Rue des Chartreux*) is regularly used as a film set. In its sober, hushed interior, serious chess-players sip drinks over endless games. Redolent of an ocean liner, Art Deco **L'Archiduc** (*6, Rue Antoine Dansaert*) was a favourite of crooners Jacques Brel and Nat King Cole, and is today popular with a sophisticated set; it serves a mean martini. **Le Java** (*31 Rue St-Géry*) is a cool but not unfriendly bar, good for a quick lunch and beer.

PRICE CATEGORIES

Prices for three-course dinner per person with a half-bottle of house wine:
€ = under €30
€€ = €30–45
€€€ = €45–60
€€€€ = over €60

THE MAROLLES

On the slope below the Palais de Justice lies the former artisans' quarter – a scruffy, earthy neighbourhood with gentrified enclaves, and the best flea market in town

This down-at-heel, working-class district has a close relationship with the Palais de Justice *(see page 136)*. Not that Marolles architecture – such as it is – owes anything to the Justice Palace's megalomaniac neo-classicism; nor does Marolliens' ribald attitude to authority have anything in common with the cold legalisms of lawyers and judges. No, it's simply that the Justice Palace, up on its Galgenberg Hill perch where public executions once took place, looms over the Marolles like a crude stone symbol of intimidation, a permanent reminder to the lower orders of who's boss. Construction of the palace towards the end of the 19th century took a big bite out of the original district, and the word "architect" has been a formidable Marollien insult ever since.

Developed during the Middle Ages to house weavers and other low-paid artisans, the Marolles expanded during the 17th century as a residential area for craftsmen labouring on the Upper City's upper-crust mansions. Frequent outbreaks of protest against miserable living conditions were equally frequently suppressed. In the 1870s, with the paving over of the Senne river, the wealthier artisans moved out to the suburbs. Then came the

Palais de Justice. As the district declined from even those low heights it had known, it became a refuge for the seriously poor and socially deprived, and for each successive wave of immigrants.

The district, which takes its name from the 17th-century Convent of the Apostolines of Mariann Colentes (no longer extant), has no precisely defined boundaries. It lies generally between Boulevard de Waterloo, Porte de Hal, Boulevard du Midi, Avenue de Stalingrad and Place du

Map on page 120

LEFT: market on Place du Jeu de Balle.
BELOW: Ploegman's, a traditional neighbourhood bar.

Cartoon on the side of a Marolles house. The tourist office can supply a map of the latest city walls that have been enlivened by comic creations.

BELOW: café on the Place Jeu de Balle.

Grand Sablon. Rue Haute and Rue Blaes, the principal through streets, run side by side from one end of the Marolles to the other.

Community spirit

An impoverished part of the city in bean-counting terms, the Marolles compensates by being rich in community spirit – an attribute nobody would ever accuse the affluent districts of sharing. Other Bruxellois look on Marolliens as a breed apart, with their own manners – or lack of them – dialect and an irreverent outlook on life. It is a small district, under pressure along its frontiers from wealthy neighbours, like the Sablon's art and antiques dealers and chic boutique, café and restaurant owners, who look on low-cost Marolles property as easy pickings for expansion.

As they penetrate deeper, the incomers are gradually eroding the Marolles' true character and creating contrasts of wealth and poverty too marked for comfort.

Marolliens resist the infiltrators as best they can, but the opposition's vastly superior financial firepower, political clout and legal resources make this a war of attrition the weaker side is slowly losing. If gentrification and property speculation are constant threats, deteriorating housing stock is even more insidious. Many residents have no funds to pay for essential repairs. Old buildings crumble; some are all but falling down.

In some parts, you will notice successful attempts at restoration, promoted by action groups trying to breathe fresh life into the district and to encourage residents to renovate. Public funds are available only sporadically. For many years the city government allocated no money at all for rebuilding, finding it easier and more lucrative to encourage private investment from builders and

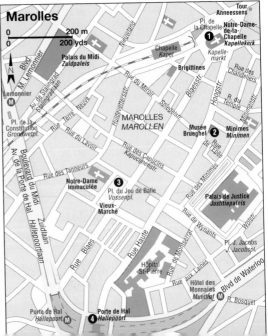

property dealers. Private investment on any significant scale by most Marolliens themselves is not a realistic proposition.

An endangered species

The genuine Marolles wants nothing to do with the Euro-city style that is the new wave elsewhere. You can still find characteristic drab little cafés and snack bars hawking mussels, watery stews and soggy French fries. In some of these places it is not uncommon to see suitcases on the floor – families who have lost their homes often lodge temporarily at neighbourhood cafés. As indigenous inhabitants die or move away, their place is being taken by immigrants from North Africa and other parts of the developing world, who now add up to more than half of the 10,000 population.

There is little doubt that true Marolliens are an endangered species whose colourful dialect, *brusseleir*, seems destined to become an intellectual curiosity, its words mouthed by people to whom the spirit that once infused them is a closed book.

The main landmarks

The Marolles is a place to wander in, uncovering its enigmatic charm by making your own chance discoveries, rather than a centre of attractions, but there are a few landmarks to suggest a possible route through. A good place to begin is **Tour Anneessens**, on Boulevard de l'Empereur, the remains of a two-storey, circular fortified tower of the city's original 12th-century wall that, astonishingly, was only rediscovered in 1957.

From here, take Rue Haute to Place de la Chapelle and its lovely church of **Notre-Dame-de-la-Chapelle ❶**, built around a 12th-century chapel that later became a place of pilgrimage for its relics of the Holy Cross. It grew over the centuries, picking up a medley of architectural styles – Romanesque, Gothic, Brabant Gothic and baroque. A small Romanesque tower in the southern transept dates from the earliest epoch, while the neo-Renaissance, onion-domed steeple is 18th-century. Look for the tympanum above the west door, which

TIP

At the far end of Rue Haute, past the busy St-Pierre Hospital, is a group of reasonably priced Spanish and Portuguese restaurants.

BELOW: the Marolles district lies in the shadow of the Upper City, to which it is now connected by lifts.

has a sculpture of the Holy Trinity (1892), by social realist Constantin Meunier. Inside, in a side chapel off the north aisle, is a memorial to Pieter Brueghel and his wife Mayken Coecke, who were married here in 1563, by his son Jan Brueghel.

Another local hero buried in the church is François Anneessens, an 18th-century guild leader whose execution in 1719 put an abrupt end to a revolt against Austrian rule.

Take Rue des Visitandines to the nearby **Eglise des Brigittines**, dating from 1665, formerly the church of a now vanished Brigittines convent. Deconsecrated in the 18th century and subsequently used as a dispensary, butcher's shop, school and dance hall, it now hosts dance, musical and other live performances.

Stylish restaurants

That's it for churches. Go up on to Rue Haute, the main shopping street. In recent years, antique shops have been wheedling their way in here from the neighbouring Sablon district, pushing out the deter-

Children rummage for toys at the Jeu de Balle market, a colourful sea of junk and gems.

BELOW: strolling down the Rue de l'Epée.

minedly proletarian Marolles shops and bringing in their train a sprinkling of fancier restaurants and bars. Rue de l'Epée and Square Pieter Brueghel form an enclave of stylish eateries. From here you can see the Palais de Justice lowering on its hill above you.

The artist Pieter Breughel the Elder (c.1525–69) lived and worked at 132 Rue Haute. The red-brick gabled town house is now the **Musée Brueghel ❷** (Wed and Sat pm only; groups by written arrangement; admission charge). The French sculptor Auguste Rodin had a studio at No. 242.

The best flea market in town

Dropping down onto Rue Blaes, another busy shopping street that has experienced the same gentrification at its Sablon end, brings you to **Place du Jeu de Balle ❸** in the heart of the Marolles, home of Brussels' most famous flea market, the **Vieux Marché**, and surrounded by motley galleries and antiquarian booksellers. At the city's premier flea market it seems that nothing is so unusual that there isn't someone who can't be persuaded to buy it.

Many pieces come from the homes of the "recently deceased", maybe including the "Hero of the Soviet Union" five-pointed gold stars with red ribbon, and certainly the dinner-sets, chairs, old books, paintings (well, pictures), clothes, shoes, radios, record players, records (those quaint old vinyl things), dolls, soft toys, racing-cars (battery-operated) and everything imaginable that comes under the headings of bric-a-brac, junk, antiques, bargain buys and rip-offs.

In short, between 7am and 2pm, all human life is here, much of it for sale. Even when the market has packed up there's a kind of post-market market, with the really dodgy,

unsaleable stuff left lying around for rummagers to rummage in.

Stalls can be found on any day of the week, but the best (and most expensive) day is Sunday, when the number often rises to 200, taking over the ragged square itself and several of the surrounding streets. Whenever you decide to go, be prepared to hunt for bargains. While you are there, take time to explore this relaxed and interesting quarter, felt by many to be the very soul of Brussels.

Café society

Early each morning, the cafés surrounding Place du Jeu de Balle attract their first customers, and generally stay busy for the rest of the day. Each café has its own character and its own type of clientele.

The Marolles hosts several of the city's most traditional *estaminets*, of which the most colourful is **La Grande Porte** (9 Rue de Notre Seigneur). **Café Alex** (224 Rue Haute), a rough-and-ready bar, is one of the last places where you can be sure of hearing the local patois, *brusseleir*; in addition to beer and a

breezy line in chat, it boasts two other Brussels passions: an Art Deco interior and a wall dedicated to comic strips. Named after Marolliens' contempt for architects (the designer of the Palais de Justice in particular), **De Skieven Architiek**, "The Crooked Architect" (50 Place du Jeu de Balle), dispenses good cheer and cheap food to an arty Flemish crowd and market aficionados.

City gateway

Facing the end of Rue Haute, on Boulevard du Midi, is the **Porte de Hal ❹**. This massive, 14th-century stone gateway is the only surviving one of the seven medieval gates in Brussels' old city wall. The other six were destroyed by Napoleon. Greatly altered in 1870, it has been restored and houses a Brussels folklore outpost of the Royal Museums of Art and History (Tues–Sun 10am–5pm – though these hours are not always strictly adhered to; July–Aug on request only; admission charge) given over to the history and traditions of Brussels. ❏

Map
on page
120

Porte de Hal, Brussels' last surviving medieval gateway.

RESTAURANTS & BARS

Restaurants

Au Stekerlapatte
4 Rue des Prêtres.
Tel: 02-512 86 81.
Open: D Tues–Sun. €–€€
Jovial restaurant with a long list of Belgian specialities and a seasonal menu, but standbys like spare ribs and steak are ever popular with a hip clientele.

La Grande Porte
9 Rue Notre-Seigneur.
Tel: 02-512 89 98. Open: L & D Tues–Fri, D Sat. €€

Appealingly shabby late-night haunt (open until 2am) in a rambling 17th-century town house. Hearty traditional dishes include Flemish chicken cooked in Kriek beer, and huge salads. Alfresco dining in summer.

Les Brigittines/Aux Marches de la Chapelle
5 Place de la Chapelle.
Tel: 02-512 68 91. Open: L & D Mon–Fri, D Sat. €
Superior brasserie offering earthy French/Belgian dishes. There's

a quirky wine list and, in a counter-intuitive touch for the Marolles, valet parking at lunchtime.

Les Petits Oignons
13 Rue Notre-Seigneur.
Tel: 02-512 47 38.
Open: L & D Mon–Sat. €€
Splendidly atmospheric eatery in a 17th-century town house. The friendly service is matched by good French cuisine. Dining on the garden terrace in summer.

L'Idiot du Village
19 Rue Notre-Seigneur.
Tel: 02-502 55 82.
Open: L & D Mon–Sat. €€
In the glow of candles

and small lamps, you dine on an updated and thoughtful form of traditional Belgian cuisine. Warm and friendly.

Cafés and bars

There are many lively cafés around the Place Jeu de Balle to stop for a drink when browsing the Marolles flea market. One of the best is the coyly kitsch **De Skieven Architek** *(No. 50).*

● ● ● ● ● ● ● ● ● ● ●
Price includes dinner and half a bottle of house wine.

€ *under* €30, €€ €30–45,
€€€ €45–60, €€€€ €60 +

THE UPPER CITY

The former enclave of the ruling classes, with its long vistas, stately architecture and formal park, is home to an outstanding national art collection

U phill from the Grand-Place is the district traditionally associated with the aristocracy and administration, royalty and government. Its monumental squares are joined by classical boulevards, and the district embraces the Belgian Parliament, government offices, the official residence of the royal family, and the overweening law courts – the monstrous Palais de Justice – which dominates the scene. Here, too, are some of the finest museums, grandest designer shops and most pretentious cafés.

Yet the Upper City is by no means a cohesive unit: Place Royale is a cold but monumental quarter with excellent museums and the Royal Palace; by contrast, the Sablon offers a sophisticated social scene, with chic cafés crammed under the Flemish gables of old Brussels.

Down the Rue Royale

An attractive route through the Upper City starts at the junction of Boulevard du Jardin Botanique and Rue Royale (metro Botanique) – a long boulevard linking the former Botanical Gardens with Place Royale – where the city gate on the Brussels to Leuven road once stood. Turning left into Rue Royale, you pass in front of the glass pavilions and rotunda of

Le Jardin Botanique ❶ (Botanical Garden). The park, which contains a fine collection of exotic flora and a grand, iron-framed greenhouse, was completed in 1830. In 1944, when the Botanical Garden outgrew the site, it transferred out of town to Domein Van Bouchout, at Meise, just north of the city *(see page 193)*.

In 1984 the glasshouses were converted to house the **Centre Culturel de la Communauté Française** (Cultural Centre of the French-Speaking Community), with facilities that

Map on page 126

LEFT: Mont des Arts.
BELOW: royal troops on parade by the Parc de Bruxelles.

Upper City

0 200 m
0 200 yds
N

Rogier

Basilique Nationale du Sacré-Coeur

Église Ste-Marie

Centre Culturel

R. Traversière

R. d. Méridien Midaggirstr.

Dwarsstr.

Adolphe Maxln.

Avenue Victoria Regina

Boulevard du Jardin Botanique

Victoria Reginaln.

LE JARDIN BOTANIQUE KRUIDTUIN

R. Royale Koningsstr.

Blvd E. Jacqmain E. Jacqmainln.

Blvd Adolphe Max

Nieuwstraat

R. de la Blanchisserie Blekerijstr.

Broekstraat

Pachecolaan

Kruidtuinlaan

Botanique Kruidtuin

R. de l'Union

Pl. Quetelet Quetelepl.

Rue de Laeken Laekenstr.

Notre-Dame-du-Finistère O.-L.-V.-ter-Finisterrae

Congrès Congres

Cité Administrative Rijksadministratief Centrum

Koningsstr.

Pl. des Barricades Barricadenpl.

Blvd Bischoffsheim

Pl. de Brouckère De Brouckèrepl.

Hôtel Métropole

Pl. des Martyrs Martelaarspl.

R. d'Argent

R. du Persil

Centre Belge de la Bande Dessinée (Comic Strip Museum)

R. des Sables

Pl. du Congrès Congrespl.

Astoria Hotel

Musée du Jouet

Pl. de la Liberté Vrijheidspl.

Av. de l'Astronomie

Centre Monnaie Muntcentrum

De Brouckère Monnaie Muntpl.

R. du Fossé aux Loups Wolvengracht

Pl. de la Monnaie Muntpl.

Théâtre Royal de la Monnaie K. Muntschouwburg

R. de l'Écuyer

R. d'Arenberg

Wolvengracht

Colonne du Congrès Congreskolom

Rue du Congrès

Cirque Royal Koninklijk Circus

Pl. Madou Madoupl.

Madou

R. Grétry Grétrystr.

Galeries Royales St-Hubert

Rue des Bouchers

Blvd de Berlaimont Berlaimontlaan

Banque Nationale Nationale Bank

R. de Ligne

Tiptstr.

IJzerenkruisstr.

Leuvenseweg

Congresstr.

Bischoffsheimlaan

Musée Charlier

R. de Tabora

St-Nicolas St-Nikolaas

Théâtre de Toone

Maison du Roi

Grand-Place Grote Markt

Hôtel de Ville Stadhuis

Kon St-Hubertus-gal.

R. de la Montagne

Cathédrale Sts-Michel-et-Gudule

R. des Colonies Kolonienstr.

Rue de Louvain

Palais de la Nation

Paleis der Natie

Rue de la Loi Wet str.

le du Lombard

Musée du Costume et de la Dentelle

Chapelle de la Madeleine

Maison des Ducs de Brabant

Carrefour de l'Europe Europakruispunt

Gare Centrale Centraal Station

Koningsstr.

Parc Park

Pl. de la Nation Natiepl.

Arts-Loi Kunst-Wet

R. de la Loi

Pl. St-Jean St-Janspl.

Fondation Jacques Brel

Pl. de l'Albertine Albertinapl.

Gare Centrale Centraal Station

Palais des Congrès Congrespaleis

Palais de la Dynastie

Musée du Cinéma

Rue Royale

PARC DE BRUXELLES

PARK VAN BRUSSEL

Théâtre Royal du Parc Parktheater

Rollebeekstr.

Parlement Bruxellois Brussels Parlement

Boulevard de l'Empereur Keizersln.

Mont des Arts Kunstberg

Bibliothèque Royale de Belgique

Pl. de la Justice Gerechtspl.

Hôtel Ravenstein

Pl. du Musée

Palais des Beaux-Arts-Bozar Paleis voor Schone Kunsten

Musée des Instruments

Musée d'Art. de Musique

Pl. des Palais Paleizenpl.

R. Guimard Guimardstr.

St-Joseph St-Jozef

Rue Belliard Belliardstr.

R. de la Science

Tour Anneessens

Musées Royaux des Beaux-Arts de Belgique

Pl. Royale Koningspl.

Pl. Royale

Musée de la Dynastie

Palais Royal Koninklijk Paleis

Palais des Académies Paleis der Akademiën

Rue du Commerce

Rue Montoyer

Pl. de la Chapelle

Rue de Rollebeek

Notre-Dame-de-la-Chapelle Kapellekerk

Musée Juif de Belgique

Pl. du Grand Sablon Grote Zavel

R. des Sablons Zavelstr.

Rue de Ruysbroeck Ruysbroeckstr.

St-Jacques-sur-Coudenberg St-Jacob-o.-d.-Koudenberg

R. de Namur

R. Bréderode Bréderodestr.

Pl. du Trône Troonpl.

Trône Troon

Sq. de Meeûs

Meeûssq.

R. des Chandeliers

MAROLLES MAROLLEN

Minimes Minimen

N.-D. du Sablon Zavelkerk

Pl. du Petit Sablon

Kleine Zavel

Conservatoire Royal de Musique

Pl. du Petit Sablon

Palais d'Egmont Egmontpaleis

R. du Pépin

Naamsestr.

Rue de la Régence

Regentschapsstr.

R. aux Laines Wolstr.

JARDIN D'EGMONT EGMONTTUIN

Pte de Namur Naamsepoort

Porte de Namur Naamse Poort

R. du Chp de Mars Marsveldstr.

Blvd du Régent Regentlaan

Av. Marnix Marnixln.

Pl. de Londres Londenpl.

Rue Caroly Carolystr.

Pl. Poelaert Poelaertpl.

Rue de la Régence

Galerie de la Toison d'Or Guldenvliesgalerij

Chaussée de Wavre Waversesteenweg

R. de Naples Napelsstr.

Palais de Justice Justitiepaleis

Blvd de Waterloo

Av. de Waterloo

Rue des 4 Bras

Waterloolaan Gulden Vlieslaan

Chau. d'Ixelles Elsensestwg

Musée Camille Lemonnier

include a library, cinema, theatre and exhibition halls. A terrace café overlooking the gardens hosts open-air concerts in summer. The park itself is a pleasant green space, despite the proximity of the *petite ceinture* (inner ring road), but is best avoided at night (though the cultural centre and its café is perfectly safe).

Before heading towards the city centre from here, it's worth continuing a little further north along the boulevard to **De Ultieme Hallucinatie** (316 Rue Royale), one of the most intriguing bars in Brussels, and a Flemish-speakers' domain. It is indeed a hallucination, an authentic Art Nouveau house complete with surreal rocky grotto and winter garden. The patrician mansion, built by Paul Hamesse in 1904, contains a friendly bar and brasserie and a swish but expensive restaurant (*see page 179*).

If you're willing to walk just a little further, or jump on a tram to the top end of Rue Royale, the lovely copper-domed **Eglise Ste-Marie** is worth seeing. Dating from 1845, the octagonal church is modelled on Ravenna's 6th-century Basilica of San Vitale.

Heading back to Place Royale along Rue Royale, you can take in a couple of other noteworthy buildings. The magnificent *belle époque* foyer and public rooms of the old-fashioned **Astoria Hotel ❷** (No. 103) are worth a look. You could even stop for a beer or coffee at its Pullman Bar, modelled on the 1920s Orient Express restaurant. Close by is **Confiserie Mary** (No. 73), a renowned praline shop, and confectioners to the Belgian royal court. At No. 13 is a surprising Art Nouveau-style flower shop, Les Fleurs Isabelle de Baecker. For those with children in tow, a little further along is the **Musée du Jouet** (Toy Museum; 24 Rue de l'Association; daily 10am–noon, 2–6pm; admission charge), a hands-on kind of place where toys from 1830 to the present day are the sole but sufficient attraction.

Continuing in the direction of Place Royale, you skirt around the edge of an old district (on your left), where almost all the houses were

Map on page 126

With its decorative detailing inside and out, the Astoria is one of the city's most graceful – and expensive – hotels.

BELOW: the floodlit National Basilica.

Koekelberg's Art Deco Church

Look westward into the middle distance along Boulevard du Jardin Botanique from Le Botanique until your gaze bumps up against the high towers and faded bronze cupola of the **Basilique Nationale du Sacré-Coeur** (National Basilica of the Sacred Heart; daily May–Oct 9am–5pm, Nov–Apr 10am–4pm; church free, admission charge for panorama) in Koekelberg. Construction of what is said to be the world's fifth-biggest church began in 1905 and was not complete until 1970.

Conceived by King Léopold II as a neo-Gothic extravaganza – Brussels' answer to the Sacré-Coeur in Montmartre, Paris, which he greatly admired – the building costs proved enormous and original plans had to be modified. As a result, a plethora of architectural styles, beginning with neo-Gothic, adorns this colossal building, enough being Art Deco to corroborate the claim that it's the world's biggest Art Deco edifice. To visit what is widely cited as the city's least loved building, take the subway to metro Simonis then tram No.19. If you're willing to make the effort to climb to the top of the dome you'll be rewarded with a panoramic view of the city.

destroyed then rebuilt with fine facades during the 19th century. Most streets converged on open spaces, which later developed into squares; the focal point of each square is usually a monument to a famous past citizen or dignitary.

Monument to nationhood

To your right is the **Colonne du Congrès ❸** (Congress Column), which commemorates the founding of Belgium in 1830, with the names of the heroes of the revolution inscribed in gold. Enthroned on the top of the shaft is a statue of the first King of the Belgians, Léopold I, a member of the German house of Saxe-Coburg-Gotha. The four vast female figures seated at his feet symbolise the human rights that had hitherto been denied to Belgians: freedom of education and religion, freedom of the press and freedom of assembly. At the base of the column, an eternal flame burns over the grave of the Unknown Soldier, a memorial to the victims of both world wars.

Further along Rue Royale at its junction with Rue de la Loi, the

Palais de la Nation (National Palace) is the seat of Belgium's fractious **Parliament**. Its two chambers, the House of Deputies and the Senate, meet behind the neo-classical facade, and you can occasionally visit to view a debate from the public gallery. The surrounding buildings house government ministries. The palace was built for the Supreme Council of the Duchy of Brabant; later, the courts of justice sat here. Originally dating from 1783, it was rebuilt in 1884–7 after being destroyed by fire.

Royal connections

Although Brussels is one of the greenest capitals of Europe, the parks in the city centre are mostly small, sedate, neatly manicured affairs. Opposite the Parliament building the **Parc de Bruxelles ❹** is a model of geometrical precision, its layout based on the shape of Masonic symbols, and a popular place for a stroll. The grounds served as a royal hunting preserve in medieval times, and its present classical landscaping dates from 1776.

TIP

Les Fleurs Isabelle de Baecker, the florist at No. 13 Rue Royale, is the only shop left in the city with an original Art Nouveau shopfront.

BELOW: keeping the Parc de Bruxelles tidy.

Refurbished and restored as far as possible to its 18th-century condition, the park is better – though no bigger – than ever. Although not very big, the cleverly laid-out park combines trails through tangled undergrowth with open avenues that offer emblematic vistas. From the big fountain beside Rue de la Loi, the central axis looks straight at the front doors of the Palais de la Nation in one direction and the Palais Royal in the other.

Badly damaged in 1998 by fire, but since refurbished to its original glory and reopened, the elegant **Théâtre Royal du Parc** stands in the northeast corner of the park, off Rue de la Loi. Opposite the Palais Royal, but still within the gardens, is a bust of the Russian Tsar Peter the Great.

On the east of the cobbled Place des Palais stands the Italian Renaissance-style **Palais des Académies**. Originally planned as the residence of Holland's Prince of Orange at a time when Holland and Belgium were united, it was completed in 1829. Converted to the headquarters of Bel-

gium's Royal Academy in 1876, it houses the Academy of Sciences, the Academy of Literature and Fine Arts and the Academy of Medical Sciences. Not far from here, across the *petite ceinture* (inner ring road) at 16 Avenue des Arts, the **Musée Charlier** (Tues noon–5pm, Wed–Fri noon–7.30pm; admission charge) occupies a villa partly designed by Art Nouveau architect Victor Horta. The house has a rich collection of Belgian artworks, furniture, tapestries, porcelain and silverware.

The central pathway of the Parc de Bruxelles leads straight to the **Palais Royal** ❺. The royal palace occupies part of the site of the seat of the Dukes of Brabant, which had been home to such rulers as Duke of Burgundy Philip the Good and Habsburg emperor Charles V *(see pages 19–21)*. In 1731, the old palace burned to the ground. The cause of the blaze has been linked to the palace cooks, apparently too engrossed in jam-making to notice the spread of the fire. Due to severe winter weather, the city's water supply was frozen and little was available to quench the

Map on page 126

The Congress Column celebrates the founding of Belgium in 1830.

BELOW: Palais de la Nation gardens.

flames. In desperation, the citizens vainly attempted to put out the fire with beer. Excavations under Place Royale have revealed the foundations and other remains of the medieval Coudenberg ducal palace, including the Aula Magna (Great Hall) of the dukes of Burgundy and the Habsburg emperors. You can visit this fascinating labyrinth of underground passageways from the Musée de la Dynastie *(see below)*. The new palace was built on part of the old site, and in the 19th century, King Léopold II had the dignified but dull building significantly remodelled in Louis XVI style, combining two patrician mansions and giving it an imperial feel. It was further renovated and enlarged at the beginning of the 20th century.

Although the royal couple spend most of their time in their more alluring palace in suburban Laeken *(see page 167)*, this is the official city residence. The palace houses the Royal Chancellery, as well as state rooms and offices, some of which are open to the public in summer. If the flag is flying, His Majesty is in residence, since this is where King Albert II conducts official business. A subdued changing of the guard takes place at 2pm.

The **Musée de la Dynastie** (Tues–Sun 10am–6pm, until 5pm Oct–Mar; admission charge), housed in the beautiful Hôtel Bellevue beside the Royal Palace, contains an exhibition documenting the history of the royal family, and has a fine display of 18th- and 19th-century objets d'art displayed in sumptuous apartments.

Diagonally opposite, across Rue Royale, the elegant **Palais des Beaux-Arts** ❻ has been restored and renamed **Bozar** *(see also page 71)*. This monumental Art Deco palace, which stretches down the hill towards Gare Centrale linking the Upper and Lower City, contains a theatre, a concert hall which is one of the city's premier venues for classical music, a banqueting hall and exhibition space. Completed in 1928, it was designed by Victor Horta *(see page 147)*, clearly well out of his landmark Art Nouveau period by this time. On the north

TIP

If you want to take time out from sightseeing, and the weather is no good for being outside, the Musée du Cinema adjoining the Palais des Beaux-Arts has daily screenings of old classics and silent films from the movie archives.

BELOW: café on the Rue Royale.

side of the palace, tucked away on Rue Baron Horta, at No. 9, is the **Musée du Cinema** (Fri–Wed 5.30–10.30pm, Thurs 2.30–9pm; admission charge), a fascinating collection for film enthusiasts, which illustrates the progress of the moving image and screens old film classics daily from 5.30pm in a revolving programme of films highlighting different genres.

Classical facades

Rue Royale ends on **Place Royale** ❼, which was built during the 18th century in Louis XVI style on the summit of Coudenberg hill. It retains the elegant proportions that characterise sections of the city rebuilt in the latter half of the 18th century on the orders of Charles of Lorraine, who governed Brussels from 1744 and under whose rule Brussels enjoyed a long period of prosperity and stability. For many years Place Royale suffered from benign neglect, but restoration of the monumental neo-classical buildings was undertaken in the 1990s.

The square is bordered on one side by **St-Jacques-sur-Coudenberg**, a graceful neo-classical church inspired by a Roman temple. In its day, it has served as a royal chapel and as a temple of reason during the French Revolution. Léopold I was crowned as first King of the Belgians here.

Surveying the scene from the middle of Place Royale is a heroic equestrian statue of Duke Godefroy de Bouillon. One of the leaders of the First Crusade launched in 1096, he succeeded, with the help of 20,000 soldiers, in recapturing Jerusalem from the Saracens in 1099. He was elected ruler of the new Crusader kingdom the same year – refusing the title of King of Jerusalem, since he would not wear a crown of gold in the city where Jesus had worn a crown of thorns, but accepting instead the title Defender of the Holy Sepulchre – and died after a reign of only a year.

From the square, there is a panoramic view over the Lower City, centred on the soaring spire of the Town Hall on the Grand-Place.

Map on page 126

Ornate staircase of the Musée de la Dynastie, which chronicles the history of the Belgian royal family.

BELOW:
trams run round the statue of Crusader Godefroy de Bouillon on the Place Royale.

BELOW:
the entrance hall of the Musées Royaux des Beaux-Arts showing *The School Parade in 1878* by Jan Verhas.

A feast of musical instruments

Downhill from the square, at 2 Rue Montagne de la Cour, the restored Old England department store, an erstwhile British firm's Art Nouveau premises, is now the home of the **Musée des Instruments de Musique ❽** (Musical Instrument Museum; Tues–Fri 9.30am–5pm, Thur 9.30am–8pm, Sat and Sun 10am–5pm; admission charge). The outstanding collection has more than 6,000 exhibits from all over the world: Bronze Age musical instruments, simple Indian flutes, handsome wind instruments. The museum has an innovative sound system: as you wander through the exhibits, headphones activated by sensors play music of the period.

A little further downhill from here, on Rue Ravenstein, the **Hôtel Ravenstein** is a mansion carved out of a remnant of the 15th-century Burgundian royal palace that did not succumb to the fire of 1731, and is a rare architectural survivor of Brussels' Burgundian period. It now houses professional institutes and the swish Relais des Caprices French restaurant *(see page 137)*. Across the way, and in a city not noted for impressive sculpture, *The Whirling Ear*, an Alexander Calder abstract, has been installed.

From Memling to Magritte

Adjoining the square are the **Musées Royaux des Beaux-Arts de Belgique ❾** (Tues–Sun 10am–5pm; tel: 02-508 32 11; admission charge), two palatial buildings housing a world-class collection of art treasures split between two galleries, one dedicated to paintings, drawings and sculpture from the 15th to the 18th centuries, the other to modern art from the 19th and 20th centuries. Together they build on the foundation of a collection of Flemish Masters that was first established at Napoleon's behest in 1801, and that has been expanded by acquisitions and recovery ever since. Among the big names represented here are Pieter Brueghel the Elder and Younger, Jan Van Eyck, Peter Paul Rubens, Antoon Van Dyck, Paul Delvaux, René Magritte and Pierre Alechinsky.

These are supported by a compelling cast of scarcely less minor performers. Most but not all of the artists featured are Belgian. *(See photo feature on pages 138–9.)*

Between the two museums, the quiet and graceful **Place du Musée** is dominated by the pleasingly proportioned neo-classical facade of the **Apartments of Charles of Lorraine**. A statue of this 18th-century governor of the Austrian Low Countries, who set up a dazzling court in Brussels, surveys the palace from a pedestal across the square.

For bibliophiles

Adjoining this extensive complex to the west is the **Bibliothèque Royale de Belgique** (cardholders only; Mon–Fri 9am–8pm; until 5pm July–Aug). Belgium's national library is part of the Albertine complex, a group of buildings built between 1954 and 1969, dedicated to the memory of King Albert I, who led the Belgian army against the Germans during World War I. The library contains some 5 million volumes. Within it are several smaller museums. The **Musée**

du Livre et Cabinet des Donations illustrates the history of books from the 10th century to the present day by way of a selection of diverse manuscripts, prints and book covers. The **Audio-Visual Archive** mainly relates to French and Belgian literature. Also worth visiting, the **Museum of Printing** includes typefaces, lithographic equipment, and bookbinding and typesetting apparatus from the 18th to the 20th centuries. Access to the state library is granted only to those with a membership card (obtainable with a photo, some form of identification and a fee of €2.50 or €15 for a year).

The other buildings in the complex, which was built on the site of the Mont des Arts, include the 1950s **Palais des Congrès** and the **Palais de la Dynastie** conference and exhibition centres. The latter's rear facade features a **Carillon Clock**, with 12 mechanical figures, one for each hour, representing key figures from Brussels' history. Every hour as the figures come out, the bells ring out a tune, which is Walloon one hour and Flemish the next.

The Mont des Arts is best-loved

Map on page 126

The Musical Instrument Museum is housed in a former Art Nouveau department store.

BELOW: Upper City grande dame.

Art in the Metro

Art in the metro is a long-established Brussels tradition. For the price of a public-transport ticket, and ideally armed with an *Art in the Metro* brochure from the tourist office, you can explore this underground exhibition of Belgian creativity.

Highlights of an artistic metro journey include stops at Horta, Bourse, Stockel and Montgomery stations. On and around Horta's platforms are sections of Art Nouveau architect Victor Horta's exquisite wrought-iron balconies. Stockel has a mural of Tintin characters. Bourse is home to Surrealist painter Paul Delvaux's homage to old Brussels trams. Belgium's traditional tramways are also celebrated at Porte de Hal, where the station walls are covered in comic-strip art by François Schuiten. Montgomery's "Magic City" design is by Folon, another master of the comic strip.

For a circuit taking in stations with works of art worth viewing, begin at De Brouckère, and stop at Bourse, Anneessens, Gare du Midi, Porte de Hal, Porte de Namur, Arts-Loi, Botanique and Rogier. An alternative itinerary goes from Gare Centrale, stopping at Gare de l'Ouest, Jacques Brel, Aumale and St-Guidon, and on the way back at Etangs Noirs and Comte de Flandre.

Anyone with a sweet tooth will find the mouth-watering patisserie displays on Place du Grand Sablon irresistible.

now for its small park, a geometric assembly of flowers, plants and walkways, softened by a children's play area. At both the front and back are grand stairways that together point the way to the Upper City.

High Gothic

Return to Place Royale and continue south along Rue de la Régence, passing the small **Jardin de Sculpture** (Sculpture Garden), which has a fountain and benches. After a short distance you reach **Place du Grand Sablon** ❿, the most delightful square in Brussels after the Grand-Place. The Sablon is graced by a beautiful High Gothic church, formally known as **Notre-Dame-des-Victoires** (Our Lady of the Victories), but more commonly called Notre-Dame du Sablon. The sumptuous church was commissioned in the early 15th century by the Brussels guild of archers, and completed in 1594. Especially noteworthy are its splendid stained-glass windows, the wall-paintings in the choir

and the carved wooden chancel (Mon–Fri 9am–6pm; Sat–Sun 10am–6pm; free). The once bed-raggled facade has been restored to its former gleaming white glory. The Sablon is particularly inviting in the evening, when the stained-glass windows of the church are illuminated.

The sloping Sablon square is lined with bijou restaurants and antique shops. It's a popular haunt for after-work drinks or Sunday morning brunch, followed by browsing in the Sablon **Antiques Market**. This is one of the most interesting and colourful of the city's regular markets, and is set up every weekend (Sat 9am–6pm; Sun 9am–2pm) on the square. The traders, whose approach is soft-sell and refined, are enthusiasts who are more than happy to expound on their speciality.

Bourgeois pursuits

A Sunday morning stroll provides a snapshot of the Belgian bourgeoisie at play: dapper bankers and genteel matrons pop into **Wittamer**, at No.

BELOW: Place du Grand Sablon (left) and Place du Petit Sablon (right).

12, pâtisserie par excellence, to collect exquisite croissants for breakfast or madeleines for tea. Across the square is an elegant covered shopping gallery, **Les Jardins du Sablon.**

The quaintly cobbled Rue de Rollebeek, leading from the Sablon to the Marolles quarter, is a popular spot for dining and browsing, given the profusion of picturesque restaurants and antique shops. At the Boulevard de l'Empereur end of the street stands the **Tour Anneessens**, a 12th-century tower from the old city ramparts *(see page 121).*

Peaceful square

Facing the Grand Sablon on the far side of Rue de la Régence lies the **Place du Petit Sablon** . This tiny, well-tended park is surrounded by an intricate wrought-iron grille adorned with 48 bronze statuettes, each representing one of the city's ancient guilds. The Art Nouveau railings were designed by Paul Hankar. The harmonious ensemble is dominated by a bronze sculpture group portraying the dukes of Egmont and Hoorn, martyrs of the resistance movement against the merciless Spanish Duke of Alva (the pair were beheaded on the Grand-Place; *see page 89*).

Behind the square stands the **Palais d'Egmont**, a 16th-century mansion remodelled in neo-classical style. Famous past residents of the palace include Louis XV and Voltaire. Today, it is the home of the Belgian Foreign Ministry. It was here in 1972 that Denmark, the United Kingdom and Ireland signed the treaties officially admitting them to the then European Economic Community. Only the slightly mournful palace gardens are open to the public (access is from Rue du Grand Cerf, south of the garden), overshadowed by the Hilton Hotel.

Symbol of power

Continue south on Rue de la Régence past the **Conservatoire Royal de Musique** (Royal Music Conservatory) at No. 30 and, next door, Brussels' 1875 **Synagogue**, which somehow managed to survive World War II, and which you can

Map on page 126

TIP

Just to the west of the Place du Grand Sablon, at 21 Rue des Minimes, is the new home of the **Musée Juif de Belgique** (Sun–Fri 10am–5pm; admission charge), an impressive collection of artefacts and books which chronicles the history of Judaism in Belgium and elsewhere.

BELOW: the antiques trade dominates the Sablon district.

Map on page 126

PC PCs: police station signs are in French and Flemish.

BELOW: *The looming Palais de Justice is built on the site of the city's former gallows.*

visit on weekdays when there is a service, provided you are discreet and do not take pictures – to the hulking **Palais de Justice** (Mon–Fri 9am–5pm, closed July; guided tours on written request; free).

The Palace of Justice, the city's law courts, was commissioned by Léopold II, the most imperial of Belgian kings. The architect, Joseph Poelaert, designed a monument to the Belgian constitution, with the law courts intentionally dwarfing every other building, whether sacred or military. The dome is 104 metres (333 ft) high; the total floor area comprises 25,000 square metres (30,000 square yds). There are 27 audience chambers and 245 smaller rooms, numerous offices, and prisoners' cells. The entrance hall alone measures 3,600 sq. metres (4,300 square yds).

The building was constructed in 1866–83, but Poelaert died, exhausted, before it was completed. In devising this eclectic design, he borrowed from virtually every period of Belgian architecture. In the end, the project became a symbol of Belgium's burgeoning industrial and colonial might. However, in recent years, the behemoth has become more a symbol of miscarriages of justice. The paedophile and corruption scandals in the 1990s, in particular, turned the courts into a focus for citizens' vocal protests against the ineptitude of the judicial system.

In the middle of **Place Poelaert**, the square on which the law courts stand, is a bronze-and-stone monument to the Belgian infantry of World Wars I and II. From the windswept esplanade, the city seems to fall away beneath you, revealing a fine view of the Brussels skyline, out as far as the Basilique Nationale du Sacré-Coeur and the Atomium.

Beneath you lies the working-class Marolles district. Employing a judicious touch of social engineering, the city authorities have linked the elegant Upper City with the Marolles via an incongruous-looking modern elevator that goes from the esplanade down to lively Place Brueghel l'Ancien (you can also go up and down on the palace's old monumental carriageway). ❏

RESTAURANTS & BARS

Restaurants

Bleu de Toi
73 Rue des Alexiens.
Tel: 02-502 43 71. Open:
L & D Mon–Fri, D Sat. €€
Close to the Sablon, this
cosy candlelit eatery
serves predominantly
French cuisine overlaid
with Belgian influences,
including their trademark
potatoes stuffed with
lobster, served in the
cosy dining room or on
the terrace in summer.

Castello Banfi
12 Rue Bodenbroeck. Tel:
02-512 87 94. Open: L & D
Tues–Sat, D Sun. €€–€€€
Chef Breeda Ruane-Kober
creates sublime Italian
food with a menu dictated
by seasonal trends and
specialities. The pleasing
results are attentively
served in an elegant Art
Nouveau-style restaurant.

La Rotonde
1 Rue de l'Enseignement.
Tel: 02-219 64 10. Open:
L & D Mon–Fri, D Sat. €€
Established in 1888,
this popular café-restau-
rant is still going strong.
The splashy 1990s "Art
Deco" interior and the
Belgian and French cui-
sine, with continental
frills, appeals to legisla-
tors from the nearby
Palais de la Nation.

La Tour d'y Voir
8–9 Place du Grand Sablon.
Tel: 02-511 40 43. Open:
L & D Tues–Sun. €€
Chic restaurant in a 16th-
century chapel above an
art gallery overlooking the
square. Exposed brick-
work, stained glass and
subtle lighting are used to
romantic effect. The
menu is rooted in classic
French cuisine, but the
chef is an improviser who
whips up dishes accord-
ing to his mood and the
whims of his customers.

Le Cap
28 Place de la Vieille Halle
aux Blés. Tel: 02-512 93 42.
Open: D daily. €
In a long, narrow room on
the ground floor of a town
house on an interesting
old square, this inexpen-
sive restaurant special-
ises in Belgian stews and
steaks, and cooks up a
good *waterzooi*. Open
until the small hours.

Le Grain de Sable
15–17 Place du Grand
Sablon. Tel: 02-514 05 83.
Open: L & D daily. €€
This restaurant could
easily be a triumph of
style over substance
were it not for the young
chef with a great sense
of adventure and the skill
to back it up. He does a
great line in salads and
other continental dishes.

Le Pain Quotidien
11 Rue des Sablons. Tel: 02-
513 51 54. Open: B, L daily. €
One of a chain of trendy
and convivial tearooms
serving excellent break-
fasts, lunch, afternoon
tea and snacks around
one big wooden table. The
loaves of bread, tarts and
jams are all home-made.

Le Relais des Caprices
1 Rue Ravenstein. Tel: 02-
512 77 68. Open: L & D
Mon–Fri, D Sat. €€–€€€
This fine French restau-
rant is one of the most
romantic establishments
in town. It is housed in a
surviving piece of the
15th-century royal
palace that was mostly
destroyed by fire in the
18th century. Candles
on the tables and an out-
side terrace in summer
complete the picture.

L'Ecailler du Palais Royal
18 Rue Bodenbroeck.
Tel: 02-512 87 51. Open:
L & D Mon–Sat. €€€
Set in a crooked 17th-
century town house,
this exclusive French
restaurant serves fine
seafood to a largely local
clientele. A marine theme
pervades the decor,
echoing a menu based
on lobster ravioli, smoked
eel, red mullet, grilled
turbot and the like.

Pablo's
51 Rue de Namur. Tel: 02-
502 41 35. Open: L & D
Mon–Sat, D Sun. €€
This relaxed Tex-Mex
place attracts a cos-
mopolitan crowd. The
food is solid and spicy,
but the margaritas and
other punchy cocktails
are the main attraction.
Live music occasionally
laid on at weekends.

The Lunch Company
16 Rue de Namur. Tel: 02-502
09 76. Open: L Mon–Sat. €
Conveniently located in a
narrow street between
Place Royale and the
shops in the Upper City,
this is a quiet restaurant
serving light lunches and
excellent afternoon tea,
coffee and cakes, in
rooms with a view of the
town-house garden.

Trente Rue de la Paille
30 Rue de la Paille. Tel: 02-
512 07 15. Open: L & D
Mon–Fri. €€–€€€
This fine and elegant
French restaurant just off
Place du Grand Sablon is
a steady if not especially
dramatic performer on
the gourmet cuisine stage
– and a regular favourite
among the city's foodies.
The menu changes sea-
sonally, and a big draw is
the line-up from the
autumn game season.

Cafés and bars

Between the Grand-
Place and the Sablon is
La Fleur en Papier Doré
*(53–55 Rue des
Alexiens)*, a snug 17th-
century *estaminet* with
a bohemian air. Magritte
was a regular at this old
Surrealist haunt.

PRICE CATEGORIES

Prices for three-course
dinner per person with a
half-bottle of house wine:
€ = under €30
€€ = €30–45
€€€ = €45–60
€€€€ = over €60

MUSÉES ROYAUX DES BEAUX-ARTS

Belgium's premier art museum is a stunning reminder of the great influence of Belgian art

The Royal Museums of Fine Arts of Belgium has two departments: Historical and Modern. Large and rambling, the sober **Musée d'Art Ancien** occupies the chambers of a restored neo-classical palace opened as a museum in 1887. On display are works from the 15th to 19th centuries, including a superb collection of Flemish masters featuring Jan van Eyck, Rogier van der Weyden, Hieronymus Bosch and Pieter Brueghel the Elder and Younger. Major artists linked to Antwerp feature strongly, notably Peter Paul Rubens and Antoon van Dyck. Great Dutch painters represented include Rembrandt, Frans Hals, Jacob Jordaens and landscape artist Jacob van Ruisdael. This museum is umbilically joined by a connecting corridor to the adjacent **Musée d'Art Moderne**, a subterranean cylindrical building descending through eight floors centred on a light well. The collection includes the works of such great artists as Courbet, Gauguin, Delacroix, Corot and Dalí, and Belgian Surrealists Magritte and Delvaux *(see opposite and page 69)*, as well as works by Ensor and the Flemish expressionists. Before starting out to explore, pick up a plan of the rooms from reception. This divides the museums into six colour-coded sections: 15th and 16th centuries, 17th and 18th centuries, sculpture, 19th century, 20th century and temporary exhibitions.

ABOVE: *Landscape with Fall of Icarus* (*c*.1558), by Pieter Brueghel the Elder, together with his *Winter Landscape with Skaters* (1565), are two of the museum's best-known masterpieces both full of life and fascinating period detail.

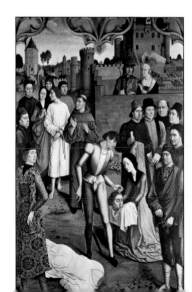

RIGHT: *Still Life with a Wreath of Flowers* (1618) by Jan 'Velvet' Brueghel, the second son of Pieter Brueghel the Elder, a versatile artist and outstanding painter of flowers.

LEFT: *Strange Masks* (1891) by James Ensor, forerunner of the Surrealists and founder member of the dynamic Les XX group in 1883. Ensor began as a realist painter, but his subject matter became progressively more bizarre as seen in his fascination with masks and skeletons.

LEFT: *The Justice of Emperor Otto* (*c*.1475) by Dirk Bouts, painted for the Leuven Town Hall, is a none-too-subtle reminder to the councillors to maintain the rule of law.

THIS IS NOT MAGRITTE

Rivalled only by Salvador Dalí as a Surrealist visionary, René Magritte (1898–1967), the Belgian master of paradox and visual puns, is one of those artists who has clearly seized the popular imagination. His eye-catching images shuffle the same themes and flit between reality and illusion: bowler-hatted men falling like soft rain on the suburbs; gravity-defying boulders suspended in space; a landscape mixing day and night *(above)*; a mermaid with the upper half of a fish and the lower half of a woman; words used instead of pictures. Perhaps his most subtle image is the simple picture of a pipe accompanied by the words *"Ceci n'est pas une pipe"* (This is not a pipe), forcing us to admit that… it is and it isn't. Yet behind the knowing commercialism, his are emotionally charged works of art, notwithstanding the blunting of ideas made seemingly banal by repetition in countless advertisements. In a way this is not so inappropriate, since Magritte himself worked for a time as a commercial graphic artist and wallpaper designer. The note of melancholy that inflects his work reflects the mood of Brussels, the city where he lived and worked, and is a reminder that Magritte believed in poetic images and the power of enchantment. Among the more than 20 works in what is the world's largest Magritte collection that you can see on floor minus 6 of the Musée d'Art Moderne are *The Secret Player* (1927), *The Empire of Lights* (1954, *above*) and *The Arnheim Estate* (1962), For more "encounters" with Magritte in places associated in one way or another with the artist, visit the Magritte Museum *(see page 173)*, the cafés La Fleur en Papier Doré and Taverne Greenwich, and the restaurant La Roue d'Or *(see page 117 for these three).*

LEFT: One of a series of powerful sculptures by Constantin Meunier (1831–1905) depicting the hardships and nobility of labourers.

THE LOUISE QUARTER AND SOUTH BRUSSELS

Shops, parks and fine houses abound in this traditional bourgeois area, but for many visitors the prime attraction is the home of Victor Horta, doyen of Art Nouveau architecture

Place Louise is the gateway to one of the city's most diverse districts, offering designer shopping, cinemas and smart cafés in a distinctly uptown setting. The so-called Louise Quarter is frequented by people who look so effortlessly elegant it seems they must surely spend their lives being measured, fitted and receipted. The adjacent commune of Ixelles, which straddles Avenue Louise, and parts of the small neighbouring *commune* of St-Gilles are more bohemian than bourgeois, and more charming for it, with delightful pockets of Art Nouveau including the Horta Museum and the elegant Art Nouveau buildings along Rue Defacqz and the surrounding streets.

Designer shopping

The city's main upmarket shopping district includes Porte de Namur, Boulevard de Waterloo, parts of nearby Place Louise, Avenue Louise and Place Stéphanie, and the elegant and expensive galleries that host a glittering array of shops: the extravagantly named **Galerie de la Toison d'Or ❶** (Golden Fleece Gallery), **Galerie Louise** and **Espace Louise**, **Galeries d'Ixelles** and **Galerie de la Porte de Namur**. Some of these galleries date from the 19th century, elegant shopping malls that reflected

the confidence of an increasingly powerful bourgeosie. At the time, they were an exciting new concept in retail trade.

Belgium's answer to Armani, Olivier Strelli, has his shop at 72 Avenue Louise. He's in good company, with Yves Saint-Laurent, Givenchy, Armani, Jil Sander, Gucci, Gianni Versace, Nina Ricci and others clustered along Boulevard de Waterloo and Avenue Louise, particularly between Place Louise and Porte de Namur.

Map on page 142

LEFT: the Louise Quarter, home of the well-heeled and well- groomed. **BELOW:** outside the Ultime Atome café, Matongé.

TIP

BeerMania carries an impressive stock of more than 400 beers. It also runs classes and tastings. (174–176 Chaussée de Wavre, metro Porte de Namur; tel: 02-512 17 88; www.users.skynet. be/beermania.)

Art galleries, boutiques, perfume and jewellery shops abound, as do restaurants, cafés, *chocolatiers* and cinemas. Even the metro station at Place Louise is refined: classical music wafting through the platforms and access tunnels, mosaics, stained glass, enamelwork and a tapestry all contribute to a carefully tailored display of good taste.

Before plunging into the chic avenues and Art Nouveau streets of this far-flung district, take sustenance at **Le Nemrod** (61 Boulevard de Waterloo) for a memorable taste of uptown Brussels. The cosy café is the preserve of bourgeois Belgians, decorated in mock-hunting-lodge style, with a blazing fire in winter, a pavement terrace in summer (heated in the cooler months), and an endless selection of beers.

Avenue Louise, long and expensive but also sober and dull for considerable stretches, was laid out in the 1840s to link the city centre with the Bois de la Cambre (*see page 146*). Originally, the broad avenue, which splits Ixelles in two, had a strip of grass and trees in the middle that until 1957 was reserved for horse-riding. Today, tramlines occupy the space.

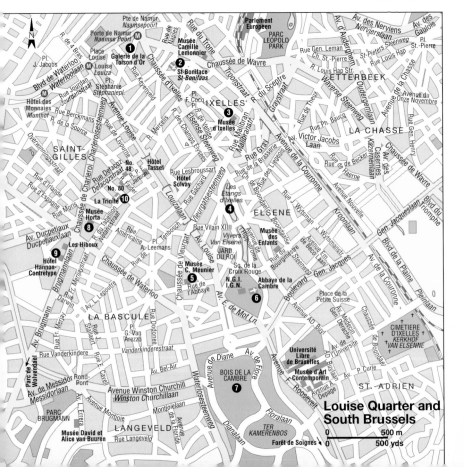

Louise Quarter and South Brussels

Map on page 142

You have a choice of either scooting along here by tram or walking. A better option is to take Chaussée d'Ixelles, which runs parallel to Avenue Louise to the north, through a scenic part of vibrant Ixelles. Originally a village, this *commune* has been part of the sprawling city since the 19th century, and is favoured not only by bourgeois Bruxellois, but also by writers, artists and intellectuals. It boasts fine houses – some of them Art Nouveau masterpieces – and a sufficiency of elegant restaurants, shops and parks.

Matongé

As a complete contrast from Avenue Louise, you could venture into the thriving, multiracial Matongé quarter between Chaussée de Wavre and Chaussée d'Ixelles. This small, lively area, named after a district of Kinshasa, is the hub of Brussels' Congolese community (the Democratic Republic of Congo, formerly Zaire, was a Belgian colony), who have been joined by other immigrants from North and Central Africa. The moment you enter this area, particularly around **Rue de Longue Vie**, you are transported into another world of market stalls and stores loaded with exotic fruit, palm oil, plantains and sweet potatoes; cafés selling African food and beers and blaring out rhythmical music; hairdressers that stay open into the small hours; and women in brightly coloured traditional dresses. Lively as it is by day, the area really comes into its own at night, when the bars and clubs fill up with regulars from all over town.

West of Rue de Longue Vie, backing on to Rue de la Paix, is the Gothic **Eglise St-Boniface ❷**. The interior is notable for its stained-glass windows – and the exterior for the bustling cafés that surround it. **L'Ultime Atome**, at 14 Rue St-Boniface, is a popular terrace café-bar and a great place for people-watching. And there are around a dozen stylish Belgian and international restaurants and cafés on this and neighbouring streets which have developed into a trendy enclave. Not far from here, in Place Fernand Cocq, is Ixelles' Maison Commu-

The grocers of Matongé stock more exotic produce.

BELOW: visions of Africa to brighten up a dull day.

nale (Town Hall), housed in a neo-classical mansion built in 1833 for opera contralto Maria Malibran and her lover, violinist Charles de Bériot.

Two museums

A few blocks south, at 71 Rue Jean Van Volsem, the **Musée d'Ixelles ❸** (Fine Arts Museum; Tues–Fri 1–6.30pm, Sat–Sun 10am–5pm; free, except for temporary exhibitions) houses works by Picasso, Magritte, Rembrandt and Rodin, among other great artists, and has a large collection of Toulouse-Lautrec's posters.

Although visiting it on this tour may be too much of a diversion, at No. 150 in adjacent Chaussée de Wavre is the house where writer, intellectual and champion of the working classes Camille Lemonnier (1844–1913) lived. Now the **Musée Camille Lemonnier** (Mon and Thurs 2–4pm, Wed and Fri 10am–noon and 2–4pm; admission charge), it is dedicated to his life and work and to that of other Belgian-French writers. It contains a recreation of his study, along with paintings and sculptures by contemporary artists, among them Constantin Meunier *(see page 145)* and Jef Lambeaux.

Ponds and green spaces

Continue along Chaussée d'Ixelles to Place Sainte-Croix, bordered by the tall 1930s **Flagey** building. The former national radio broadcasting station, with an art deco facade, was built to look like a passenger liner, hence its nickname *Le Paquebot*, which means steamboat. After years of restoration and refurbishment it has been transformed into a musical and cultural centre, complete with a trendy glass-fronted café, art-house cinema and performance venue.

Directly ahead is the tall brick church of Sainte-Croix, and to its right, trees and a line of ponds called **Les Etangs d'Ixelles ❹** in the valley of the Maelbeek stream. You can choose either bank of the ponds, but as the left bank has busy traffic and a tramline it is more restful to take Avenue Général de Gaulle, which begins with a monument to the Spirit of Flanders. In summer, elegant town houses on the opposite side are

BELOW: bourgeois elegance; a typical residential street in the Louise Quarter.

almost invisible behind a canopy of leaves from many different kinds of trees, yet this is close to one of Brussels' busiest districts.

Farther along, another green area, the **Jardin du Roi**, given to his subjects for their rest and enjoyment by King Léopold II, opens up on your right. Across Avenue Louise from here, at 59 Rue de l'Abbaye, is the house-cum-studio where realist sculptor and painter Constantin Meunier (1831–1905) lived. Now the **Musée Constantin Meunier ❺** (Tues–Fri and alternate weekends 10am–noon and 1–5pm; free), it displays around 170 sculptures and 120 paintings and drawings by this underappreciated artist, whose dark works evoked the hard lives of ordinary people in the industrial age. The pieces on display include a series of bronzes, one of which depicts a horse-borne prawn fisherman of the kind you can still see working at the Belgian North Sea resort of Oostduinkerke.

Continue southward past a sculpted African's head, a monument to Ixelles' colonial pioneers in the Congo, to Square de la Croix Rouge, which is graced by a sculpture of Henri Dunant, the Swiss founder of the Red Cross.

If you are with children, note that a diversion (though a long one for small feet) to 15 Rue du Bourgmestre on the other side of Les Etangs d'Ixelles brings you to the **Musée des Enfants** (Children's Museum; Sept–Apr Wed, Sat and Sun; May–June Wed and Sat; July Mon–Fri – all 2.30–5pm; admission charge), where a changing programme of hands-on, themed exhibitions allows children to explore their world. It can be a godsend for frazzled parents.

Cistercian abbey

From here, the arched entrance to the former Cistercian **Abbaye de la Cambre ❻** lies directly ahead. Lily-covered ponds, cool arbours, glades and a French-style ornamental garden laid out on five different levels form a tranquil haven flanked by busy Avenue Louise. They attract large numbers of visitors at weekends, but on weekdays they are an

Map on page 142

The pampered pooch, a popular accessory with equally well-groomed owners.

BELOW: weekend market by the Ixelles ponds.

TIP

The best way to get around the far-flung Louise Quarter and South Brussels is to hop aboard one of the city's yellow-and-blue trams.

oasis of calm. The 14th-century Gothic abbey church of Notre-Dame de la Cambre has magnificent stained-glass windows behind the altar, and smaller ones in the cloister that record the names of abbesses from 1201 until 1794, when the Revolutionary French abolished the abbey. The restored abbey building itself dates from the 18th century. Many of the old buildings have been restored, and today they house the National Geographical Institute and the Brussels Decorative Arts College.

Walks and picnics

Outside again, climb the stairs to the ornamental garden, leave by the gate just beyond a little fountain, and turn right to Avenue Louise. A short stroll to the end of the avenue brings you to the **Bois de la Cambre ❼**. Brussels' biggest park is the city's green lung, a place where people go in good weather to sunbathe, play on the grass and wander around. On Sundays in July and August, live music adds to the relaxed atmosphere. Riding-paths criss-cross the park – unfortunately

main roads with fast-moving traffic also slice through it.

Follow almost any path to the Théâtre de Poche, the nearby café terraces and roller-skating arena, and beyond to a small lake. A tiny electrically operated ferry makes a two-minute voyage to **Robinson's Island**, which used to have a charming café-restaurant called the Châlet Robinson, until fire reduced it to a smoking ruin. There is a proposal to rebuild it, however, and in the meantime an "emergency service" provides refreshments from a tent. You can hire rowing boats and pedal boats on the island.

On the east side of the park is a complex of buildings that house the Université Libre de Bruxelles (Brussels Free University), founded in 1834. The ULB campus's Salle Allende, at 24 Avenue Paul Héger, houses the **Musée d'Art Contemporain** (Museum of Contemporary Art; Mon–Sat 11am–4pm; free), which has a small but quite notable collection of modern art, mostly by Belgian artists like Roger Somville, Pierre Alechinsky and others. Considerably further out, at 1850 Chaussée de

BELOW: picnicking in the grounds of Abbaye de la Cambre.

Wavre, the university's **Jardin Jean Massart** (Mon–Fri 9am–5pm; free) is a research garden founded in 1922 that covers 5 hectares (12.5 acres), and is a pleasant, scented place to stroll around. It contains around 2,000 plant species and a variety of habitats.

Well to the east of the park, on the far side of Brussels Free University, the **Cimetière d'Ixelles** is the resting place for the architect Victor Horta *(see below)*, writer Camille Lemonnier and artist Constantin Meunier (both referred to above), as well as other artists, writers, musicians and notable people. Well to the east of the park, on the far side of Brussels Free University, the Cimitière d'Ixelles is the resting place for the architect Victor Horta *(see below)*, writer Camille Lemonnier and artist Constantin Meunier (both referred to above), as well as various other artists, writers, musicians and Brussels luminaries.

If you are a keen walker, you might want to continue south from the Bois de la Cambre, across busy Chaussée de la Hulpe, into the adjoining **Forêt de Soignes** *(see page 184)*, which

Map on page 142

extends over 4,380 hectares (17 sq. miles) almost as far as Waterloo to the south and Tervuren to the east.

Victor Horta's masterpiece

Although not in Ixelles, but in the neighbouring **St-Gilles** *commune*, which shares some of Ixelles' characteristics, the **Musée Horta ❽** (Tues–Sun 2–5.30pm; admission charge) at 23–25 Rue Américaine is easily reached from Avenue Louise (at Place Stéphanie) on the 91 and 92 tram. With some justification, Brussels considers itself the world capital of Art Nouveau architecture and interior design. Victor Horta (1861–1947), a master of free-flowing curves and naturalistic images in glass, iron and wood, was its most famous local practitioner. The museum is in the twin houses and studio the architect designed for himself and lived in until 1919. The facade is interesting enough, but not hugely different from that of its neighbours. The inside, though, is another matter. The house is a testament to his style, with an elegant terrace and winter garden and a

Gravestone in the Cimetière d'Ixelles, final resting place of the great and the good of Brussels.

BELOW:
Bois de la Cambre.

Art Nouveau Hôtel Hannon, built for a wealthy industrialist and amateur photographer, is now a photographic gallery.

BELOW: Victor Horta designed his own home, now a museum, down to the last detail.

graceful spiral staircase surmounted by a glass canopy. The house abounds in exquisite fixtures and fittings, from stained-glass windows to the original furniture, and contains exhibits of his best known architectural achievements.

A wealth of Art Nouveau

The *commune* of St-Gilles is a treasury of Art Nouveau architecture, and many of the highlights are within easy walking distance of the Horta Museum.

North of the museum, near Avenue Louise, is a cluster of other notable sites. The slight curves on the facade of the **Hôtel Tassel**, from 1893, at 6 Rue P. E. Janson, may not look like a revolution, but it was Victor Horta's first excursion into Art Nouveau, and gave him experience and confidence on which he would capitalise in future works. More significantly, the house is credited with initiating Art Nouveau as an architectural style (though it was partly based on antecedents imported from England). Near by, **80 Rue Faider** from 1900 is a development of the

style by Albert Roosenboom, Horta's pupil. Look for the fine wrought-iron balcony railing, sgraffito mural and other touches. At 48 Rue de Livourne is Octave van Rysselberghe's **Hôtel Otlet** from 1894, a low-key interpretation of Art Nouveau by an architect previously noted for his cool academic style, and with an interior by Henry van de Velde.

One block north of here, Rue Defacqz, which runs between Avenue Louise and Chaussée de Charleroi, is the most charming part of the district. The surrounding streets boast exuberant, daring Art Nouveau buildings and a gentrified bohemian ambience. Quirky boutiques and funky galleries are interspersed with Art Nouveau town houses designed by Paul Hankar. The architect's last home, at **71 Rue Defacqz**, has a geometric facade and Japanese decorative influences. In 1897, he designed **Hôtel Ciamberlani** at no. 48 as a painter's studio, with large rounded windows and sgraffito work displaying floral and animal motifs (the house next door at no. 50 is also by Hankar).

Southwards, just off Avenue Brugmann (which continues on from Chausée de Charleroi) at 1 Avenue de la Jonction, is the superb **Hôtel Hannon** , a town house built in 1903 by architect Jules Brunfaut and embellished by two French practitioners of the Art Nouveau style. Restored in 1985 after years of neglect, the residence has fine Tiffany stained-glass windows, a bas-relief of a woman spinning, frescoed stairways and many other decorative features. It now houses the **Contretype** photographic exhibition space (Wed–Fri 11am–6pm, Sat–Sun 1–6pm; admission charge), which has a changing programme of creative photography displays.

Just around the corner, at 55 Avenue Brugmann, is another town house, **Les Hiboux** (The Owls), by

Map on page 142

Edouard Pelseneer, from 1899, noteworthy for a fine sgraffito of two owls above the entrance.

Further afield, on the far side of Avenue Louise at No. 224, is another Horta building, the **Hôtel Solvay**. Dating from 1894, this mansion built for the Solvay family is something of an Art Nouveau masterpiece, since Horta had free rein to work both the exterior and the interior according to his own vision.

While in the area, visit the **Eglise de la Trinité ⓲**, a pretty baroque church at the end of Rue du Bailli, a few blocks east of the Horta Museum. It incorporates elements from another church, the Eglise des Augustins (1620–41), which until it was demolished in 1895 stood in what is now Place de Brouckère in the city centre. There's also a **Street Market** every Wednesday from 2 to 7pm in adjacent Place du Châtelain, where you can buy fresh food, flowers, clothes and more. This square is the focal point of a cluster of fine restaurants and trendy cafés that extends into neighbouring streets.

South to Uccle

West of the Bois de la Cambre, in the sprawling, leafy *commune* of Uccle, you can visit the **Musée David et Alice van Buuren** (Sun–Mon 1–6pm, Wed 2–6pm; admission charge), a wonderful collection of paintings, sculpture and objets d'art, both ancient and modern, displayed in the 1930s Art Deco house of a wealthy Dutch banker and his wife, who were keen art collectors, which is surrounded by extensive gardens. It is south of Rond-Point Winston Churchill, at 41 Avenue Léo Errera.

Yet further south, the small but handsome **Parc de Wolvendael** was known more for its endearing bronze sculpture of Tintin and Snowy than for its Louis XV pavilion and its association with minor royal weddings in the distant past. But Hergé's timeless comic-book heroes have been removed for safe-keeping to the Centre Culturel d'Uccle, next to the park at 47 Rue Rouge, and you can see them there during performances and by appointment (tel: 02-374 04 95). ❏

TIP

At 14 Rue Defacqz in St-Gilles is a memorable building, the Hôtel Wielemans. Designed in Andalusian Art Deco style and replete with *azulejos* tiles, the restored mansion houses the Art-Media Foundation (Tues–Sun 10am–6pm), which stages temporary art exhibitions.

BELOW: elegant town house terrace in St-Gilles.

RESTAURANTS & BARS

Restaurants

Amadeus
13 Rue Veydt. Tel: 02-538 34 27. Open: L & D Tues–Fri and Sun; D only Mon, Sat. €€
A fashionable and romantic Art Nouveau bar/brasserie/wine bar/oyster bar in keeping with the artistic mood of the quarter. The welcoming town house built around a courtyard was once French sculptor Rodin's studio, and the cuisine is primarily French too.

Au Bon Coeur
27 Rue Joseph Claes. Tel: 02-538 96 69. Open: L & D daily. €
Try this cheap and cheerful Greek restaurant near Gare du Midi for platefuls of delicious ribs grilled with oregano, *salade paysanne*, and perfect french fries, all washed down with jugs of plonk.

Au Vieux Bruxelles
35 Rue St-Boniface. Tel: 02-503 31 11. Open: L & D Tues–Sun. €€
This favourite Brussels institution, established in 1882, may look a little out of place, surrounded by bright, shiny, trendy new restaurants – but it is likely to still be here when others have faded away. The predominantly seafood menu includes mussels in many guises.

Blue Elephant
1120 Chaussée de Waterloo. Tel: 02-374 49 62. Open: L & D daily. €€

Although this internationally famous temple to Thai cuisine lies outside the historic centre, the enchanting setting, distinct flavours and charming waiting staff in traditional dress make the journey worthwhile.

Brasserie Georges
259 Avenue Winston Churchill. Tel: 02-347 21 00. Open: L & D daily. €€€
A bustling Parisian-style brasserie next to the leafy Bois de la Cambre. Given its location, it attracts affluent families and a post-yuppie crowd for Sunday lunch. Apart from traditional Belgian dishes, the specialities are steak, seafood (oysters and shellfish are delivered daily from Brittany, Normandy and Zeeland), game and cassoulet.

Ce Soir On Dîne à Marrakech
408 Avenue Brugmann. Tel: 02-347 76 01. Open: L & D Tues–Sun. €
A Moroccan fairy-tale place in the Uccle district. Waitresses dressed in Berber jewellery and headgear and displays of hand-woven rugs and spice jars set the Middle Eastern mood. Nor do the spicy dishes disappoint, with couscous, tagine and grilled meats served on terracotta plates.

Cose Cosi
14–16 Chaussée de Wavre. Tel: 02-512 11 71. Open: L & D daily. €€

An engaging Italian restaurant in the heart of the Matongé district that promises a fun night out. The cuisine is classic Italian but the clubby decor is colonial Kenyan, with kitsch leopard-skin benches and hunting trophies.

Gri-Gri
16 Rue Basse. Tel: 02-375 82 02. Open: L & D Tues–Sun. €
This small but lively restaurant serves African specialities in a room sparsely decorated with African masks. It evokes the Congo, but extends the African theme to embrace the Ivory Coast, Senegal, Chad and Angola, with a chef from each country to ensure authenticity.

La Châtelaine du Liban
7 Place du Châtelain. Tel: 02-534 92 02. Open: L & D daily. €
Located in the fashionable Châtelain district in St-Gilles, this is currently the best Lebanese restaurant in town. The decor is low-key but the Middle Eastern cuisine exuberant and creatively presented with mezze, tabouleh, grills and more on the good-value menu.

La Maison du Boeuf
Hilton Hotel, 38 Boulevard de Waterloo. Tel: 02-504 13 34. Open: L & D daily. €€€€
The Brussels Hilton is a cut above the average costly hotel restaurant in this city, thanks to master

chef Michel Theurel's clever way with French cooking. Much more than beef is prepared with delicate and inventive style.

La Porte des Indes
455 Avenue Louise. Tel: 02-647 86 51. Open: L & D Mon–Sat, D Sun. €€–€€€
High-class Indian restaurant from the same stable as the Thai Blue Elephant *(see above)*; in an elegant old house beautifully decorated with Indian antiques. The service from waiters in traditional dress is friendly but discreet, and the cuisine gives full consideration to the subcontinent's delicate flavours and sophisticated mix of spices.

La Quincaillerie
45 Rue du Page. Tel: 02-538 25 53. Open: L & D Mon–Fri, D Sat–Sun. €€
Although a bit conscious of its modish good looks, this fine example of an upmarket brasserie set in a converted hardware store in the fashionable Châtelain district is hugely popular. Its success is down to its cheerful staff, strong wine list, reliable oyster bar and a justified reputation for French *cuisine du terroir*.

La Truffe Noire
12 Boulevard de la Cambre. Tel: 02-640 44 22. Open: L & D Mon–Fri, D Sat. €€€€
This small but perfectly formed restaurant features gourmet French and Italian cuisine at

prices to match. Truffles (both black and white) are used in sauces, on bruschetta or simply grated over fresh pasta. The ambience is modern and there's a garden for summer dining.

Le Doux Wazoo
21 Rue du Relais. Tel: 02-649 58 52. Open: L Mon; L & D Tues–Fri; D Sat. €
A popular small restaurant in the university quarter. The menu features mussels and other traditional Belgian specialities, with the occasional more unusual French and Belgian dish such as duck stew, and is accompanied by a good wine list.

Le Fils de Jules
35–37 Rue du Page. Tel: 02-534 00 57. Open: L & D Mon–Fri, D Sat–Sun. €€
For all its chic interior à la Philippe Starck, this restaurant retains a neighbourhood feel. Sound southern French and Spanish wines accompany the *cuisine du terroir* of the French Landes region and the Basque Country. Dishes range from the artery-clogging *magret de canard* stuffed with foie gras to a healthy Basque-style sea bream and langoustine salad.

Les Perles de Pluie
25 Rue du Châtelain. Tel: 02-649 67 23. Open: L & D Sun–Fri, D Sat. €€
Occupying an elegant town house in trendy Châtelain, the food and decor of this excellent Thai restaurant, which mounts changing exhibitions of Thai art, are equally memorable. Spicy seafood dishes are a house speciality.

Les Salons de l'Atalaïde
89 Chaussée de Charleroi. Tel: 02-537 21 54. Open: L & D Sun–Thur, D Fri–Sat. €–€€
In a former auction house, this modish restaurant/brasserie/bar makes full use of its cavernous space. A baroque ground floor decorated with frescos and esoteric signs leads to an upstairs dining room kitted out à la Moroccan harem. The vaguely French, vaguely fusion cuisine, is satisfying if not inspirational. Choices range from mint tea and pastry to seafood, steaks and salad.

L'Ile de Gorée
28 Rue St-Boniface. Tel: 02-513 52 93. Open: L & D Tues–Sat, D Sun. €€
One of the stars of the enclave of chic, stylish restaurants and bars around the Eglise St-Boniface, this sweet-natured yet cool African restaurant does more than merely play with nostalgic colonial images and tastes. It provides a taste of modern Francophone Africa. Sophisticated and inventive.

L'Ultime Atome
14 Rue St-Boniface. Tel: 02-511 13 67. Open: B, L & D daily. €–€€
The good-looking waiting staff in this bustling bar-restaurant dispense cool cheer and vaguely Continental food to a young and arty crowd until after 1am. The picture-windows are a great vantage point from which to observe the comings and goings on the street outside.

Villa Lorraine
75 Avenue du Vivier d'Oie. Tel: 02-374 31 63. Open: L & D Mon–Sat. €€€€
In one of the country's best and most prestigious restaurants, close to the leafy Bois de la Cambre, master-chef Freddy Vandecasserie and son Patrick create memorable, classic French cuisine with the accent on fish and other seafood. You dine in beautiful surroundings in an ambience of graceful distinction, and can bask in the glorious Villa's garden in summer.

Cafés and bars

Standing out among the colourless cafés in this designer shopping district is **Le Nemrod** (*61 Boulevard de Waterloo*), a cluttered, overheated mock hunting lodge beloved by bourgeois Bruxellois, who feel perfectly at home amongst the stuffed beasts, foreign Eurocrats and fashion victims. The bar and bistro rated the best by beer connoisseurs is **Chez Moeder Lambic** (*68 Rue de Savoie*) in lively St-Gilles, the right address for *les blondes*, *les brunes* and *les blanches*. Arguably the most romantic bar in Brussels is **L'Archipel** (*163 Chaussée de Charleroi*), a literary bar and *café-chanson* in the district favoured by struggling artists and bourgeois students. **Café Belga** (*Place Ste-Croix*) in the far-flung Flagey building – Brussels' old broadcasting house turned art house – is one of the city's hippest haunts.

THE EUROPEAN QUARTER AND THE CINQUANTENAIRE

EU offices may loom large here, but this part of the city offers great museums, leafy plazas and an array of fine Art Nouveau buildings

To the east of the city centre, beyond the *petit ring* (the wide boulevards that enclose central Brussels) lie some intriguing areas. The Cinquantenaire district, surrounded by a superb park, is home to a series of prestigious museums, the only rivals to the royal art collections in the Upper City. The adjoining "neighbourhood of squares" is an elegant Art Nouveau quarter. Sandwiched between these two districts and the city centre is the European Quarter, the preserve of the Commission, the Council of Ministers and the European Parliament. The Schuman metro station serves both the Cinquantenaire and the European Quarter.

Compared with the elegance of the Cinquantenaire, the European Quarter is no urban showpiece. In keeping with a curious form of institutional irony, the cultural arm of the Commission professes a belief in mixed neighbourhoods, where residential, working and recreational areas blend harmoniously. Yet, unlike the Grand-Place area, gift-wrapped in Gothic facades, the European quarter reveals only odd islands of charm in a sea of ugliness. A victim of poor planning, this is a soulless, anonymous district devoted purely to servicing the institutions. After office hours or at weekends, the drab thoroughfares of Rue de la Loi and Rue Belliard resemble a ghost town.

For all the self-aggrandisement of the European institutions, the Eurocrats realise that Brussels, as the symbol of the new Europe, needs to move closer to the people, and to become a more pedestrian-friendly city. The capital also belatedly admits that Brussels deserves an elegant European quarter, Europe's equivalent of Washington, DC. The city planners have therefore come up with inspired ideas to link the

Map on page 154

LEFT: autumn brings colour to the Parc du Cinquantenaire.
BELOW: fountain sculptures.

TIP

The European Quarter is chaotic and widespread, and confusing to non-Eurocrats. Visiting on an organised tour is a good way to make sense of it, to distinguish the landmarks, and to gain access to many buildings. Architectural and thematic visits, generally restricted to exteriors, can be booked through the city tourist office.

cold European quarter with the livelier historic city, both spiritually and literally, by means of pedestrian walkways, bridges and lifts. But cynical citizens are still waiting to see how many of these projects leave the drawing board. The idealistic aspiration is still worth aiming for – to transform the Eurocrats into local citizens, and local citizens into citizens of Europe.

Towers of babble

The unsightly building adjoining Rond-Point Robert Schuman is the **Palais de Berlaymont** ❶ (guided tours for groups of at least 15 persons, on written request only, eight weeks in advance; tel: 02-299 16 22; free) – nicknamed "Berlaymonstre" (Berlay-monster). As the seat of the Commission, the European Union's executive arm, this 13-storey X-shaped building is the nerve centre of the EU. The august commissioners once occupied a smart building at 45

Avenue d'Auderghem, but since the 1999 controversy over the ethical (or otherwise) conduct of some of their number, they have been exiled to the departments they control and are scattered across the city. In Berlaymont's shadow is the **Bâtiment Charlemagne**, a glass-and-steel affair which houses the International Press Centre, home base for the legions of hacks from around the world who earn their daily bread by reporting on the EU and all its works, a purgatorial assignment where the devil is most certainly in the detail. These "showcase" buildings have been inserted close to rows of Art Nouveau houses, which are almost visibly ashamed to be seen in the same company.

Across Rue de la Loi (a frenetically busy street on weekdays), at No. 175, stands the **Consilium** or Justus Lipsius building (but better known locally as the "Kremlin"), named after a 16th-century Flemish

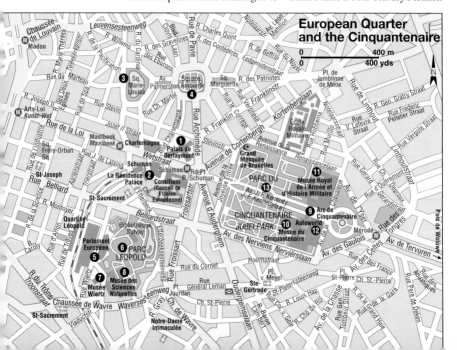

European Quarter and the Cinquantenaire

scholar. This mammoth pink-granite Euro-bunker is the formal seat of the Council of Ministers, although many top-level meetings of this body are held in other countries. Although only finished in 1995, it is already too small, since it was designed for a Europe of 12 rather than the then 15 member states, far less the current (2005) 25, or 2007's projected 27, to say nothing of possible future growth.

Brussels uprooted thousands of hapless Bruxellois to create this zone. In the surviving surrounding and often dilapidated neighbourhoods, many private owners refuse to sell, in the hope that property prices will soar if the European institutions want the area; by the same token, there is no incentive to restore property, since it could be confiscated or demolished at any moment, as has happened elsewhere.

To restore your spirits, or to drink to European unity, join the Eurocrats in one of the friendly bars and restaurants on Rue Archimède. What some might call a nest of Towers of Babel, and others a melting pot of languages and cultures, has spawned a cosmopolitan neighbourhood in which new restaurants and cafés are forever springing up.

Art Deco gem

Further west along the charmless Rue de la Loi stands **La Résidence Palace ❷**, built on the edge of the city's former aristocratic quarter. In its heyday, this chic cruise liner of a building was one of the most luxurious apartment blocks in Europe, inspired by the great British liners such as the *Queen Mary*. In the 1930s, the serviced apartment block boasted its own rooftop restaurant, luxury boutiques, post office, entertainment complex, health and sports facilities, and dumb waiters linking every apartment to the communal kitchens. If the building was miraculously spared in the depredations of the building boom, it was because the Eurocrats themselves appreciated a dip in the glorious Pompeian Art Deco swimming pool or enjoyed attending the odd function in the Art Deco theatre. Decorated with Lalique glasswork, these 180 apartments,

Map on page 154

Europe's civil servants are entitled to a special number plate.

BELOW: Square Marie-Louise, one of two chic squares spared by the bulldozers.

some with 22 rooms, are let on an annual basis to Eurocrats.

From here, a short stroll along Boulevard Charlemagne leads to the remains of Brussels' patrician quarter, including well-kept Art Nouveau residences.

The chic squares

In the 1870s this "area of the squares" was the most sought-after residential quarter, and remained prestigious until the 1930s. The squares were designed with the "new nobility" in mind, the *haute bourgeoisie* made up of diplomats, bankers and top civil servants. Centred on **Square Marie-Louise ❸** and **Square Ambiorix ❹**, these form the main visual pleasures salvaged from the urban wasteland. The finest town houses use the full range of Art Nouveau materials, from wrought iron and glass to precious woods and brick. Avenue Palmerston (named after the British prime minister who was foreign secretary at the time of Belgian independence), which links the two squares, has several Horta houses,

Maison Saint-Cyr's fairy-tale facade is a riot of swirling wrought iron and intricate woodwork.

BELOW:
Palais de Berlaymont.

including the **Van Eetvelde Residence** (1895–8) at No. 4, and the **Hôtel Deprez-Van de Velde** (1896) opposite. Baron van Eetvelde, an industrialist who grew rich exploiting the wealth of the Congo, decorated his home with precious materials from the Belgian colonies, from onyx to mahogany and teak; a crystal winter garden links two sections of the house.

The adjoining Square Marie-Louise remains pleasing, with its English-style gardens, duck pond and a complex water system which feeds the fountains. Square Ambiorix is even more delightful, and graced with one of the loveliest Art Nouveau houses in Brussels. **Maison Saint-Cyr** at No. 11, designed by Gustave Strauven, is a tiny, thin town house with a sweeping circular window – a remarkable achievement for a 20-year-old. Strauven's virtuosity is all the more remarkable given his limited resources, which restricted him largely to brick and iron. The city tourist office has information on walks that cover this area, but the only way to see any of the intriguing

interiors, including that of the Residence Palace, is to go on an ARAU Art Nouveau or Art Deco tour, organised regularly in English or French *(see Travel Tips, pages 224–5)*.

The spell is broken by a return to the ugly traffic artery, Rue de la Loi. However, a turning left down Rue de la Science leads to **Square Frère Orban**, a neo-classical oasis designed for courtiers and top civil servants employed by the Belgian state. Inspired by London's Bloomsbury district, the grassy gardens are lined with severe patrician town houses.

Folly of the gods

From here, uninspiring Rue Belliard leads to the Quartier Léopold, now home to the European Parliament and support buildings. Centred on Gare Léopold, the area between Rue Wiertz and Rue de Trèves was a diverse, living neighourhood until the 1980s, but since the bulldozers arrived, the district has been transformed, with yet more mammoth administrative buildings. Although the matching buildings officially serve the European Parliament, the complex resembles a self-sufficient city. Apart from thousands of offices and conference rooms, the Eurocrats enjoy libraries, restaurants, shops, a sports centre, and a no doubt much-needed "meditation chamber". A small electronic car is used to deliver the post along these labyrinthine corridors. This formerly shabby station area became for a time the largest building site in Europe, with a project to bury the railway station under a pair of oppressive institutional buildings. With typical Brussels logic, the station facade has been kept as a fine example of Façadisme *(see page 45)*, but the train station itself has been moved underground.

The **Parlement Européen** ❺ (European Parliament; visitors' entrance 43 Rue Wiertz; audio-guided tours Mon and Thur 10am and 3pm, Fri 10am; tel: 02-284 34 57; free), is housed in a huge complex opposite Gare Léopold. At night, this futuristic glass-and-chrome building can be seen from afar thanks to its curious lighthouse effect. The Parliament is dubbed *"caprice des dieux"*, the folly of the gods, because of its

Map on page 154

TIP

Rue Archimède, the road that runs between the Schuman roundabout and Square Ambiorix, is the site of several lively bars popular with the expat crowd that stay open until the small hours and show international football and rugby matches.

BELOW: the press room.

A Triceratops at the Institute of Natural Sciences, one of the city's most appealing museums for children. The huge animated models of Iguanodon dinosaur skeletons are the top attraction.

unwieldy size, lofty aspirations and resemblance to a French cheese of the same name. Inside are four debating chambers, including the main parliamentary chamber – a semicircle seating 750, complemented by a public gallery for 500 spectators.

This building makes liberal use of mirrored windows and marble, glass, granite and chrome, and includes sections which, after skilful horse-trading, were produced within different member states. In keeping with cosy national stereotypes, the German sections are supposed to be satisfactory while the Portuguese parts leave much to be desired. Even so, given the quality of the facilities, model members of the modern Euro-state have little need to visit the outside world. And, as the locals wryly remark, the expanse of windows in these glittering blue-green behemoths "keep the army of cleaners in business".

On the far side of the Parliament stands **Parc Léopold ❻**, a somewhat bedraggled park that was once home to the city zoo, a function it still performs today, albeit for semi-caged

Eurocrats in search of space. A group of educational institutes at its eastern end includes the Sociological Institute's **Bibliothèque Solvay** (Solvay Library) from 1902, which has a remarkable barrel-vaulted ceiling flanked by wrought-iron arches and mahogany wainscot.

Monumental displays

Off the southern edge of this complex, at 62 Rue Vautier, the **Musée Wiertz ❼** (Tues–Fri and alternate weekends 10am–noon and 1–5pm; free) affords a fascinating insight into the works of Belgian artist Antoine Wiertz (1806–65), exhibited in his former home and studio. His monumental, often macabre and erotic, canvases depict mostly mythological and religious themes. Well known in his day, Wiertz aspired to the greatness of Rubens, his spiritual master, but though undeniably talented, the proud Romanticist falls far short of the great master's genius.

More popular by a long chalk is the nearby **Musée des Sciences Naturelles ❽** (29 Rue Vautier; Tues–Fri 9.30am–4.45pm, Sat–Sun

and school holidays except July–Aug 10am–6pm; admission charge). The star performers in this sprawling museum are 29 complete – and mobile – iguanodon skeletons more than 65 million years old, discovered in southern Belgium. The whale gallery has 18 skeletons, including one of a blue whale. You can plunge into the ocean in a deep-sea diving vessel which transports visitors to a depth of 1,000 metres (3,300 ft) to witness mortal combat between a sperm whale and a giant squid. With other displays on insects, shells, coral and minerals, a trip to this museum is worthwhile, especially if you have children in tow. (Note that some galleries are closed for renovations until 2007.)

Léopold's legacy

As its name suggests, the Cinquantenaire (metro Schuman or Mérode) was created in 1880 to celebrate the Golden Jubilee of the Kingdom of Belgium. The prestigious complex, built over a military parade ground, was the jewel in the crown along the triumphal way linking the Royal

Park and the royal domain of Ter-vuren *(see page 181)*. Léopold II, the builder-king, intended the avenue to link the sites connected with the World Exhibition of 1897. Designed by the French architect Charles Girault, it links the two wings of the **Palais du Cinquantenaire**. Though not quite completed for the Golden Jubilee, it was ready in time for the 1897 World Exhibition held at the eastern end of the Quartier Léopold.

The Cinquantenaire is dominated by the neo-classical **Arc du Cinquantenaire ⑨**. At 45 metres (148 ft) high and 60 metres (197 ft) wide, the triumphal arch is visible from afar. The colossal monument, emblematic of the heavy, imperialistic style of architecture Léopold was so keen on, is a triple arch crowned with a four-horse-chariot sculpture group representing Brabant Raising the National Flag, faced with mosaics, and flanked by twin colonnades. Access to the viewing platform is via the Musée d'Histoire Militaire *(see page 160)*.

In summer the area becomes a drive-in movie theatre, with the arch providing the framework for a vast

Map on page 154

A short stroll from Cinquantenaire Park, Paul Cauchie's house, designed by the Symbolist painter himself, is another Art Nouveau gem and worth a detour (5 Rue des Francs, metro Mérode).

BELOW: playing football in the shadow of Le Cinquantenaire's arches.

outdoor screen (anyone turning up in a vintage car can watch the film for free). And on the last Sunday in May, ordinary Bruxellois put on their running shoes and join top international performers for the annual Brussels 20-km (12-mile) race through the city's streets, which starts at Bois de la Cambre and finishes at the arch.

War and civilisation

The Cinquantenaire complex houses three excellent museums. Foremost among them is the vast **Musée du Cinquantenaire** ❿ (Tues–Fri 9.30am–5pm, Sat–Sun 10am–5pm; admission charge) – it has more than 140 exhibition rooms, so be sure to pick up a free floor plan on your way in. This superb museum gives a grand overview of the diversity of world civilisations, from classical antiquity to the 19th century (though Africa is conspicuously absent, the continent is 'covered' in the Central Africa Museum in Tervuren).

Highlights of the collection include the 5th-century Syrian mosaic and a bronze sculpture of the African-born Roman emperor Septimius Severus.

The section devoted to non-European civilisations is rich in Incan, Mayan and Aztec artefacts. European decorative arts are also well represented, featuring everything from medieval furniture, altarpieces, and some superb 15th-century tapestries to modern ceramics.

The already huge museum was recently expanded to include restored interiors designed by the greatest Art Nouveau architects, including Horta, as well as new sections devoted to film and photography.

On the other arm of the colonnade is the **Musée Royal de l'Armée et d'Histoire Militaire** ⓫ (Tues–Sun 9am–noon and 1–4.30pm; admission charge), which displays weapons, military equipment, war posters and a host of other militaria from the past three centuries of Belgian history, with a strong focus on World War I and the battles fought on Belgian soil. Exhibits include uniforms, sabres and cannon from the Brabant revolution, as well as weapons used in both world wars. One whole section is dedicated to the history of the air force, including

BELOW:
the Army Museum.

a display of some 100 aircraft dating from the early years of military flight, including the World War II British classics, the Spitfire and the Hurricane. There's also a military library, containing some 70,000 volumes, as well as documents, photographs, prints and maps. From the top floor of the museum you can access the viewing platform of the Arc du Cinquantenaire.

Classic cars

Across the courtyard, **Autoworld** ⓬ (Apr–Sept daily 10am–6pm; Oct– Mar Mon–Fri 10am–5pm, Sat–Sun 10am–6pm; admission charge) takes you on a fascinating journey through the highways and byways of automotive history, tracing the development of the motor car from 1886 until the 1970s. Apart from the permanent displays, the museum regularly mounts special exhibitions. Its array of 450 top models from 12 different countries makes Autoworld among the finest museums of its kind in the world. Apart from a large number of Belgian vehicles, the pride of the

museum is the extensive display of vintage cars from around the world – many still in working order.

Jubilee park

The surrounding **Parc du Cinquantenaire** ⓭ (Jubelpark) is a popular spot for jogging, sunbathing and walking the dog. Near the entrance at the end of Rue de la Loi, in the park's northern corner, is the **Grande Mosquée de Bruxelles** (visits by appointment; tel: 02-735 21 73), one of the few mosques built for the city's sizeable Muslim community, which is also an Islamic cultural centre.

Near by stands Victor Horta's unfinished **Pavillon des Passions Humaines**, from 1899. This neoclassical temple was built to house a series of relief sculptures by Jef Lambeaux (1852–1908); showing the human passions, they scandalised polite society for their alleged obscenity. Lined up around the park's periphery are eight female statues representing the then nine Belgian provinces (West Flanders and East Flanders provinces are rep-

TIP

The long Avenue de Tervuren was laid out by Léopold II to link the Cinquantenaire with his Palais des Colonies, now a museum, built to glorify his acquisition of the Congo. The 44 tram runs along its length from Square Montgomery, past *fin de siècle* buildings and the Transport Museum *(see page 162)* through the Forêt de Soignes *(see page 184)* to the African Museum in Tervuren *(see page 181)*.

BELOW: vintage cars in Autoworld.

resented by a single statue; since Brabant split into separate Flemish and Walloon provinces there are now 10 provinces). Other sculptural monuments include one to Belgium's former colony, the Congo, and another to Africa in general.

East of Cinquantenaire

After the Cinquantenaire park, Avenue John F. Kennedy becomes Avenue de Tervuren; note the row of late-19th-century town houses on the right side of the street. You can make a detour southeast into the Woluwe St-Pierre *commune*, to visit the **Bibliotheca Wittockiana** (21–3 Rue du Bémel; Tues–Sat 10am–5pm; admission charge), which is both a museum of the history of bookbinding and a 3,000-volume library, with sections on genealogy and heraldry. Or, if you happen to be a fan of Robert E. Lee and Stonewall Jackson, you can head northeast into Woluwe St-

Lambert to the unlikely-sounding **Confederate Museum** (40 Rue de la Charette; visits on request only; free), a documentation centre for US history in general, but with a focus on the Civil War (1861–5).

More universally appealing is the **Musée du Transport Urbain** (364b Avenue de Tervuren; Apr–first week Oct, Sat–Sun and public holidays 1.30–7pm; admission charge), a fine collection of vintage horse-drawn and electric trams. To reach the museum, walk or catch the 81 tram from the Cinquantenaire to Square Maréchal Montgomery. From here the 39 or 44 tram will deliver you to the museum door. When it is open, some of the ancient open-sided trams shake and sway their way from the museum to the Musée Royale de l'Afrique Centrale in Tervuren – the price of a ticket includes entrance to the museum *(see page 181)*.

Fans of old books and newspapers should head to the Transport Museum

Parc de Woluwe, part of the green belt to the east of the city.

BELOW: Las Castañuelas tapas bar *(see listing, opposite).*

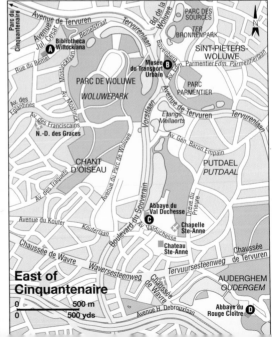

East of Cinquantenaire

on the first Saturday of the month between 8am and 5pm, when there is an antiquarian book market.

Across Avenue de Tervuren from the Transport Museum is another of Brussels's signature green spaces: the **Parc de Woluwe** and its **Etangs de Mellaerts** – these ponds, in a park laid out under the direction of Léopold II, are used for boating and fishing (and sometimes for ice-skating in winter).

Beyond this park, on the far side of Boulevard du Souverain, in the *commune* of Auderghem, is another attractive green space, with more ponds and at its heart the **Abbaye du Val Duchesse** ❸. This abbey was founded in 1262 by Duchess Aleyde of Brabant, and was the home of the oldest Dominican congregation in the Low Countries. In the surving building of later provenance, now a conference centre, in 1956, European experts worked out the text of the founding treaties of the Common

Market and Euratom. Near the abbey is the Romanesque **Chapelle Ste-Anne**, dating from the 12th century.

Further southeast from here (but actually still close to Avenue de Tervuren, which has followed a curving southeasterly course to about this point), is the former **Abbaye du Rouge Cloître** ❹ (Abbey of the Red Cloister), down a steep winding path off the neighbouring Chaussée de Tervuren, which merges with Avenue de Tervuren at a point further east). You can have a drink or a meal outside here, look around the gardens and the artists' workshops.

Back at Avenue de Tervuren is the dramatic **Palais Stoclet**, at No. 279–281 (you can walk there or try to spot it from the tram; it is on the right side of the road going out of town). This private residence of 1911 by the Austrian architect Josef Hoffman defies categorisation, and subsequently influenced different schools of modern architecture. ❑

Abbaye du Rouge Cloître.

RESTAURANTS & BARS

Restaurants

La Brace
1 Rue Franklin. Tel: 02-736 57 73. Open: L & D Mon–Sat. €–€€
So popular is the best of the Italian eateries on this street that the service can sometimes be brusque – or maybe this is just the natural order of human relations in the European quarter. Anyway, the pizzas, pasta and other Italian dishes are pretty good.
Las Castañuelas
132 Rue Stévin. Tel: 02-280 00 81. Open: L & D Mon–Sat. €€

A good tapas bar in the Schuman area just up the hill from the EU head-quarters. You can dine outdoors on a veranda terrace in summer.
L'Atlantide
73 Rue Franklin. Tel: 02-736 20 02. Open: L & D daily. €
An excellent choice for lunch in the Schuman area, serving authentic Greek dishes such as feta cheese and spinach pasties, and calamari.
Le Rocher Fleuri
19 Rue Franklin. Tel: 02-735 00 21. Open: L & D Mon–Sat. €
Near Rond-Point Schu-man in the European

Quarter, this Viet-namese restaurant is great value for money and serves a delicious all-you-can-eat buffet.
Le Stévin
29 Rue St-Quentin. Tel: 02-230 98 47. Open: L & D Mon–Fri. €€–€€€
A favourite with Euro-crats, this restaurant, in a fairly grand town house with a garden at the back, serves very good French-Belgian food.

Cafés and bars

Irish bars seem to have cornered the drinking market in the European Quarter. There's **Kitty O'Shea's** (4 Boulevard Charlemagne) and

James Joyce (34 Rue Archimède), both close to the Commission's Berlaymont head-quarters, and **The Wild Geese** (2–4 Avenue Livingstone), just off Square Marie-Louise. Escape from the EU and all its works to **La Terrasse** (1 Avenue des Celtes), on the far side of the Cinquantenaire. This more than decent neighbourhood café serves up some fine Trappist beers and continental food.

● ● ● ● ● ● ● ● ● ●
Price includes dinner and half a bottle of house wine.
€ under €30, €€ €30–45,
€€€ €45–60, €€€€ €60 +

THE CAPITAL OF ART NOUVEAU

Brussels, along with Barcelona, Vienna, Prague and Glasgow, was a major centre of the new movement that swept Europe in the 1890s

At the turn of the 20th century, Brussels had outgrown its medieval walls and the city was experiencing an economic boom. Prosperity from the Belgian Congo meant an influx of precious materials, from marble to ivory and exotic woods. While Paris opted for sweeping boulevards and mansion blocks set around inner courtyards, the Belgians were less enthusiastic about apartment living. The bourgeoisie preferred individual homes, from small châteaux and villas in the city suburbs to *maisons de maître*, distinguished town houses. While Catholics and conservatives opted for Gothic Revival or Flemish Renaissance styles, free-thinkers chose Art Nouveau, a style that was part of a progressive social movement, with a commitment to public building as well as private commissions. The main architects of the new style were Victor Horta *(pictured above)*, Antoine Blérot, Ernest de Lune, Paul Hankar and Henry van de Velde. Such innovators were generously supported by enlightened patrons, who commissioned architects to create eclectic town houses as "portraits" of their owners.

In Art Nouveau, the line subordinates all other elements, imposing musical rhythms and organic shapes. Architects favoured corner plots as stage sets for experimentation with exuberant facades, bow windows, loggias and intricate balconies. Many facades feature *sgraffito* (incised mural decoration) depicting floral and figurative motifs. The use of "plebeian" materials resulted in iron and glass adorning rich mansions, alongside marble and rare woods.

ABOVE: Floral tribute. Hankar's florist's *(see right)* shows a wonderful contrast between the floral motifs of the graceful ironwork and the fresh flowers within.

RIGHT: Magasins Wolfers. Horta turned out another masterpiece for goldsmith Philippe Wolfers, who commissioned the architect to design his shop and studio in Rue d'Arenberg (1909).

LEFT: Monument to a mayor. The Art Nouveau monument by the Grand-Place is dedicated to Charles Buls, Mayor of Brussels from 1891 to 1899, who instigated the restoration of much of the city.

ON THE ART NOUVEAU TRAIL

Musée Horta *(see page 147)* is a capsule of Art Nouveau, designed by Belgium's greatest modern architect. Horta's Hôtel Tassel (6 Rue P E Janson) is considered the manifesto of Art Nouveau (1893), while the Comic Strip Museum *(see page 109)* is one of his finest works.

The Cinquantenaire and St-Gilles neighbourhoods are studded with Art Nouveau mansions, including works by Horta *(see pages 148 and 156)*. In the Brugmann district, Hôtel Hannon, 1 Avenue de la Jonction, displays temporary photographic exhibitions. The frescoed setting (1903) is enhanced by a superb spiral staircase, Tiffany stained glass and mosaics.

In the Upper City, Paul Hankar's gorgeous florist's (13 Rue Royale) is the only surviving Art Nouveau shopfront (1898). At No. 316 in the same street is De Ultieme Hallucinatie, Hamesse's patrician mansion, and a delightful bar *(see page 127)*.

Urban heritage group ARAU organise guided tours of notable Art Nouveau buildings, mostly private residences which are otherwise closed to the public *(see Travel Tips pages 224–5)*.

LEFT: Iron and glass. Horta's pupil, Gustave Strauven, was just 20 when he designed the flamboyant Maison St-Cyr on Square Ambiorix.

RIGHT: Total design. Horta pioneered the concept of total design: "For my house, I drew and created each piece of furniture, each hinge and door latch, the carpets and wall decoration."

BELOW: Musical store. Old England (1899), the restored Art Nouveau department store, now houses the Musical Instruments Museum.

ABOVE: The last detail. The bright, curvaceous dining room of Horta's house (now part of the Musée Horta in St-Gilles, *see page 147*): stained glass, enamelled brick walls, mosaics, ironwork and floral motifs were all his design.

ROYAL LAEKEN AND HEYSEL

This area has diverse attractions: breezy royal parkland, glorious glasshouses and oriental follies, plus the Atomium and Bruparck's model village and tropical watersports

L aeken *commune* in the northern suburbs has strong associations with Belgium's royal family. The secluded Domaine Royal de Laeken (Laeken Royal Estate) both complements and far outshines the royal family's official palace in the city centre. The Belgian royal family are not noted city-lovers, and infinitely prefer to live in the secluded country setting of Laeken. The magnificent botanical gardens and greenhouses, which rival the English equivalent in Kew, have earned the domain the title of "glass city". As a colonial power, Belgium revelled in the profusion of exotic plants shipped in from the Congo. Apart from the leafy estate itself, Laeken's appeal lies in its exotic oriental constructions and theatrical hothouses.

Royal Palace

The royal estate revolves around the **Château Royal ❶**, concealed behind railings on Parc Royal. Although the palace is not open to the public, the grounds are dotted with curious monuments and memorials, and the famous hothouses. The Laeken Estate was created in the 1780s by Marie-Christine and Albert of Saxe-Teck, rulers appointed by Emperor Joseph II of Austria. Albert, a keen amateur architect, is said to have drawn the initial sketches for the palace and its

extensive gardens. At the end of the 18th century, Laeken was considered one of the loveliest estates in Europe. Not that Austria had long to enjoy it. In 1795, France annexed Belgium and the Austrians left, escaping with a prestigious art collection that formed the basis of Vienna's Albertina collection of paintings and drawings.

The Royal Palace was built by Montoyer during the second half of the 18th century but was remodelled in Louis XVI style under Léopold II. The occupying French forces planned

Map on page 168

LEFT: orchids, bananas and date palms thrive in the winter garden.
BELOW: the Atomium, a shining symbol for the city.

King Léopold II, the "architect king", was notorious for his exploits with his dancer Cleo.

to turn it into a public hospital. However, in 1804, Napoleon Bonaparte rescued the palace from total ruin, and used it as his residence until his withdrawal from Belgium in 1814 – his subsequent defeat at Waterloo in 1815 ensured there would be no comeback.

It was here, in 1812, that Napoleon signed the declaration of war against Russia. William I of Orange-Nassau became the next owner as ruler of the United Kingdom of the Netherlands and Belgium, but he had only a brief period to revel in the splendours of his stately home. In 1830, Belgium gained its independence, and Laeken became the residence of Léopold I of Saxe-Coburg (an uncle of Queen Victoria), the first King of the Belgians.

Royal Park

Léopold II (1835–1909), the second king, was responsible for the creation of the fine park at Tervuren *(see page 181)* and his impact on Laeken was equally great. This "architect king", who was responsible for many of the fine 19th-century buildings that grace Brussels and other Belgian cities today (with more than a little help from the resources he looted from the Belgian Congo), extended the palace

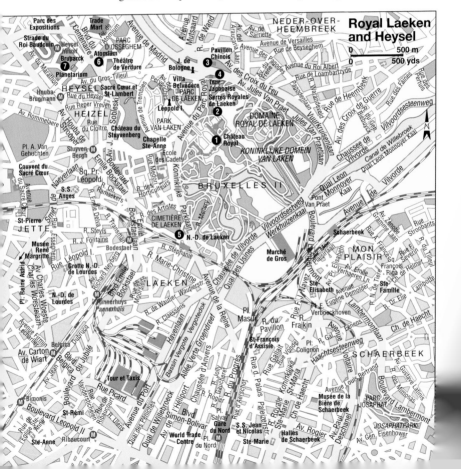

and had magnificent avenues built from the estate to the capital. The park was embellished by two superb oriental "follies", a Chinese pavilion and a Japanese pagoda, relics of the Paris World Fair in 1900. Set on the otherwise rather gloomy traffic artery Avenue Jules Van Praet, the pavilion and the pagoda lend the park an exotic air *(see page 171)*.

The king's plans to expand the domain of Laeken foundered on his death, and further development was halted by the outbreak of World War I. However, Léopold's greatest achievement at Laeken was the creation of the so-called "glass city".

Royal greenhouses

The **Serres Royales** ❷ (Royal Greenhouses; several weeks in late Apr–early May, when flowers are in bloom *(see page 170)*; enquire at tourist office on Grand-Place, dates and times announced Jan; admission charge) form a remarkable complex that has remained virtually intact since its completion in 1895. Léopold II's predecessors had toyed with more modest schemes. A Chinese tower

with adjoining orangery had been built by the ruling Austrian archdukes. Napoleon, too, had entertained grandiose plans for exotic hothouses, but these came to nothing following his separation from the Empress Josephine. The orangery as it stands today was built under William I of the Netherlands. Léopold I also had a number of lesser greenhouses erected to supply the palace with orchids and pineapples. But nothing was on the scale planned by Léopold II, beginning in 1876, inspired by his love of grandiose projects and the luxuriant vegetation of the Congo.

The royal greenhouses, one of the best-preserved iron-and-glass structures in Europe, are attributed to the prominent architect Alphonse Balat and a young Victor Horta. The techniques required to build metal-framed glass buildings had reached new heights of sophistication, permitting the construction of fairy-tale palaces which combined the romantic cult of the exotic with a longing for nature, exemplified by the sinuous forms of Art Nouveau.

The resulting greenhouses present

Map on page 168

The Fountain of Neptune on the royal estate is a replica of a 16th-century original in Bologna, Italy.

BELOW: statuary and greenhouses in the botanical gardens.

*An armed guard
keeps unwanted
visitors from the
royal door.*

RIGHT:
King Albert shows off
his hidden talents.

an architectural treasure that comprises a huge central dome, topped by an ironwork crown and flanked by a secondary chamber, cupolas, turrets and vaulted glass tunnels.

Palm trees and winter gardens

The interlinked greenhouses allow you to stroll from one end to the other, covering a distance of 1 kilometre (about half a mile). In the middle, a palm-tree complex meets a series of magnificent winter gardens, linked by an airy gallery. The palm-houses include a playful succession of passages and galleries abounding in startling perspectives.

The winter gardens, however, are designed according to strictly formal lines: a row of hothouses is laid out along a central axis, the pièce de résistance being an impressively vast dome-shaped hothouse.

The plants inside are rare and precious, perfectly in tune with the architecture. Léopold II particularly loved palms, which now curve majestically into the centre of the dome. These are joined by fuchsias

and figs, geraniums, azaleas and begonias, as well as tropical plants and camellias, the king's favourite flowers. Many species are of historical importance: most of the 44 orange-tree species are more than 200 years old. Bananas and myriad varieties of palm grow between wall ferns, overshadowed by broad palmyra palms. Ferns and orchids flourish alongside camellias which formed part of the original Victorian planting. Today, they constitute the most valuable collection of their kind in the world.

Léopold II's wish was that the greenhouses should be open to the public once a year; and this tradition has been honoured ever since. Each year, in late April and early May, when thousands of flowers blossom in an array of rainbow colours, the Royal Greenhouses open their doors. A night tour may be the highlight of a visit to Brussels. The spectacle only lasts a couple of weeks, but draws thousands of local citizens and tourists alike, who revel in the heady atmosphere of lush palms and exotic blooms.

The Role of the King

The rights and duties of the King of Belgium were laid down by the country's 1831 constitution and have remained unchanged since. According to Article 65, the king is responsible for nominating and dismissing his prime minister. In practice, of course, the choice lies in the hands of the political parties and the king has no real power. However, every day King Albert II signs documents and exercises his right to be informed on all matters of state. Article 64 rules that all documents signed by the king also require the signature of a minister to make them valid (the minister bears sole responsibility for the content). In addition to attending to paperwork, King Albert represents the state on all occasions, including internationally.

The royal couple's official residence is the Palace of Laeken. A black, red and gold striped flag fluttering from the palace roof indicates that they are at home. The official office and audience rooms are in the Palais Royal. It is here that Albert conducts most of his state work, receiving overseas ambassadors and representatives of European Union organisations and foreign firms.

Visitors drift dreamily amid the steamy fragrances of camellias and orchids, admiring the illuminated patterns of ferns and fuchsias.

Oriental follies

Outside the Royal Estate, in an unprepossessing location that is now a roundabout at the junction of several busy roads (you virtually take your life in your hands to get a close-up look), is the Fontaine de Neptune (Neptune Fountain), a replica of the fountain created by the sculptor Jean de Bologne in 1566 for Piazza del Nettuno in Bologna.

The nearby **Pavillon Chinois** ❸ (Chinese Pavilion) and **Tour Japonaise** ❹ (Japanese Tower), on opposite sides of Avenue Jules Van Praet, lend the park an oriental air (both Tues–Fri 9.30am–5pm, Sat–Sun 10am–5pm; admission charge, combination ticket available). Léopold II commissioned them in the early 1900s, as part of a whimsical plan to fill the gardens with exotic architecture, which was in vogue at the time. Both structures were designed by Parisian architect Alexandre Marcel, who had the panels of the pavilion constructed in China and transported to Belgium for assembly. It now contains a priceless collection of oriental porcelain from the 17th to the 19th centuries. The richly decorated tower is a monument-museum housing exhibitions illustrating different facets of Japanese culture.

Uphill from here, on the other side of Avenue du Parc Royal, is the **Parc de Laeken**, a wooded rolling park with ornamental gardens. In its eastern reaches stands the royal **Villa Belvédère**, which was built in 1788 for the Vicomte de Walckiers and is now the residence of the Prince de Liège; across on the western side is the **Château du Stuyvenberg**, a residence for foreign VIPs. Between these two palaces, which are both closed to the public, is a monument to Léopold I.

Léopold II engaged Balat and his fellow French architect, Girault – famous for his buildings for the World Exhibition in Paris – for the spectacular **Théâtre de Verdure**

Map on page 168

TIP

The shady Parc de Laeken with its views over the city is a good place for a picnic on a fine summer's day.

BELOW:
the Chinese Pavilion was made in Shanghai and shipped over to Belgium in pieces.

(Theatre Greenhouse) in the Parc d'Osseghem, which adjoins the Parc de Laeken on the side closer to the Atomium.

Sea link

The **Port of Brussels** extends from near the city centre to the Royal Estate's southern boundary. As early as 1434, Duke Philip the Good had granted Brussels the right to canalise the Senne river, which was in danger of silting up. In 1477, Mary of Burgundy authorised construction of a lateral canal alongside the Senne, to link up with the Rupel river near Willebroek, and from there ships could continue into the Scheldt river at Rupelmonde and thence to Antwerp and the sea beyond. The canal was completed in 1562. Between 1829 and 1836, the Willebroek Canal was deepened; and after further work, plans were developed in 1902 for the construction of a sea canal. World War I delayed the scheme; the new canal finally opened in 1922 to seagoing vessels with a draft of almost 6 metres (20 ft).

Today, the various port operations employ 8,000 people, and generate an annual €170 billion from a throughput of 18,000 metric tons of cargo: raw materials, finished and semi-finished products, and waste materials. It has to be admitted that not much of this effort contributes greatly – or at all – to the city's scenic aspect, but port operations do have a certain specialised interest, as you can see on a boat tour of the port and the canals leading north and south of the city with **Brussels by Water**, 2b Quai des Péniches (tel: 02-203 64 06). Used cars are auctioned between 7.30am and 1pm on Sundays at the Quai des Usines. There are good bargains to be had among the old bangers.

On the west side of the port installations lies the vast and crumbling **Tour et Taxis** facility. This early-20th-century complex of architecturally interesting bonded warehouses alongside railway freight sidings never made it into the 21st century as a going concern – at least not in its original role. A renewal project saved the crumbling monument from demolition, and is busy transforming it into a dynamic

BELOW:
Tour et Taxis, at the centre of the port area regeneration project.

district of refurbished facilities given new life in a variety of cultural, nightlife and social guises, accompanied by homes and offices.

Royal crypt

The church of **Notre-Dame de Laeken** ❺ (open for services only), outside the southwestern edge of the Royal Estate, at the junction of Avenue de la Reine and Avenue du Parc Royal, was designed by Joseph Poelaert in neo-Gothic style, and built between 1854–72 in memory of the first Queen of the Belgians, Louise-Marie. Many of the country's royals are buried in the crypt of this royal church. Also of interest in the church is a 13th-century statue of the Virgin, said to have miraculous powers, and the early-Gothic-style choir.

Other prominent Belgians buried in the adjacent cemetery, the **Cimetière de Laeken**, include the playwright Michel de Ghelderode, the architects Joseph Poelaert, Alphonse Balat and Léon-Pierre Suys, and the violinist Charles de Bériot. The tombs and chapels are decorated with works of art, the most impressive of which is the copy of Rodin's *The Thinker*.

In the neighbouring *commune* of Jette, Magritte's former house at 135 Rue Esseghem has been transformed into the **Musée René Magritte** (Wed–Sun 10am–6pm; admission charge) to celebrate the life and works of the father of Belgian Surrealism. Exhibits include original works, documents, objects, letters and photographs illustrating his commercial work.

The Atomium

The Heysel plateau, adjoining the Royal Estate to the northwest, groups together an array of attractions that make this one of the most popular, if least traditionally attractive, parts of the city. To get there, take the metro to Heysel station, or trams 23 or 81 from the city; by car take exit 8 off the ring road.

Many cities have a distinctive identifying symbol: Paris has the Eiffel Tower, London has Big Ben, New York the Statue of Liberty. If they don't, they can always create one, which is what Brussels did for

Map on page 168

BELOW: in Laeken Cemetery, a copy of Rodin's *The Thinker* marks the grave of artist and collector Jef Dillen (1878–1935).

the 1958 World Expo in the city. The result was the **Atomium ❻** (Apr–Aug daily 9am–8pm; Sept–Mar daily 10am–6pm; admission charge), a gigantic model of an iron crystal that dominates the Heysel plateau, and is as impressive in its way as any of the three mentioned above. This curious monument was designed to symbolise the potential of Belgian industry in the post-war period. It took four years to plan and build. The concept of its designer, André Waterkeyn, a professional engineer, was to monumentalise one of the fundamental building blocks of matter.

The Atomium's nine giant, aluminium-coated spheres connected by tubes, towering above Boulevard du Centenaire, represent the atomic structure of an iron crystal, with nine atoms magnified 165 billion times. (There were nine Belgian provinces in 1958, and each sphere also represented one – since Brabant's 1990s fission into separate Walloon and Flemish units, there have been 10 provinces. Iron being made of less transient stuff, the Atomium still has only nine spheres.) It looks like a *Star*

Wars set, as if all you need do is li the blue touchpaper, step back a the next stop is Alpha Centau Savour the impact of your fi glimpse, because you'll never anything quite like it anywhere e

A few vital statistics: the Atomi is 102 metres (335 ft) high; e sphere has a diameter of 18 met (59 ft); the tubes connecting sphe are 3 metres (10 ft) in diameter; es lators that transport you from c sphere to another inside the conne ing tubes are 35 metres (115 ft) lo and the lift linking the bottom sph with the top one is reputedly Europ fastest, whisking you to the top in seconds at 5 metres (16 ft) per s ond; there's a great view over Br sels from up here. After dark, the n spheres are illuminated by lights po tioned 1.5 metres (5 ft) apart. Th are switched on alternately, the po of light revolving around the sphe illustrating the motion of electr around an atomic nucleus.

Since the Expo, Brussels has sp a good deal of time scratching its c lective head and asking: "Now w do we do with it?" What they ha

BELOW:
an illustration of the Grand Palais for the cover of a news journal published in 1935.

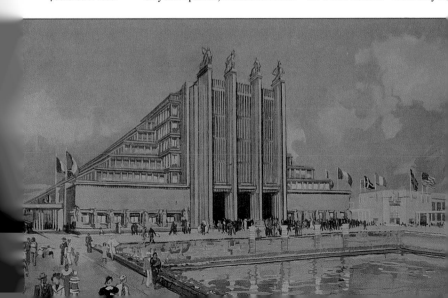

done is put an exhibition space inside, and a pretty good restaurant, Chez Adrienne, in the top sphere; an observation deck in the same sphere gives a fine view across Brussels. Note that at the time of writing the Atomium had been closed for refurbishment since late 2004 and was due to re-open some time in 2006, at which time there may be some variation on both the opening times provided here and the interior arrangements.

Grand exhibition halls

At the top of Boulevard du Centenaire, the **Parc des Expositions**, built for the 1935 World Fair, was extended for the 1958 World Fair and since then has grown apace. The enormous halls are in permanent use for trade fairs, exhibitions and international congresses, which are vital to the city's economy. At the park's heart is the 1935 **Grand Palais**, an exhibition hall with a big fountain and pools out front.

Whistlestop tour of Europe

On the west side of Boulevard du Centenaire, across a car park, is **Bruparck ❼**, which has become hugely popular since it opened in 1988. **Mini-Europe** (Apr–June and Sept 9.30am–5pm; July–Aug 9.30am–7pm and to 11pm mid-July to mid-Aug; Oct–early Jan 10am–5pm; admission charge) is its most interesting component, presenting the European Union's finest architectural and engineering creations with commendable realism, at 1:25 scale. This is Brussels' most important attraction as far as visitor numbers go.

There are more than 350 models – the Leaning Tower of Pisa, the Palace of Westminster, the Acropolis, the Arc de Triomphe, the canals of Amsterdam, the Brandenburg Gate, the Channel Tunnel, the Seville Bullring and Brussel's own Grand-Place to name but a few. To give an idea of the scale, London's Big Ben (which

actually chimes) is 4 metres (13 ft) high. The park is veering increasingly towards interactive attractions, making it a fun place for children. You can reawaken Mount Vesuvius, for example, or destroy a piece of the Berlin wall. And you can watch an Ariane rocket taking off and a TGV train speeding through France. A tour of the park takes around 2 hours.

Tropical pools, moules and movies

The **Océade** (generally Mon–Fri 10am–6pm, Sat–Sun and public holidays 10am–10pm; closed Mon Apr–June, Mon–Tues Sept–Mar; admission charge) is an aquatic theme park with giant flumes, wave machines, palm trees, plastic beaches, poolside bars and so on. It's fun at any time, but especially on a cold, grey winter's day, when you can pretend to be in the Bahamas.

You can have a coffee, a beer or a meal at **Le Village**, a faux-Flemish enclave of cafés, restaurants, fast-food outlets, souvenir shops, and children's attractions that include an old-fashioned carousel. One of the

Map on page 168

The Bruparck leisure complex may not be everyone's cup of tea, but the kids love it.

BELOW: make waves at the Océade water funpark.

Sporting Passions

What does it take to prove that all internationally famous Belgian sporting heroes are not necessarily male, nor do their surnames have to end with the letter "x" (think Eddy Merckx and Jacky Ickx)? Well, when Belgium decided to make a racket in the world of tennis, it produced not one but two heroines: Kim Clijsters and Justine Henin-Hardenne. And, this being Belgium, one of them is Flemish (Kim) and the other Walloon (Justine). Although at the start of 2005 both young tennis aces were languishing on the sidelines due to injury and illness, Justine Henin-Hardenne made a dramatic comeback by winning the French Open in June 2005.

The Belgian Open and Antwerp Classic (in which the winner receives a diamond-studded racket) are Belgium's premier tennis events. Tennis is popular, with many public and private tennis courts all over the country.

Before Kim and Justine, Eddy "the Cannibal" Merckx, the outstanding racing cyclist of the 1960s and '70s, was one of the few Belgian sporting personalities whose name was familiar abroad. Merckx won every major international cycling race, gaining the coveted Tour de France trophy no fewer than five times.

Cycling arouses strong passions in Belgium, and a new generation of Belgian enthusiasts, among them Merckx's son Axel, try hard to emulate his example in local annual competitions like the Tour de Belgique, Toer van Vlaanderen (Tour of Flanders), Flèche Wallonne (Walloon Arrow), Paris–Brussels race and the prestigious Eddy Merckx Grand Prix, as well as in the big international events. It is without doubt the favourite national sport. Hardly a day goes by without a cycling race somewhere supported by thousands of enthusiastic spectators along the route.

For Belgium's Formula One Grand Prix race, you have to go a long way out of town, to Spa-Francorchamps in the Ardennes. One of the sport's most testing and scenic circuits, it winds through the Ardennes hills and forests. No Belgian driver has managed to emulate the great Jacky Ickx's eight Formula One Grand Prix victories in 116 races between 1967 and 1979. Thierry Boutsen came closest with three wins in 163 races between 1983 and 1993, but he never had the opportunity to drive for an elite team. Ickx also dominated the Le Mans 24-hour race, winning it a record-breaking six times.

Bruxellois with limited sporting ability like nothing better than retiring to the city's bars to indulge in a quiet game of billiards. The professional standards some players reach are demonstrated by a string of world championships won by the nation's experts.

Other popular sports include golf (Belgium has more than 60 courses) and cross-country skiing, which is practised in winter in the Ardennes hills. During the summer months, sailing and surfing are both popular pastimes on the coast. Rugby is played predominantly in the French-speaking provinces, where it is a favourite spectator sport.

And then there's football. Brussels' own Anderlecht side is generally in contention when national and European honours are to play for – but it never quite gets there on the European arena. ❏

LEFT: Justine Henin-Hardenne celebrates her win against fellow Belgian, Kim Clijsters, at the US Open Tennis Tournament women's finals 2003.

best restaurants is a branch of the Chez Léon chain, the place for *moules*. There are plenty of other so-so restaurants if seafood does not appeal. You can even dine aboard a train restaurant car, on a single segment stretch of track outside a make-believe railway station.

Also in the Bruparck complex is the huge **Kinepolis** multiplex cinema, which has 26 screens showing mostly mainstream films in their original language (usually English). A giant IMAX wrap-around screen projects short 3D films with full sensurround sound and effects.

Stargazing and soccer

The **National Planetarium** (Mon–Fri 9am–4.30pm, Sun 1.30–4pm; admission charge) is just outside Bruparck, at 10 Avenue de Bouchout, which leads westwards from the Atomium. North of here is the magnificent **Stade du Roi Baudouin** (King Baudouin Stadium). This replaced the demolished old Heysel Stadium, scene of the 1985 tragedy in which 39 Italian soccer fans were crushed to death when part of the sta-

dium collapsed as Juventus of Turin supporters were trying to get away from attacking hooligan supporters of Liverpool during a European Cup final. The Belgian police took some of the blame for being unprepared and disorganised, and have since acquired a reputation for erring on the side of hard-handedness when dealing with football-related disorder. International matches are generally played at the stadium, and the performances by the national team – dubbed the "Red Devils" – are on the whole creditable, though by no means good enough to scale the heights.

Schaerbeek

Back towards Brussels, the once fashionable *commune* of Schaerbeek is now a deprived and run-down area with a large and poorly integrated immigrant population. A few traces of its more prestigious past can be seen in the grand domestic architecture, particularly in the zones around Parc Josaphat, the striking Maison Communale (Town Hall) on Place Colignon, and the downhill approach on Avenue Huart Hamoir to the

Map on page 168

 TIP

Should you happen to be going by train from Gare du Nord and have some time to kill, visit the Musée des Chemins de Fer Belges (Belgian Railway Museum; Mon–Fri and first Sat in month 9am–4.30pm; free), an exhibition of some 30 Belgian locomotives and coaches, the earliest dating from 1835.

BELOW: Europe's greatest landmarks in miniature.

Map on page 168

Les Halles de Schaerbeek – the converted market hall is a thriving French-speaking cultural centre.

BELOW: Parc Josaphat has ponds, sculptures, and free concerts during the summer.

equally striking, temple-like Schaerbeek railway station. It is a vision of faded elegance. Magritte lived here for a time.

Parc Josaphat is one of the few reasons to visit Schaerbeek (though not at night). This naturalistic space is filled with flowers, plants and birds, and has a couple of duck ponds and a scattering of sculptures. Close to the west side of the park, at 31–33 Avenue Louis Bertrand, the **Musée de la Bière de Schaerbeek** (Wed and Sat 2–6pm; admission charge) covers the history and practice of brewing in Belgium, and has a collection of more than 1,000 different Belgian beer bottles.

La Maison Autrique (Wed–Sun noon–6pm; admission charge), an Art Nouveau Horta residence from 1893 at 266 Chaussée de Haecht, has been transformed into a convincing dream world. By means of ingenious installations, comic-strip artist François Schuiten has turned the windows into cinema screens projecting the fantasy life of the house. This is contemporary Brussels at its best: creating a new vision of the city while retaining the authenticity of the existing building.

The nearby **Halles de Schaerbeek**, former covered markets and warehouses at 22 Rue Royale Ste-Marie, represent a cutting-edge French-speaking cultural centre. Inside is a series of exciting performance spaces. This is the place for Latin music, hip-hop and rock, as well as *chanson française* and circuses.

Downhill from here – in more than one sense – the streets bordering Gare du Nord immediately to the north and east of the station are best avoided. They house Brussels' main red-light district. This area is sleazy and far from safe. On the other side of the station is the city's little Manhattan, a cold place of office towers – among them the city's World Trade Centre – that has all the charm of a missile silo, and winds that howl mournfully around the corners. An effort of sorts has been made to humanise the district a bit with a thin green strip of park along Boulevard Emile Jacqmain, but somehow it seems like a lost cause. ❑

RESTAURANTS & BARS

Restaurants

Bruneau
73–75 Avenue Broustin. Tel: 02-427 69 78. Open: L & D Thur–Mon. €€€€
Evergreen hangout for gastronomes in the Ganshoren district, close to the giant Koekelberg Basilica. Master-chef Jean-Pierre Bruneau and his accomplished assistants serve inventive contemporary French and Belgian dishes, including a delicious ravioli with celery and truffles, and a rich roast turbot.

De Ultieme Hallucinatie
316 Rue Royale. Tel: 02-217 06 14. Open: L & D Mon–Fri, D Sat (restaurant); L & D Mon–Fri, D Sat–Sun (brasserie). €€€ (restaurant) € (brasserie).
Both places here are renowned for their good food and Art Nouveau surroundings. The gourmet restaurant in a former Masonic lodge serves French haute cuisine with a Flemish flavour, embracing such classics as *moules marinières*, poached brill, and tagliatelle with smoked salmon. The lively brasserie incorporates a winter garden and a weird grotto.

King Hwa
40 Chaussée de Louvain. Tel: 02-230 15 79. Open: L & D Tues–Sun. €
Excellent Chinese restaurant in St-Josse which offers an enormous choice of dishes from all regions of China, and adds a few from Vietnam for good measure. It may not be the best of its class in any single style, but it does a professional job on them all and is great value for money.

La Bonne Humeur
244 Chaussée de Louvain. Tel: 02-230 71 69. Open: L & D Thur–Sun. €
It may look like a workaday café, but this small no-frills, family-run, neighbourhood restaurant has people – primarily Bruxellois who know what they're about – queuing in the street to eat their excellent *moules-frites*. Go early, as the kitchen closes at 9.30pm.

Le Saint-Germain
1 Place Rogier. Tel: 02-203 20 03. Open: L & D Mon–Fri. €€
Time was when this venerable brasserie looked lost and lorn amid a clutter of dingy sex clubs. The latter have been swept away and the restaurant benefited as the neighbourhood went up in the world. Now you can enjoy its sober service and stylish presentation of Belgian and French dishes.

Passage to India
223 Chaussée de Louvain. Tel: 02-735 31 47. Open: L & D daily. €
This unpretentious and friendly establishment is probably the best in this enclave of Indian restaurants on this section of the long Chaussée de Louvain. It offers a fairly broad range of classic Indian dishes, alongside a few more unusual items, such as Bangladeshi freshwater fish. Evening candlelight adds a touch of romance.

Cafés and bars

Easily the best café in this area is **De Ultieme Hallucinatie** (316 Rue Royale), which also happens to have a fine restaurant on the premises *(see above)*. Two good bets in Schaerbeek are the bustling **'t Narrenschip** *(185 Rue Rogier)*, which stocks around 100 beers and features live music, and **Le Jugement Dernier** *(240 Chaussée de Haecht)*, a neighbourhood café-plus, which serves around 260 different beers.

PRICE CATEGORIES

Prices for three-course dinner per person with a half-bottle of house wine:
€ = under €30
€€ = €30–45
€€€ = €45–60
€€€€ = over €60

RIGHT: De Ultieme Hallucinatie.

AROUND BRUSSELS

There's a choice of excursions in all directions: the university town of Leuven and the battlefield of Waterloo to the south, the lovely towns of Lier and Mechelen to the north and country walks all around

Whichever direction you choose to take, it is easy to escape the bustle of the capital. North, south, east and west, the surrounding provinces of Flemish Brabant and Walloon Brabant offer a wide variety of excursion options. Idyllic little towns, fairy-tale castles and historic churches all bear witness to the country's colourful history.

Tervuren

On the eastern fringes of Brussels is the old Flemish town of **Tervuren** ❶, 10 km (6 miles) from Brussels via the Avenue de Tervuren (Tervurensesteenweg), a long boulevard laid out by King Léopold II. During the 17th and 18th centuries, **Tervuren Park** – over 200 hectares (500 acres) of gardens and lakes – was the setting for glittering court balls. Its manicured lawns, boating lakes, flowerbeds and trees make it a favourite destination for excursions from the capital. Originally a hunting lodge, Tervuren Palace was rebuilt as a royal residence by Albert and Isabella at the beginning of the 17th century. It was demolished in 1781 by Emperor Joseph II; only **St Hubert's Chapel**, built in 1617, and the 18th-century **Palace Stables** remain.

On the edge of the spacious park is the **Musée Royal de l'Afrique Centrale/Koninklijk Museum voor**

Midden Afrika (Royal Museum of Central Africa; 13 Leuvensesteenweg; Tues–Fri 10am–5pm, Sat–Sun 10am–6pm; admission charge). King Léopold II's original Congo collection, displayed in a palatial neoclassical colonial villa, forms the core of the exhibition. The collection grew so quickly that the king decided to commission the present building, a dignified structure in the style of Louis XVI, to accommodate it. On the opposite side of the road, a massive stone elephant points the way.

Map on page 182

LEFT: Villers-la-Ville.
BELOW: Mellaerts Park, Woluwe-St-Pierre.

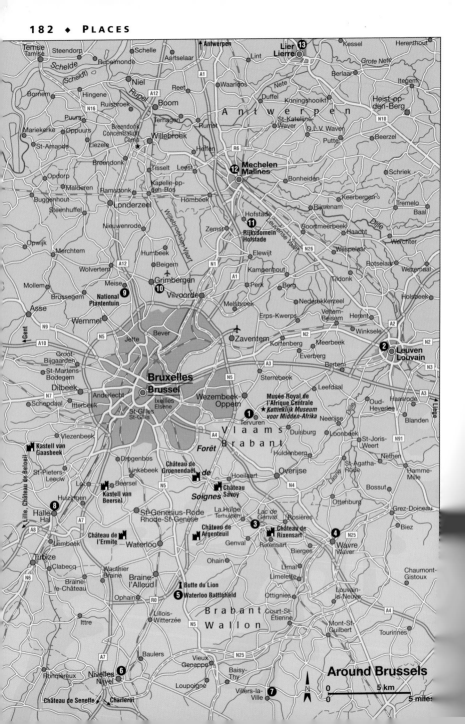

Around Brussels

0 ————— 5 km
0 ————— 5 miles

The museum is Belgium's monument to its colonial glories in the Congo and to the Belgian pioneers who "opened up" this and other parts of the "Dark Continent". Also included are mementoes of Henry Morton Stanley, of "Dr Livingstone, I presume…" fame. In these enlightened times the museum has moved beyond simple imperialistic images, but you can see some of the rifles and artillery pieces that no doubt played a persuasive role in the opening up.

In a setting worthy of a royal country retreat, which it once was, the building itself is a stunning piece of architecture in the grandiose style that went down well in 1910, with a superb, naturally lit rotunda as an entrance foyer. Since the Congo gained its independence in 1960, the exhibitions have broadened to include much of Africa and aspects of ethnography on a global scale. The exhibition halls feature modern African sculpture, as well as crafts, archaeology and wildlife, and explore environmental and development issues such as the problem of desertification and the destruction of rainforests.

Exhibits on display include Central African ivory carvings, dancers' masks, weapons, everyday tools, cult objects and sculptures. Among the most interesting items is a huge pirogue – a canoe carved from a single tree trunk. The zoological, geological, mineralogical and botanical sections provide a wealth of information about Central Africa, and children of all ages love the dioramas, displaying stuffed crocodiles, antelopes, water buffaloes, rhinoceroses, zebras, lions, giraffes and elephants, all set in mock-ups of their natural habitats.

Forest walks

Back outside, you can wander around the gardens and among the ornamental pools. Following the line of the main pool across Keizerinnedreef and Spaans Huisdreef takes you to a cool forest walk, then, on the left, to a lake called the Vijfer Van Vossem. A few minutes' walk in the other direction, along Keizerinnedreef, brings you to a waterside café called Aan de Bootjes. In good weather it is pleasant to sit on

Map on page 182

The elephant points the way to one of the finest museums of African art in Europe.

BELOW:
colonial days recalled in the Royal Museum of Central Africa.

TIP

The Forêt de Soignes
is a lovely place for
walking and
picnicking at any time
of year, but it is
definitely at its best in
the autumn, when the
trees and forest floor
are bathed in golden
and russet hues.

RIGHT: the Forêt
de Soignes in all
its autumn glory.

the terrace and nurse a cherry-based beer or a glass of wine while watching the pleasure boats on the lake.

After visiting the museum, Tervuren itself is worth a wander round. The historic centre, in particular **Kasteelstraat**, has fine examples of 18th- and 19th-century town houses. Art Nouveau architect Henry van der Velde designed and lived in **Het Nieuwe Huis** (3 Albertlaan).

Before leaving the town, take a stroll in the **Kapuzinenbos**. Léopold II had a little footpath laid between Tervuren and the village of Jezus-Eik; it is a lovely woodland route, skirting the domain of a former Capuchin monastery. An **arboretum** was planted here in 1902; its trees are grouped according to place of origin (Europe, America, China and Japan).

This forest adjoins the great **Fôret de Soignes** (*see below*), which is more or less a southward continuation of the city's Bois de la Cambre (*see page 146*), but much more rugged and overgrown. Many paths wind through it, and it is a favourite place of escape for city denizens at weekends and during the summer.

Leuven

The pleasant medieval town of L ven ❷ (Louvain), 25 km (16 mil east of Brussels, has the oldest u versity in the Low Countries. Leuv was founded as a trading settlem on the site of a Viking fortre destroyed and later rebuilt by Co Lambert I during the 11th centu Thanks to its strategic position on Dijle river, commanding the ro from the Rhine valley to the sea, settlement grew rapidly in imp tance, and in the 12th century r eived its charter. During the 12th 13th centuries, the town's weav industry made it one of the m important cloth-manufacturing c tres in Europe. The monasteries churches still bear witness to the mendous wealth of the Counts Leuven, who, in 1190, also beca Dukes of Brabant.

In 1378 the guildsmen and pe ants revolted against the aristocra and one noble was killed as attempted to flee the mayhem. A reprisals by the Duke of Luxe bourg, many weavers emigrated England, where the textile indust

The Fôret de Soignes

In Roman times, the Forêt de Soignes was just part of a dense forest that covered most of Belgium. It later became a hunting preserve for wild boar and stags, belonging to the Dukes of Brabant and their successors, including Habsburg emperor Charles V. Today the rolling forest stretches over 4,380 hectares (10,823 acres) – only one-third of its 19th-century extent – almost as far as Waterloo in the south and Tervuren in the east. Criss-crossed by a network of paths, the forest, which is mostly made up of beech trees but also includes oak and conifers, is a popular place for walking, cycling and horse-riding. Nestling in a valley at its heart are the ruins of the ancient **Abbaie de Groenendael**, with an arboretum sheltering around 400 forest species. On the southern edge of the forest, 17th-century Renaissance **Château de Rixensart** (*see page 192*) houses a collection of antique furniture, Gobelin tapestries and Beauvais wall hangings. To find out more about the history and ecology of the Soignes Forest, visit the **Information Centre** (4 Drève du Rouge Cloître; Tues–Sun, May–Oct 2–6pm, Nov–April 2–5pm; tel: 02-629 34 11/02-660 64 17), in its northern reaches near the Chaussée de Wavre.

were beginning to thrive; the town, robbed of its *raison d'être*, ceded its dominant position to Brussels.

Leuven's most famous sites, the Stadhuis (Town Hall) and Sint-Pieterskerk (the church of St Peter), are grouped round the Grote Markt. The **Stadhuis** was built by Mathieu de Layens between 1448 and 1463 for the Duke of Burgundy, Philip the Good. The three-storey building, a masterpiece of Brabant Gothic architecture, has 10 pointed-arched windows per floor and six exquisitely carved octagonal turrets. The niches in the facade house statues of famous local personalities. Reliefs, carved between 1852 and 1872, illustrate Biblical themes. In 1890 the facade suffered damage from lightning, but was restored to its original form.

Within the town hall, you can tour the jury room, once furnished with paintings by Dirk Bouts (1415–75), a powerful influence on German 15th-century painting, who died in Leuven. Two of these works, designed to serve as a model of fair judgement for the magistrates, now hang in the Musée d'Art Ancien in Brussels.

Opposite the town hall stands the late-Gothic **Sint-Pieterskerk**. The cruciform basilica with ambulatory and chapels was never finished because its foundations proved unstable. An exuberantly baroque pulpit, dating from 1742, is adorned with reliefs depicting Peter's denial and the conversion of St Norbert. Three arches, which were completed in 1488, separate the choir from the nave. The church's most valuable treasures are two paintings by Dirk Bouts. His triptych of the Last Supper is one of the period's masterpieces. The Apostles are gathered round a table, listening to Christ, a much larger figure than his onlookers and the only one looking out of the picture. The second painting is *The Martyrdom of Erasmus.*

Not far from the Grote Markt, Oude Markt is a busy cobbled square lined with cafés and restaurants that are generally filled with students. A market is held here every Friday. To the east of the square, Parijsstraat, then Schapenstraat, lead to the **Groot Begijnhof**. Founded around 1230, this was once the biggest *béguinage*

Map on page 182

The Stella Artois brewery in Leuven is a big employer.

BELOW: the roof of Leuven's 15th-century town hall.

in the land, housing around 300 Beguines – women who lived like nuns but without taking the vows. *(For more about béguinages, see page 108)* The cluster of red-brick homes by the Dijle river are now used for student accommodation.

Leuven University produced the first Latin version of Thomas More's Utopia *in 1516.*

A university divided

The Catholic **University of Leuven** traces its history back to the "Studium Generale Louvaniense", founded in 1425 by Pope Martin V at the request of Duke Jean IV of Brabant. Its 12 teachers were brought from Cologne and Paris. Pope Adrian VI of Utrecht, Erasmus of Rotterdam and Justus Lipsius, who founded the discipline of classical and antiquarian studies, were renowned scholars with close links to the university. When German troops invaded in World War I, over 300,000 books in the archive went up in flames. In May 1940 the new university library – a gift of the United States, containing a million books – was also destroyed.

For many years the university was at the centre of the bitter feud between Belgium's Flemings and Walloons – both faculty and students were split along linguistic and community lines. The problem was resolved in 1962, when the proud old university was divided into the Flemish Katholiek Universiteit Leuven and the French-speaking Université Catholique de Louvain. The Dutch-speakers remained triumphally in occupation of "their" university, while the French-speakers decamped to a new campus at **Louvain-la-Neuve** (New Leuven) on Walloon soil southeast of Brussels, which opened in 1969. Even the library was divided 50/50 between the two universities: books were shared by allotting those with an even catalogue number to one, and those with an odd number to the other.

Louvain-la-Neuve is a campus community with a garden-city atmosphere enlivened by its student population, and worth a visit if you like modern architecture: some university buildings were designed by top Belgian architects. Everyday life is dominated by the university. The town planner, Raymond Lemaire, designed an attractive, open space. Since the

BELOW: Stadhuis, Grote Markt, Leuven.

diameter of the campus is only about 2 km (1¼ mile), it is easy to commute on foot between residential, study and leisure centres. The town centre contains banks, shops, offices and the railway station, on the line from Brussels to Namur.

Park Abbey, founded in 1129 by Premonstratensian monks from Laon, lies a short distance outside the town.

Lake of dreams

A popular weekend outing for the Bruxellois is a stroll around the pleasant **Lac de Genval** ❸ (Genval Lake), combined with a refreshment break at one of the lakeside terraces. It lies southeast of the city on the Wavre road, midway to Louvain-la-Neuve and about a 40-minute journey by train from Brussels' Gare Centrale. Genval Lake is not big. You can walk around it along Avenue du Lac in about 40 minutes at an easy pace, but the location is idyllic and the lakeside is dotted with imposing houses and villas overlooking the water. When the lake, fed by the Argentine stream, was created in 1904, the first villas built replicated

famous buildings. For example, the pavilion Rendezvous d'Amour is based on an original at Versailles, while the chalet Le Rütli and the villa Guillaume Tell are based on Swiss buildings associated with William Tell. A high fountain, the Genvaloise, gives the lake the aspect of a miniature Lake Geneva.

Turn right off lakeside Avenue du Lac and follow the signs a short distance to the **Musée de l'Eau et de la Fontaine** (Water and Fountain Museum; 63 Avenue Hoover; Sat–Sun and public holidays 10am–6pm, Mon–Fri irregularly 9.30am–noon and 1.30–4.30pm; admission charge). This is a curious little place, with a collection of fountains, both functional and decorative, as well as old water-pipes, pumps, filters and other hydraulic equipment, plus displays on the problems of water pollution and distribution.

Watersports at Wavre

More light relief can be found just outside **Wavre** ❹, at the Walibi and Aqualibi amusement parks (both Easter holidays daily 10am–6pm;

Map on page 182

TIP

Genval Lake's shoreline is dominated by the Château du Lac, a four-star hotel with an excellent restaurant, a bar – the Kingfisher Inn – and its own bottled mineral water from four nearby springs.

BELOW: Lac de Genval.

TIP

The road through
Sint-Agatha-Rode,
Sint-Joris-Weert,
't Zoet Water and
Heverlee, in the scenic
Dijle river valley,
makes a fine driving
or cycling excursion.

May Wed–Sun 10am–6pm; June–
July daily 10am–6pm; Aug daily
10am–8pm; Sept–Oct Sun 10am–
6pm; admission charge). The former
is famed for its white-knuckle rides
among 40 or so different rides and
shows, and the latter is a subtropical
water theme park.

Beyond Genval, running north
across the Wallonia–Flanders line
towards Leuven, is the scenic **Dijle
River Valley**, a place of attractive little villages, châteaux (kasteelen) and
farms, with lakes and river views
along the way.

Waterloo

One of the most popular "attractions"
in Belgium, visited annually by a
million tourists from around the
world, is the **Waterloo Battlefield
❺**, 21 km (13 miles) south of Brussels *(see The Battle of Waterloo,
pages 26–7).* Here, in June 1815, an
Allied army of British, Dutch, Belgians, Hanoverians and Prussians
decisively defeated the French
emperor Napoleon Bonaparte. The
defeat led directly to his abdication
for a second, and final, time.

The Battle of Waterloo did n
actually take place at Waterloo, b
in rolling farmland a few kilomet
to the south. So do not get off the b
(line W from Gare du Midi in Bru
sels) in Waterloo, a busy suburb
Brussels, expecting to find the batt
field in its streets. Ask the driver
let you off instead a few kilometi
south, at the **Butte du Lion** (Li
Mound), a huge conical mound c
ated in 1825 from soil taken from
battlefield, at the spot near the cen
of the Allied army's position whe
the Prince of Orange was wounde
The hill takes its name from a ca
iron sculpture of a lion, its rig
forepaw resting symbolically or
globe. The sculpture, 4.5 metres (
ft) long, 1.5 metres (5 ft) high, a
weighing 28,000 kg (61,700 lb
stands on a stone pedestal.

Napoleon's troops never made
to this point. But they gave it th
best shot, causing the Duke
Wellington, who commanded a cor
bined force of British, Hanoveriar
Dutch and Belgians, to call t
bloody slaughter "the nearest r
thing you ever saw in your life". T

BELOW: the French
infantry prepare for
a last-ditch effort.

timely arrival of Marshal Blücher's Prussian army clinched the matter, transforming near-victory for the French into their defeat and rout.

Strategic overview

Before exploring the battlefield, study the tactical picture at the **Visitor Centre** (Apr–Sept daily 9.30am–6.30pm; Oct–Mar 10am–5pm; tel: 02-385 19 12; admission charge) beside the bus stop, which gives you a good idea of the sheer scale of the battle. You can also pick up a free map of the area and buy a ticket that gives access to all the battle-related attractions.

Climbing the Lion Mound's 226 steps may leave you feeling like one of the French infantrymen who sweated up the slopes hereabouts. The view from the summit is worth the effort, even if you need an active imagination to fill the peaceful farmland below with slashing cavalry charges, thundering artillery and 200,000 colourfully uniformed, struggling soldiers.

Next door to the Visitor Centre, a round building houses a spectacular painted **Panorama de la Bataille** (Panorama of the Battle; Apr–Sept daily 9.30am–6.30pm; Oct–Mar 10am–5pm; admission charge). Maquettes of troops, horses and equipment ranged round the viewing gallery add realism. Across the road, the **Musée des Cires** (Waxworks Museum; Apr–Nov daily 10am–5pm; Dec–Mar Sat–Sun 10am–5pm; admission charge) has worn-looking waxen images of the main players and, though interesting, is not essential viewing unless you are fascinated by all things Napoleonic.

Monuments and memorials

A path beside the Panorama, Chemin des Vertes Bornes, runs past the Lion Mound to some of Waterloo's most dramatic scenes. Beside the memorial to Lieutenant Augustin Demulder, a young cavalryman from nearby

Nivelles who fell in Napoleon's cause, massed waves of French horsemen under Marshal Ney ("the bravest of the brave") broke against unyielding Allied infantry deployed in squares. A little farther, in the midst of now tranquil fields, another memorial records the position of British batteries that poured canister and grapeshot into Napoleon's elite Old Guard, thrown forward by the emperor in a desperate charge at the battle's late-afternoon climax. At the end of the path, **Hougoumont** manor-farm still bears the scars of heroic assault and valiant defence; the owners are happy for visitors to wander around the grounds.

Back at the cluster of buildings beside the Visitor Centre, there's no shortage of cafés and restaurants, with names like Le Hussard, Bivouac de l'Empéreur, Les Alliés, etc. None are exactly crack outfits, but in typical Belgian style it is hard to do badly even in humble eateries.

Walking along Route du Lion in front of the Visitor Centre, parallel to the Allied frontline, can be about as dangerous today as it was in 1815,

Map on page 182

The Lion Mound Visitor Centre has an audio-visual reconstruction of the Battle of Waterloo alongside a huge circular canvas portraying its decisive moments.

BELOW: Waterloo sunset.

thanks to Belgian drivers' take-no-prisoners style; extreme caution is needed when crossing Chaussée de Charleroi at the end of the road. Beside the crossroads are monuments to the Belgians and Hanoverians; to Colonel Gordon, a mortally wounded aide to Wellington; and to General Picton, shot down at the head of his division.

A little way downhill is **La Haie-Sainte**, a fortified farm that played a crucial role in the battle. In the field across the road, British cavalry slaughtered a wavering French infantry column, got carried away by victory and charged on to the enemy guns, which promptly blew them to pieces. If your blood is up, you can make a trek along Chaussée de Charleroi to **La Belle Alliance**, where Wellington and the Prussian Marshal Blücher shook hands on their victory; and to **L'Aigle Blessé** (The Wounded Eagle), a monument that marks the spot where the Imperial Guard went down in a blaze of glory so that Napoleon could escape. Even more distant, at 66 Chaussée de Bruxelles, is Napoleon's headquar-

ters, now the **Musée du Caillou** (Apr–Oct, 10am–6.30pm; Nov–Mar, 1–5pm; admission charge). Many exhibits are associated with the emperor, including his map table and campaign bed; there is also a bust of Napoleon by Chaudet. Other items, such as spent musket balls, were gleaned from the battlefield.

Back at Waterloo, the **Musée Wellington** (daily Apr–Sep 9.30am–6.30pm; Oct–Mar 10.30am–5pm; admission charge) is housed in the Duke of Wellington's headquarters, a Brabant coaching inn where he wrote his victory dispatch. You can see weapons and other paraphernalia of the battle.

Walking country

The region south of Brussels is ideal for country walks. Nestling at the heart of this rolling landscape lies the town of **Nivelles** ⑥, 35 km (22 miles) from the capital. The town's history is closely linked to that of the 7th-century **Abbey of St Gertrude**, the oldest monastery in Belgium. According to legend, following the death of the Frankish ruler Pepin the

Map
on page
182

Elder, his widow Itta retired with their daughter Gertrude to a villa overlooking the Thines valley. After the death of her mother and with an unsuccessful marriage to Dagobert I, Gertrude founded the monastery, at the instigation of Amand, Bishop of Maastricht.

Nowadays, the abbey church, constructed in various phases from the 11th century onwards, is regarded as one of the finest Romanesque churches in Belgium. It consists of a main nave and two aisles, separated from each other by square and cruciform pillars. Its porch is flanked by two small towers, the "Tour Madame" and the "Tour de Jean de Nivelles". The latter contains a bronze statue donated by the Duke of Burgundy, Charles the Bold, that has become a symbol of the town.

Only a handful of figures and fragments of architecture survived a fire in the church in 1940. There are a number of features worth seeing, however. Reliefs depicting incidents in the life of Samson – including a scene in which Delilah is cutting his hair, and one in which he is blinded by the Philistines – adorn the North Door. The South Portal contains a statue of the Archangel Michael with outspread wings.

A 13th-century silver reliquary contains the remains of St Gertrude. Each year, on the Sunday after the Feast of St Michael, the bones of St Gertrude are carried in procession along a 12-km (7-mile) route through the town and its immediate surroundings, a tradition which has been observed since the 12th century.

Nivelles village grew up around the abbey and became one of the country's most famous weaving towns, prospering until well into the 17th century.

Cistercian ruins

East of Nivelles, in **Villers-la-Ville ⑨**, are the ruins of the Cistercian abbey founded in 1146 by St Bernard of Clairvaux (1090–1153). The monastery was self-sufficient. Its monks worked the land, and the order's estates were extensive. During the Low Countries' wars of independence against the Spanish, part of the complex was destroyed. It was rebuilt, only to be dissolved under Austrian rule and finally destroyed by the French in 1794.

During the 19th century the ruins were sold piecemeal. Not until the 20th century was any interest shown in restoring what remained of the buildings and sculptures, which by this time were in danger of total decay. Today all that remains are Romanesque sections of the earliest buildings and the abbey church's pointed arches.

Pilgrimage town

Further west, 15 km (9 miles) south of Brussels, lies the pilgrimage town of **Halle ⑧**. Its **Basilique de Notre Dame**, a fine example of Brabant Gothic dating from the 14th century, contains notable treasures. The tower recalls those of many Belgian town

While writing Les Misérables, *Victor Hugo stayed in Mont St-Jean, scene of Napoleon's defeat, to research and write his description of the battle.*

BELOW: Abbey of St Gertrude, Nivelles.

Châteaux

Given Brussels' role as a crossroads of Europe, château-building has always been an engrossing affair, pursued by the princely powers of the day. Depending on the taste of the time and the nationality of the builders, the châteaux range from medieval castles to symmetrical French classical pleasure palaces and bourgeois Flemish Renaissance red-brick affairs.

The **Château de Rixensart**, south of Tervuren, overlooks gardens supposedly designed by the French landscaping genius, Le Nôtre (1613–1700). This 17th-century Flemish Renaissance gem has belonged to the noble Mérode family since the 18th century. The château's location close to Genval makes for a pleasant conclusion to a summer's day on the lakeside terraces at the Lac de Genval.

Those seeking a real moated, medieval castle should head for **Kasteel van Beersel**, 10 km (6 miles) southwest of Brussels, one of few remaining fortified strongholds in Brabant. Indeed, such authentic military castles are rare in Belgium. Beersel's appeal also lies in its rustic setting and in its imposing crenellations, turrets and pointed

slate-covered roofs. The early-16th-century fortress was once impregnable, thanks to an impressive drawbridge and marshy terrain. The crenellations, nightwatchmen's walk and wild grounds provide ample opportunity for children to frolic. Families with young children may like to follow a visit to the castle with an exploration of neighbouring **Huizingen**, a village noted for its pleasant park, complete with golf course and amusement park.

Alternatively, **Kasteel van Gaasbeek**, 15 km (9 miles) southwest of Brussels, is a Flemish castle dating from feudal times. Although it has been remodelled over the centuries, the château is graced with a richly furnished interior and encircled by classical gardens and wilder parkland.

Château de Beloeil, in Hainaut province, southwest of Brussels, boasts some of the loveliest classical gardens in Belgium, as well as the most lavish interior. The French, Le Nôtre-style grounds play games of perspective, enhanced by water gardens, canals and statuary. They were anglicised during the 18th century in keeping with the Romantic spirit of the times. The château itself is essentially classical, a 17th-century pleasure palace set on two islands and linked by a bridge. Although charming, it is eclectic rather than authentic, since it was remodelled after a fire in the 19th century. However, the classical lines of the structure were retained, and embellished with an interior adorned with a magnificent library, art collection and Flemish tapestries. Every summer, the splendid gardens host Nocturne de Beloeil, gala evenings of classical concerts in the torchlit grounds.

The harmonious **Château de Seneffe**, near Nivelles, was inspired by Italian and French classicism and English Palladianism. The 18th-century château is surrounded by manicured grounds and graced by an orangery and neo-classical theatre. General Von Falkenhausen, the military ruler of Belgium during the German occupation, knew an imposing location when he saw one: Seneffe was promptly chosen as the Nazi headquarters. ❏

LEFT: school trip to the Kasteel van Beersel.

Map
on page
182

halls. Inside, an extensive collection of sculptures traces the development of Belgian sculpture across the centuries. Of particular note are a statue of the Madonna and Child beside the west door and a series of Apostles in the choir above the arches. Above the high altar is a wooden statue of Our Lady, carved during the Middle Ages and believed to possess miraculous powers, which is the object of pilgrim processions at Whitsun and at the beginning of September. In the **Chapelle de Trezgnies**, an exquisite Renaissance alabaster altar by Jehan Mone from 1522 is adorned with carved reliefs depicting the seven sacraments.

Neighbouring **Huizingen** has a park whose magnificent gardens display over 1,200 species of plants. It is worth making a short detour from here to the medieval moated **Kasteel van Beersel** *(see opposite)*, set in woodland. The castle, restored in 1920, has three 14th-century towers that soar high above the moat.

Near by, not far from the village of Vlezenbeek, another castle worth seeing is the feudal **Kasteel van Gaasbeek** *(see opposite).*

Northern highlights

Just north of Brussels are several places of interest that can easily be combined on one excursion. The **National Plantentuin ❾** (National Botanical Garden; daily 9.30am–5pm; summer and winter times may vary slightly; greenhouses close earlier; park free, admission charge for greenhouses; De Lijn bus 250 from Gare du Nord in Brussels) at Meise occupies a beautiful country estate, the Domein Bouchout, that covers 93 hectares (230 acres). It was moved here in 1944 when the collection outgrew its former location at Le Jardin Botanique in Brussels *(see page 125)*. It's a great place for a stroll, and has masses of exotic plants and trees, both outdoors and indoors. The arrangement of the plants in the large, partly landscaped greenhouses takes into account their geographical origins. Scientific collections of plants and a library of botany are housed in the Herbarium, which is not open to the general public. In the middle of the park is a much-renovated 12th-century castle beside a lake; it served as the occasional residence of Empress Charlotte. From April to October, the park's Oranger café is open.

Just 7 km (4 miles) from Meise on the road to Vilvoorde, in the handsome old village of **Grimbergen ❿**, is **Grimbergen Abbey**. Noteworthy in its baroque Sint-Servaas church are the confessional, pulpit and choir pews, as well as a ceiling fresco in the vestry. The Mira Observatory (mid-July–Aug Mon–Fri 10am–5pm; Sept–June Mon and Fri–Sat 2–10pm, Tues and Thurs 9am–10pm, Wed 9am–6pm; admission charge) next to the abbey, at 22 Abdijstraat, provides an introduction to astronomy and the chance to use some of its instruments.

Heading northeast towards Mechelen is **Rijksdomein Hofstade ⓫**

Grimbergen Abbey, not far from the Botanical Garden, is the source of the strapping Trappist Grimbergen beers, which are sold in a café in the abbey grounds.

BELOW:
the National Botanical Garden at Meise.

(open daily; free; beach and parking charges in summer). An artificial beach around the big lake here is considered by many to be an acceptable substitute for the distant beaches of the Flemish coast, and it gets busy in summer. The lake and its surroundings also form a nature reserve that hosts many birds.

Spiritual centre

Mechelen ⓬ lies 22 km (14 miles) north of Brussels, in Antwerp province, where the Dijle river, a tributary of the Scheldt, splits into two. Excavations of pile dwellings have revealed that a village existed here as long ago as Celtic times. St Rombout founded an abbey in 756, but no further settlement developed until the 11th century.

The town experienced its Golden Age between 1507 and 1530 when it was the seat of Margaret of Austria, regent for the future emperor Charles V. She sponsored a brilliant court culture – a kind of Camelot-on-the-Dijle – by inviting and being patron to prominent artists, musicians and scholars, among them Erasmus. A

BELOW: 16th-century architecture in Mechelen.

statue of Margaret occupies the middle of the Grote Markt, ringed by fine buildings, including the 14th-century Gothic **Lakenhalle** (Cloth Hall), which now houses the municipal art collections, and the 16th-century late-Gothic **Paleis van de Grote Raad** (Palace of the Grand Council), which is now the Stadhuis (Town Hall). After her successor, Maria of Hungary, decided to transfer her residence from Mechelen to Brussels, the town became an archbishopric in 1556, with a primate whose authority extended across the Low Countries.

The 97-metre (310-ft) tower of the 14th/15th-century **Sint-Rombout-skathedraal** (St Rombold's Cathedral), named after a local saint who founded the abbey here during the 8th century, dominates the square, and indeed the entire town. Begun in 1452, it was intended to reach a height of 168 metres (538 ft). However, in 1578 William of Orange had the stones reserved for its completion carried away to build the fortress of Willemstad.

Two **Carillons**, each with 49 bells, hang in the belfry. The ancient art of campanology was revived in the 20th century in Mechelen by Jef Denijn, who established the **Koninklijke Beiaardschool** (Royal Carillon School), at 63 Frederik van Merode-straat, the world's only school of bell-ringing. Carillon concerts take place on Monday evenings in summer.

The interior of St Rombold's baroque black, white and red marble indicates the town's former prosperity. A richly decorated choir blends with the three Gothic naves. The high altar, in the shape of a Renaissance arch, is the work of the local sculptor Luc Fayd'herbe. Above it stands a statue of St Rombold. Other treasures include a painting of the Crucifixion by van Dyck. Twin tombs recall two famous princes of the church: Cardinal Granvelle, the first bishop of Mechelen, and Cardinal Mercie

spiritual leader of the Belgian Resistance during World War I, who died in 1926, and to whose memory there is a black marbled chapel.

Today, Mechelen is a thriving industrial town and one of the country's leading ecclesiastical centres, as the seat of the Catholic Primate of Belgium. The country's last major tapestry maker, remnant of a once powerful industry, is the **Koninklijke Manufactuur van Wandtapijten** (Royal Tapestry Manufacturer), which produces modern tapestries and restores old ones in a 15th-century former abbey at 7 Schoutestraat. The **Hof van Busleyden Museum** (Tues–Sun 10am– 5pm; admission charge), in an early-16th-century mansion at 65 Frederik van Merodestraat, has paintings, tapestries, sculptures and furnishings from medieval to modern times.

The **Justitiepaleis** (Justice Palace), built between 1507 and 1529, is one of the oldest Renaissance buildings in the country. Originally built by Rombout Keldermans as a palace for Margaret of Austria, it later became the residence of Cardinal Granvelle. The Grand Council convened here from 1616 until 1794. Also of note is the **Sint-Janskerk** (church of St John), from the 15th century, housing the altarpiece *The Adoration of the Magi* by Peter Paul Rubens.

Mechelen was once surrounded by 12 gateways, of which only one, the twin-towered **Brusselpoort** (Brussels Gate), remains today.

Northwest of Mechelen, at a distance of about 10 km (6 miles) on N16, north of the town of Breendonk at Fort Breendonk, is the **Breendonk Concentration Camp** (Apr–Sept 9am–5pm; Oct–Mar 10am–4pm; admission charge). During the Nazi occupation of Belgium in World War II, the fort served as a transit centre for Jews, Resistance fighters and other "undesirables".

Lier, "the loveliest town"

At the confluence of the Grote and Kleine Nete rivers lies **Lier** **⓭**. This town's main claim to fame lies in two famous sons: the writer, Felix Timmermans (1886–1947) and Louis Zimmer, the inventor of the astronomical clock.

Map on page 182

Mechelen's Toy Museum houses a major collection of old and new toys and games (21 Nekkerspoelstraat; open Tues–Sun 10am–5pm).

BELOW: the astronomical clock in Lier.

Map
on page
182

Stained glass at Kasteel van Gaasbeek, a feudal castle with a richly detailed interior.

BELOW:
Lier town centre.

Timmermans is one of the most important Belgian folklore writers and painters. In his novels and stories he created a colourful, often idealised picture of life in Brabant, characterised by gentle humour and naive piety. He described Lier in many of his books and considered it to be the loveliest town in the country.

Part of the ancient fortifications, the **Zimmertoren** (Zimmer Tower; daily 9am–noon and 1–4pm, July–Aug 5pm; admission charge) houses the **Astronomical Clock** and the **Planetarium**, both the work of Louis Zimmer. The clock, 4.5 metres (14 ft) high, was built into the tower in 1930 as a present to the town. Although only 13 dials are visible from outside, inside the tower a further 57 dials show the time in every part of the world, as well as astronomical phenomena, including the phases of the moon and the path of the stars.

In the centre of the town, the **Grote Markt**'s principal building, the rococo **Stadhuis** (Town Hall), built in 1740, has no fewer than 3,600 windows. A Gothic belfry from 1369 is connected to it. You can view paintings by Dutch and Belgian masters at the **Museum Wuyts van Campen en Baron Caroly** (Tues–Sun 10am–noon and 1–5pm; admission charge), at 14 Florent Van Cauwenberghstraat, which houses works by Rubens, Teniers, Pieter Brueghel and van Dyck as well as modern works.

Near the Grote Markt, the late-Gothic church of **St Gummarus**, from the 15th and 16th centuries, has fine stained-glass windows in the choir, depicting Emperor Maximilian of Habsburg and his wife, Mary of Burgundy. The window entitled *The Coronation of the Virgin* in the southern aisle recalls the style of Rogier van der Weyden. The triple-arched choir screen from 1536 represents the evangelists and fathers of the church.

Other interesting features include the baroque shrine (1682) of St Gummarus by Dieric Somers, containing the relics of the town's patron saint. Its tower, which is 80 metres (256 ft) high, contains a carillon of 48 bells.

Maximilian's son, Philip Handsome, and the Infanta of Spain, Joanna, the daughter of Ferdinand of Aragon and Isabella of Castile, married in this church in 1496, marking the beginning of the influence of Spain in the Low Countries.

When Philip died in 1506 after only a year on the Spanish throne, Joanna was deemed insane and kept in confinement by her father (hence her nickname Joanna the Mad). Their son Charles had only to wait for his grandfather to die before succeeding as king of Spain. Thanks to the wheeling and dealing of his grandfather, who died in 1519, aged 61, Charles was also crowned Holy Roman Emperor.

Lier's **Beguine Convent**, founded in the 13th century, is the best-preserved in Belgium. Passing through the entrance you arrive in front of the Flemish Renaissance convent church from the 17th century. ❏

RESTAURANTS & BARS

Restaurants

GENVAL

Genval les Bains
Château du Lac Hotel, 87
Avenue du Lac. Tel: 02-655
73 73. Open: L & D daily.
€€–€€€
Set in an 1890s château
hotel on the banks of the
Lac de Genval, t his
brasserie is cool and
refined. Seafood domi-
nates the menu, which
mixes light fusion dishes
with good old Belgian
standbys, such as Ostend
shrimp croquettes.
There's a summer terrace
with lake view, and an
open fire for cold days.

GROOT-BIJGAARDEN

De Bijgaarden
20 Isidoor Van Beverenstraat.
Tel: 02-466 44 85. Open: L &
D Mon–Fri; D only Sat. €€€€
A legendary French
restaurant on the north-
west outskirts of Brus-
sels, next to Groot-
Bijgaarden Castle that
sports a brace of Michelin
stars. It offers some of
the country's very best
food, served in formal but
delightful surroundings.
Outdoor terrace and gar-
den in summer. Smart
dress is expected.

LA HULPE

Salicorne
41 Rue Pierre Broodcoorens.
Tel: 02-654 01 71. Open:
L & D Tues–Sat. €€€
Out in the Brussels' sub-

urbs, this restaurant in a
country villa serves traditional French specialities
with a contemporary
touch, many of them
flavoured with the distinctive taste of truffles and
foie gras. The main dining
room is bright and ele-
gant, and there is an
attractive garden for
summer dining.

LEUVEN

Ming Dynasty
9 Oude Markt. Tel: 016-29
20 20. Open: L & D
Wed–Mon; D only Tues. €€
Chinese restaurants
don't get much better
than this one on Leuven's
bustling main square.
The food is from all
regions and the style is
light and refined; the
Peking duck – always a
sure indicator of success
or failure – is excellent.

Sire Pynnock
10 Hogeschoolplein. Tel: 016-
20 25 32. Open: L & D
Mon–Fri; D Sat; L Sun €€€
This French and continen-
tal restaurant is located in
a graceful townhouse in
the centre of Leuven, with
several differently styled
dining rooms. On Tuesday
evenings there's a special
vegetarian menu.

MEISE

L'Auberge Napoléon
1 Bouchoutlaan. Tel: 02-269
30 78. Open: L & D daily. €€€
Round off your visit to the
scented greenhouses and
open spaces of the

Nationale Plantentuin
(National Botanical Gar-
dens) with a meal in this
fine traditional restaurant
across the street. In
manorial, wood-beamed
surroundings, you dine on
sophisticated but not
stuffy French and Belgian
cuisine.

OUD-HEVERLEE

Spaans Dak
2 Maurits Noëstraat. Tel: 016-
47 33 33. Open: L & D
Wed–Sun. €€€
The "Spanish Roof" is
scenically set among the
Zoet Water (Sweet Water)
lakes outside this village
6 km (2 miles) south of
Leuven. Its interior is as
elegant as you might
expect of a mansion that
once belonged to the
16th-century Habsburg
emperor Charles V. The
focus of the continental
menu is on Mediter-
ranean dishes.

OVERIJSE

Barbizon
95 Welriekendedreef, Jezus-
Eik. Tel: 02-657 04 62. Open:
L & D Thurs–Mon. €€€€
Very luxurious, long-established French restaurant
in a country mansion
located in a pleasant village just southeast of
Brussels. Among the light
and inventive dishes is
the speciality *homard en
chemise* (crusted lob-
ster), but the cuisine goes
beyond classical French.
The garden terrace is a

great place to dine in
summer.

WATERLOO

L'Opéra
178 Chaussée de Ter-
vuren. Tel: 02-354 86 43
Open: L & D Mon–Fri; D
only Sat. €€–€€€
At this fine restaurant and
wine bar you dine on
sophisticated regional
Italian dishes so good
they might have you
singing by the end of your
meal. The modern decor
of the large dining room
incorporates lavish
amounts of white marble.

Cafés and bars

To wet your whistle in
cosy traditional surroundings, head for **Domus** *(8
Tiensestraat)* in Leuven,
an Old Flemish tavern
popular with students
and with 70 beers on
their drinks list. Equally
traditional and welcoming
is **In de Pattatezak** *(48
Oude Mechelsestraat)* in
the northern suburb of
Strombeek-Bever; people
pile in from all around for
the beers and the great
spaghetti bolognese.

PRICE CATEGORIES

Prices for three-course
dinner per person with a
half-bottle of house wine:
€ = under €30
€€ = €30–45
€€€ = €45–60
€€€€ = over €60

BRUGES, GHENT AND ANTWERP

Three excursions to three landmark Belgian towns: pristine Bruges, the pride and joy of Flanders; Ghent, a vibrant city with a historic centre often compared to Venice; and Antwerp, birthplace of Rubens, a major port and a hotbed of new fashion designers

Only after seeing **Bruges**, the grande dame of Flemish cities, can you begin to understand Flanders. In the 14th and 15th centuries, when the powerful Dukes of Burgundy held court here, the prosperous city was the last word in pomp and splendour; the largest, richest and most powerful merchant city north of the Alps.

In the 15th century, Bruges' fortunes started to decline. With the silting up of the Zwin inlet in the Eastern Scheldt estuary, the city was cut off from the open sea. Furthermore, the reign of the Dukes of Burgundy came to an abrupt end through the death of the young Mary of Burgundy in a riding accident in 1482. Her husband, Maximilian of the Austrian House of Habsburg, moved the ducal residence to Ghent, and transferred Bruges' trading privileges to Antwerp. This sealed the city's fate. For the next 500 years, Bruges was *la ville morte*, the dead city. Not until the closing years of the 19th century was the city, by then badly dilapidated, rediscovered with all its original medieval charm.

The Bell Tower

The best panoramic view of this unique city can be seen from the top of **Belfort** ❶ (Bell Tower; Tues–Sun 9.30am–5pm; admission charge). It

is a 366-step climb to the tower's observation deck, but worth the effort. This mighty tower, 88 metres (290 ft) high and a landmark symbol of the city, ascends from the medieval Hallen (Market Halls), where in times past Bruges merchants used to store the textiles that secured the city's prosperity.

The market square and Town Hall

In front of the Belfort and Hallen lies a broad market square, the

Map on page 200

LEFT: view of Bruges' historic centre, with not a modern rooftop in sight. **BELOW:** the cloister garden of the Prinselijk Beginhof.

TIP

If you plan on visiting all of Bruges' main museums, it's worth investing in a combination ticket available from the Groeninge, Arentshuis, Gruuthuse and Memling museums.

Markt ❷, with a sculpture memorial to two Flemish liberation heroes, Jan Breydel and Pieter de Coninck, at its centre. They led an army of peasants and craftsmen in the Battle of the Golden Spurs in 1302, in which the French cavalry were decisively defeated – when the fighting came to an end, the rebels collected 700 golden spurs.

The splendid neo-Gothic edifice of the West Flanders provincial administration building dominates the east side of the square. Along its other faces are narrow-gabled guildhouses, many of them given over to

restaurants and cafés. While sitting on one of their terraces, you can listen to folk melodies played on a carillon of 47 bells pealing out from the bell tower.

In the neighbouring – and equally significant – central square, the Burg, is the **Stadhuis ❸** (Town Hall; Tues–Sun 9.30am–5pm; admission charge). Built in 1376, it is the oldest and among the most beautiful town halls in Belgium. Originally, the facade was ornamented with statues of important figures in Flanders' history all brightly painted by the great master,

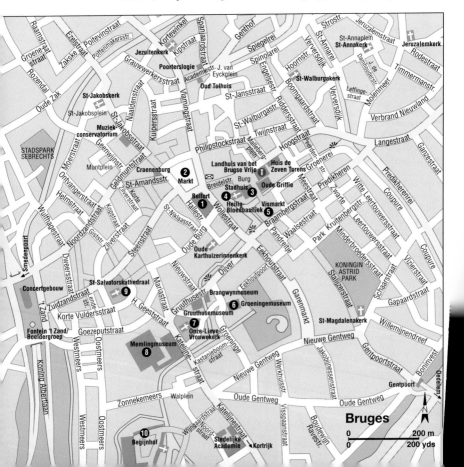

Bruges

0   200 m
0   200 yds

Map on page 200

Jan van Eyck, who worked for a period in Bruges. Unfortunately the sculptures were destroyed in the wake of the French Revolution. Replacements for them have gradually been erected over the past few decades, although they remain a sober white. Particularly lovely is the figure of the Virgin (to the outer left in the bottom row, just where the narrow Blinde-Ezelstraat begins). This is the Madonna of Oudenaarde, also known as the Madonna with the Inkwell. The highlight of the interior is its vaulted ceiling, made entirely of carved oak. The walls are painted with relatively recent frescos, dating from the 19th century and depicting important events in the city's history.

The Renaissance building next to the town hall is the former Office of the Town Clerk, the **Oude Griffie**; and next to this, the **Landhuis van het Brugse Vrije** (Palace of the Liberty of Bruges), which now houses the city tourist office. In the palace's Renaissance Hall is a splendid chimneypiece made of black marble, carved oak and alabaster; it depicts the Habsburg emperor Charles V and his parents and grandparents, and celebrates his victory at Pavia over King François I of France.

Basilica of the Holy Blood

To the west of the Stadhuis stands the **Heilig-Bloedbasiliek** ❹ (Basilica of the Holy Blood; Apr–Sept daily 9.30am–noon and 2–6pm; Oct–Mar 10am–noon and 2–4pm, closed Wed pm; basilica free, admission charge for museum). Returning from a crusade to the Holy Land in 1149, Count of Flanders Dietrich of Alsace brought a small phial containing a drop of blood said to have been washed from the body of Christ by Joseph of Arimathea. To commemorate the arrival of the relic, the Holy Blood Procession takes place every year on Ascension Day; it is the most important festival in Flanders *(see page 203)*. The reliquary, one of the finest pieces of medieval gold craftsmanship in existence, can be seen inside the church in the Museum of the Holy Blood.

Rent a bike: it's the most practical and efficient way to get around. Cyclists can pedal in both directions in more than 50 one-way streets.

BELOW: the Markt.

Fresh fish from the North Sea has been bought and sold at the colonnaded Vismarkt since 1820.

Food with a view

The narrow Blinde-Ezelstraat leads off the square to the **Vismarkt** ❺ (Fish Market). Here, on Tuesday to Saturday mornings, you can watch fresh fish from the North Sea ports being washed, gutted and traded. A few steps further along, past the delightful **Café Mozart**, you come to the Huidevettersplein, lined with eating establishments. The view over the waters of the Burgundian Cross is stunning, and painters often set up their easels here. Winston Churchill was one of many who have painted the scene.

The banks of the Dijver, the branch of the Reie which flows from here towards the mighty church of Our Lady, are dotted with berths for motor launches. The sightseeing tours of the waterfront and canal network of Bruges are highly recommended. On a warm and sunny day there is no better or easier way to see the city.

Old Masters

Bruges' municipal art gallery, the **Groeningemuseum** ❻ (Tues–Sun 9.30am–5pm; admission charge),

has a small but outstanding collection of early Flemish paintings. Works by Jan van Eyck feature strongly: they include his *Canon van der Paele* and a portrait of his wife. Hans Memling, Gérard David, Pieter Pourbus, Rogier van der Weyden and Hieronymus Bosch are among the other great artists represented.

The **Onze-Lieve-Vrouwekerk** ❼ (church of Our Lady; Mon–Fri 9–12.30pm and 1.30–5pm; Sat 9–12.30pm and 1.30–4pm; Sun 1.30–5pm; church free, chapel of Charles and Mary admission charge) close by, built from the 13th to the 15th century, is the largest Gothic church of the Low Countries, though at 122m (400 ft) its spire is fractionally lower than Antwerp cathedral's. The tombs of Mary of Burgundy and her father, and several Old Master paintings are among the chief highlights; another sight not to miss is the Michelangelo *Madonna and Child*. The sculptor executed this piece for the cathedral of Siena, but when it was completed he found that the cathedral could not pay him. Snapped up by a wealthy Bruges

Map on page 200

merchant, the Madonna came to Bruges, the only work by Michelangelo to have left Italy during his lifetime.

The adjacent **Memlingmuseum** ❽ (Mariastraat; Apr–Sept daily; Oct–Mar closed Wed) has pride of place among Bruges' museums. It is housed in the 13th-century St-Janshospitaal. The only evidence of the building's original function is the dispensary, which dates from the 15th century, and some wards. In the room once assigned to terminal cases some of the most important works of the German-born painter Hans Memling, who lived in Bruges from 1465 until his death – most notably the *Marriage of St Catherine* and the *Shrine of St Ursula*. The latter, depicting six scenes from the life of the saint, is considered to be one of the most important art treasures in Belgium.

The other major church in Bruges also houses masterpieces from the Burgundian era. The Gothic choir stalls in the **St-Salvatorskathedraal** ❾, the city's diocesan church, founded by Saint Elegius in 646, still bear the crest of the Knights of the Golden Fleece. Philip the Good, Mary of Burgundy's grandfather, established this order on the occasion of his marriage to Isabella of Portugal. Jan van Eyck, incidentally, had pleaded for Isabella's hand by proxy.

Beguine convent

One of the city's most enchanting and tranquil hidden corners is the **Begijnhof** ❿ (Beguine Convent; daily; free), founded in 1245. Its occupants are no longer beguines *(see page 108)* but Benedictine nuns. Concealed behind white walls, the convent's small houses are arranged over a broad expanse of lawn dotted with poplars. The Beguine convent stands in an area where lacemaking is still practised. On warm days, you can see old women and young girls sitting in the surrounding alleyways deftly working the fine threads.

Before you leave Bruges, follow the course of the Reie for a look at the medieval city gates: **Gentpoort**, **Kruispoort**, **Ezelpoort** and **Smedepoort**, which date from the early 15th century.

"The difference between Bruges and other cities is that in the latter, you look about for the picturesque, and don't find it easily, while in Bruges, assailed on every side by the picturesque, you look curiously for the unpicturesque, and don't find it easily."
– ARNOLD BENNETT

BELOW: bearing the cross in the Holy Blood procession.

Holy Blood Procession

Once a year, on Ascension Day, Bruges plays host to the Holy Blood Procession, the most important religious festival in Flanders. The procession centres around a precious religious relic: a crystal phial, supposedly containing the blood of Christ. While the official story has it that this phial was awarded to Dietrich of Alsace by the Patriarch of Jerusalem for bravery in the Second Crusade against the Saracens, other historians place its origins in Constantinople, and suggest that its presence in Bruges is the result of the ransack of the ancient capital of the Byzantine Empire. Whatever the truth, the phial of blood is a precious relic; as such, it is kept throughout the year in a silver reliquary and venerated every Friday, in the morning and evening.

The relic is paraded around the streets of the old centre of Bruges in a day-long ceremony. The parade is divided into two parts: in the first, a number of biblical scenes are enacted, while the second part re-enacts the return of Dietrich with the relic. Hundreds of inhabitants of Bruges take part in the re-enactments, which continue a tradition from the Middle Ages – a time when reading was uncommon amongst the peasantry, and visual forms were used to teach Christian tales and beliefs.

GHENT

Ghent (Gent) owes its historical importance to the cloth trade. The city flourished during the Middle Ages, and for a period around the start of the 15th century it was the second-largest city north of the Alps after Paris. The capital of East Flanders province is spread across 13 islands at the confluence of the Scheldt, Leie and Live rivers. It is a good city to explore on foot, as the historic centre is compact, and most of the notable sights are within walking distance of each other.

The belfry tower, topped with a gilded dragon, is a symbol of freedom.

The Belfort and Stadhuis

A good place to get a feel for its layout is atop the 90-metre (300-ft) **Belfort ❶** (Bell Tower; mid-Mar– mid-Nov daily 10am–12.30pm and 2–5.30pm; admission charge). In the Middle Ages this tower, crowned with a gilded dragon, was a symbol of the freedom of the citizens of Ghent and the power of its guilds. In

the same complex, the Gothic **Lakenhalle** (Cloth Hall) housed the inspection commission for the cloth weavers who assured Ghent's economic well-being.

Near by, the impressive 16th-century **Stadhuis ❷** (Town Hall; guided tours in summer, Mon–Thur 3pm; admission charge) is built partly in the Flemish late-Gothic style, with additional Renaissance features. Its ornate facade is embellished with sculpted figures and ghoulish ornaments. In 1576, the Pacification of Ghent, which ended (for a time) the disputes between Catholics and Protestants in the Low Countries, was signed in one of the building's most beautiful rooms.

The Ghent altarpiece

Ghent's most important artistic work, Jan van Eyck's masterly triptych altarpiece, can be found in **Sint-Baafskathedraal ❸** (St Bavo's cathedral; daily 8.30am–6pm; until

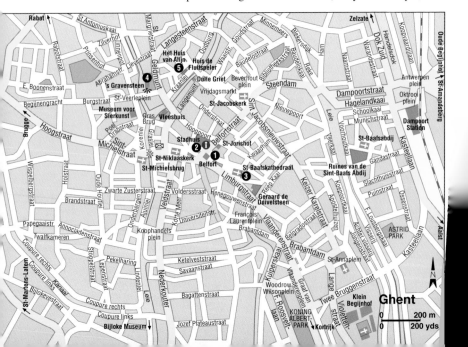

Ghent

0 ___ 200 m
0 ___ 200 yds

5pm Oct–Mar; cathedral free, admission charge for crypt). Known as the *Adoration of the Holy Lamb*, it is an allegorical glorification of Christ's death. During every major European conflict the Ghent Altarpiece has been stolen; Napoleon took it to Paris, the Germans stole it during World War II. But it always found its way back to the city – except for the panel depicting the wise judges, which had to be replaced by a copy after it was stolen in 1934.

On the banks of the Leie

The rows of guild houses and warehouses along **Korenlei** and **Graslei**, the two streets lining the Leie between Sint-Michielsbrug (St Michael's Bridge) and Grasbrug (Grass Bridge), have splendid Gothic and baroque facades, richly ornamented with stepped or curving gables, false fronts and lavishly decorated cornices. On one side of the narrow **Customs House** (1682) is the **House of the Grain Measurer** (1698), a building of red brick and white stone, with decorative stepped gables; on the other side is the

Romanesque **Stockpile House** built 550 years earlier. Closer to St Michael's Bridge is the **House of the Free Boatmen** (1531), with the figure of a ship cast above the doorway.

Ghent's gloomy castle, **'s Gravensteen** ❹ (daily 9am–6pm; until 5pm Oct– Mar; admission charge), protected on one side by the waters of the Leie, was modelled on the castles constructed by the Crusaders in Syria and the Holy Land. At first, it served as a residence and a fortress; after the 14th century, however, even the Counts of Flanders became uncomfortable in the sinister surroundings, and the building was turned into a dungeon, its inner courtyard used as a place of execution.

On the opposite side of 's Gravensteen, **Het Huis van Alijn** ❺, the city's Folk Museum (Tues–Sun 11am–5pm; admission charge), is housed in 18 small Flemish houses. The museum conveys a picture of life in Ghent around 1900 through the recreation of typical environments, such as a cooper's workshop, a chemist's laboratory and a town inn.

Map on page 204

TIP

During the summer, a walk around Ghent at night can be magical, as many of the city's buildings are floodlit. For the rest of the year, the buildings are only lit on Friday and Saturday evenings.

BELOW:

views under and over St Michael's Bridge.

Tiles painted with seafaring scenes on display at the Steen Maritime Museum.

ANTWERP

Antwerp is many things to many people: a major port, a diamond centre, an industrial nucleus, the city of Rubens, a hotbed of new fashion designers, a haven for gourmets and an elegant shopping centre. The city on the Scheldt is a marvellously vibrant place.

Around the main square

As with most Flemish cities, all the action is around the main square, the Grote Markt, with its 16th-century guild houses and Flemish Renaissance town hall. The elegant ensemble is overlooked by the soaring spire of the **Onze-Lieve-Vrouwekathedraal ❶** (cathedral of Our Lady; Mon–Fri 10am–5pm, Sat 10am–3pm, Sun and church holidays 1–4pm; admission charge), the place first-time visitors should begin their sightseeing. With seven aisles, 125 pillars and a 123-metre (403-ft) high tower, this is Belgium's largest and

arguably its most beautiful Gothic church. Construction took from 1352 to 1521. Inside are masterpieces by Rubens: the *Crucifixion*, the *Descent from the Cross*, and the *Assumption of the Virgin*.

The old lanes and squares around the cathedral are full of atmosphere. Look out for the **Vlaeykensgang**, a romantic little alleyway, restored to resemble its 16th-century original. The nearby square, Oude Koornmarkt, is lined with a variety of restaurants and bars.

Northwest of the cathedral, the **Grote Markt** is dominated by the stately Renaissance **Stadhuis ❷** (Town Hall; Mon–Wed and Fri–Sat; guided tours until 3pm; admission charge), with its marble facade and richly decorated rooms. Built between 1561 and 1565, it combines Flemish and Italian stylistic elements. Most of the square's splendid guild houses, which have been painstakingly restored over the

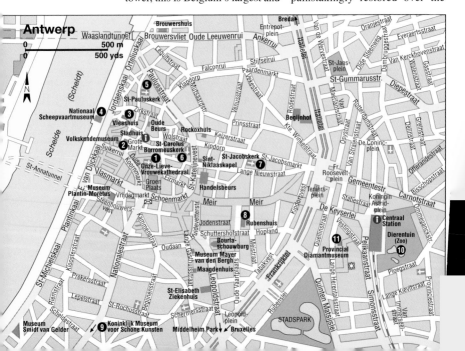

years, date from this period. They were built by the wealthiest and most influential of the guilds, including the archers, grocers, carpenters and tailors.

On Gildekamersstraat, behind the Town Hall is the **Vleeshuis** ❸ (Tues–Sun; admission charge). The "house of the butchers' guild", its "bacon streaks" of red brick and white sandstone carefully restored to their original glory, is one of the most remarkable secular buildings in all Antwerp. Today it houses a museum of arts and crafts and local history, which incorporates a fine collection of musical instruments. Concerts are held regularly here.

On the waterfront

On the nearby riverfront, stands the oldest building in Antwerp: the Steen, a 12th-century castle now home to the **Nationaal Scheepvaartmuseum** ❹ (National Maritime Museum; Tues–Sun 10am–5pm; admission charge). Here, Antwerp's centuries-old connection with the sea and shipping is documented through model ships, old maps and charts, and navigational instruments.

Right next to the Steen, the Flandria line's white tour boats dock, offering tours of the Scheldt of either 50 or 80 minutes' duration.

A couple of blocks inland, the magnificent 16th-century **Sint-Pauluskerk** ❺ (church of St Paul's; May–Sept daily 2–5pm), is a harmonious combination of elements of Gothic, Renaissance and baroque. The former Dominican church contains many paintings by Rubens, Jordaens and van Dyck.

On the Rubens trail

Back in the historic centre, another city jewel is the **Sint-Carolus Borromeuskerk** ❻ (church of St Charles Borromeo; Mon–Sat 10am–12.30pm and 2–5pm; admission charge), built between 1614 and 1621. Rubens is said to have designed the main facade. Thirty-nine ceiling paintings by the artist were destroyed by fire in 1718, but three of his altar paintings survived.

East of the church looms the Gothic **Sint-Jacobskerk** ❼ (St Jacob's church; Apr–Oct daily 2–5pm; Nov–Mar Wed–Mon 2–5pm; admission charge), where Rubens is buried. Containing paintings by virtually all the great Flemish masters, valuable sculptures and ornate items of gold and brass, the church outdoes even the cathedral in artistic wealth.

On the other side of the Meir, you can follow in Rubens' footsteps to the **Rubenshuis** ❽ (Tues–Sun 10am–5pm; admission charge). In his house, built in 1610, the studio where he worked and taught and the living apartments have been carefully restored. Ten works by the artist are displayed, including an accomplished early work, *Adam and Eve in Paradise*. The imposing portico which divides the inner courtyard from the garden makes an appearance in many of Rubens' pictures.

Map on page 206

The Rubens chapel in St Carolus church.

BELOW:
the city on the Scheldt.

Map on page 206

TIP

The Meir and and De Keyserlei are Antwerp's two main shopping streets. The so-called "shopping mile" is invariably busy, as are the many cafés dotted along its length that serve weary shoppers.

BELOW: Rubenshuis – the former home of the great painter and now a museum dedicated to his art.

The **Koninklijk Museum voor Schone Kunsten** (Royal Museum of Fine Arts; Tues–Sat 10am–5pm, Sun 10am–6pm; admission charge) on Leopold de Waelplaats in the south of the city is an outstanding museum with over 1,000 works by old masters, including some 20 paintings by Rubens, representing every period of his artistic output. Among the most notable masterpieces to look out for are *The Adoration of the Magi* by Rubens, *The Entombment of Christ* by Quentin Matsys, and *The Seven Sacraments* by Rogier van der Weyden. More recent painting is also represented in the museum, with some 1,500 paintings and sculptures dating from the 19th and 20th centuries, including works by René Magritte and Paul Delvaux.

Antwerp Zoo

If you're wanting a break from all that art and architecture, **Antwerp Zoo** (daily 10am– dusk; admission charge), next to the railway station, is worth a visit, especially if you are travelling with children. More than 6,000 animals of 950 different species live in conditions as near to their natural habitats as possible.

Jewish Quarter

East of the station, between the Avenue Frankrijklei, the zoo and Koning Albert Park, lies the **Jewish Quarter**. Antwerp has Europe's largest Orthodox Jewish community, served by 22 synagogues. Fifteen thousand Jews in the city live in observance of strict religious laws. When the sabbath begins on Friday evenings a host of candles illuminates the windows of this district. In **Pelikanstraat** and the streets around it, there are many small shops which sell kosher groceries, Hebrew books and menorahs.

The Jewish community is extensively involved in Antwerp's thriving diamond trade. One of the city's four diamond exchanges is located on Pelikanstraat. The **Provincial Diamantmuseum** (31 Lange Heren-talsstraat, Nov–Apr 10am–7pm, May–Oct 10am–6pm; admission charge) offers a glimpse into the world of hot rocks and diamond cutters. ❏

RESTAURANTS & BARS

Restaurants

BRUGES

Bistro De Stove
4 Kleine Sint-Amandstraat.
Tel: 050-33 78 35. Open:
L & D Fri–Tues. €€–€€€
Tucked away on a side
street just north of the
Markt, this family-run
eatery is a lot less for-
mal than some of
Bruges' better restau-
rants, but ranks right up
there when it comes to
taste. Seafood is a
strong performer on the
menu, but meat dishes
are available too.

't Bourgoensche Cruyce
41–43 Wollestraat. Tel: 050-
33 79 26. Open: L & D
Thurs– Mon. €€€
For one of the best,
most atmospheric
eating experiences in
town, try this graceful
and friendly little restaurant in a bijou Bruges
hotel. The antiques-
filled dining room over-
looks the canal in the
heart of town. The
menu offers a refined
interpretation of French
and Flemish cuisine.

Kasteel Minnewater
4 Minnewater. Tel: 050-33
42 54. Open: L & D daily. €€
Given its location on the
banks of the beautiful
Minnewater lake at the
edge of the old centre,
this restaurant is
extremely good value for
money. The Belgian and
French cuisine does full

justice to the elegant
surroundings. You can
dine outside when the
weather is fine.

GHENT

Brasserie Pakhuis
4 Schuurkenstraat. Tel: 09-
223 55 55. Open: Mon–Sat
11:30am–midnight. €€
Perhaps a little too con-
scious of its own modish
good looks, this Franco-
Italian brasserie in a
restored former indus-
trial warehouse – all
cast-iron pillars, wrought-
iron balustrades, and
oak and marble tables –
delivers on the plate.
The oyster and seafood
platters are especially
noteworthy. Snacks are
served outside of regular
mealtimes.

Keizershof
47 Vrijdagmarkt. Tel: 09-223
44 66. Open: L & D
Mon–Sat. €€
You may feel a bit lost
in this rambling restau-
rant spread across
three floors of a 17th-
century building on
Ghent's central square,
but the waiters always
manage to find you. The
decor and service are
cool and breezy, and the
food is a combination of
modern continental and
traditional Belgian.

Vier Tafels
6 Plotersgracht. Tel: 09-225
05 25. Open: D only Mon;
L & D Tues–Sun. €€
In the heart of the
medieval Patershol

district, near S' Graven-
steen this restaurant
serves up its quota of
Flemish food, in dishes
like *waterzooï* (fish
stew), but complements
the traditional with an
intriguing range of world
cuisine. Among the
more unusual offerings
are reindeer, ostrich,
kangaroo and crocodile.

ANTWERP

De Rooden Hoed
25 Oude Koornmarkt.
Tel: 03-233 28 44.Open:
L & D daily. €€–€€€
The location of this,
Antwerp's oldest restau-
rant, across from the
cathedral makes it a firm
fixture on the tourist circuit, but it is hard not to
like it. It's a cavernous
place filling several
rooms, and it packs
them in, but standards
have not slipped. The
seafood dishes are
especially good.

Sir Anthony van Dijck
16 Oude Koornmarkt.
Tel: 03-231 61 70. Open:
L & D Mon–Sat. €€€
Located just off the
Grote Markt in the
indelibly romantic
surroundings of the
16th-century Vlaeykens-
gang courtyard, which
has been restored as a
haunt of bijou boutiques
and cafés, this polished
brasserie brings more
than a touch of class to
its classic Belgian and
French dishes.

Cafés and bars

All three Flemish cities
are filled with great
cafés, in styles ranging
from the utmost tradi-
tional to ultra modern.
Bruges' **'t Brugs Beertje**
(5 Kemelstraat) stands
out in the former cate-
gory, not least for the
300-plus beers it
stocks.For something a
little quirkier, have a
drink in **De Veersteende
Nacht** *(11 Langestraat)*
a shrine to the comic
strip. Live jazz is played
on some nights. In
Ghent, you might want to
try the *jenever* (gin) specialist **'t Dreupelkot**, *(12
Groentenmarkt)*, where
this traditional Belgian
tipple is given due care
and attention. There's
no better place to sam-
ple De Koninck, the beer
that's Antwerp's pride
and joy, than at the
antique watering hole **De
Engel** *(3 Grote Markt)*, in
the heart of the city. Or
for an atmospheric dock-
land experience, seek
out the cosy **Café
Beveren** *(2 Vlasmarkt)*.

PRICE CATEGORIES

Prices for three-course
dinner per person with a
half-bottle of house wine:
€ = under €30
€€ = €30–45
€€€ = €45–60
€€€€ = over €60

TRANSPORT

GETTING THERE AND GETTING AROUND

GETTING THERE

By Air

Brussels National Airport (tel: 0900-70 000; www.brusselsairport.be) is at Zaventem, 11 km (7 miles) northeast of the city centre. As the seat of the European Union, Brussels is well served by international airlines. By air, it is an hour from Paris, London, Amsterdam and Frankfurt. The modern terminal is user-friendly and has restaurants and bars, shops, a business centre and children's play areas. *(For information on getting into the city from the airport, see Getting Around, page 211).*

Taken together, British Airways, BMi, Virgin Express and SN Brussels Airlines operate virtually an hourly service during the day between Brussels and London, and less frequently from other cities around Britain. Aer Lingus and SN Brussels Airlines fly between Dublin and Brussels. Ryanair flies from several cities in Britain and Ireland to Charleroi (or Brussels Charleroi, as the airline calls it), which is about an hour by bus from Brussels.

There are direct daily flights to Brussels from several cities in North America and Canada, among them New York, Washington, Chicago, Atlanta and Toronto. There are regular links with all major European cities.

Airlines

British Airways
Tel: 02-717 32 17 (Brussels)
Tel: 0870-850 9850 (UK)
www.britishairways.com

BMi
Tel: 02-771 77 66 (Brussels)
Tel: 0870-607 0555 (UK)
www.flybmi.com

Virgin Express
Tel: 02-752 05 05 (Brussels)
Tel: 0870-730 1134 (UK)
www.virgin-express.com

SN Brussels Airlines
Tel: 02-754 19 00 (Brussels)
Tel: 020-7559 9787 (UK)
www.flysn.com

Ryanair
(To Charleroi)
Tel: 0902-88 007 (Belgium)
Tel: 0906-270 5656 (UK)
Tel: 1530-787 787 (Ireland)
www.ryanair.com

Aer Lingus
Tel: 02-275 01 75 (Brussels)
Tel: 0818-365 000 (Ireland)
www.aerlingus.com

American Airlines
Tel: 02-711 99 77 (Brussels)
Tel: 800-433 7300 (US)
www.aa.com

Delta Airlines
Tel: 02-711 97 99 (Brussels)
Tel: 800-241 4141 (US)
www.delta.com

United Airlines
Tel: 02-713 36 00 (Brussels)
Tel: 800-241 65 22 (US)
www.united.com

Air Canada
Tel: 02-627 40 88 (Brussels)
Tel: 888-247 2262 (Canada)
www.aircanada.ca

By Sea

From the UK, P&O Ferries operates a daily service between Hull and Zeebrugge; the overnight journey time is about 13 hours. Superfast Ferries sails every other day between Edinburgh (Rosyth) and Zeebrugge; the overnight journey time is about 17 hours. A free bus service that coincides with ferry arrivals and departures shuttles between the harbour and Zeebrugge railway station, from where there are hourly trains to Brussels. Zeebrugge is close to the start of the E40 (A10) motorway from Ostend to Brussels.

P&O Ferries, tel: 02-710 64 64 in the UK; 050-54 34 11 in Belgium; www.poferries.com
Superfast Ferries, tel: 08702-340870 in the UK; 050-25 22 92 in Belgium; www.superfast.com

By Coach

Coaches depart several times daily from London's Victoria

Coach Station and are operated by Eurolines (tel: 08705-808080 in the UK; 02-274 13 50 in Brussels; www.eurolines.com). The journey takes about 8 hours.

By Car

From the UK, **EuroTunnel** (tel: 08705-353535; www.eurotunnel.com) provides a 35-minute drive-on service for cars on shuttle trains through the Channel Tunnel between Folkestone and Calais, from where there is a good motorway connection to Brussels. The fare varies greatly depending on the time of travel; night or early-morning crossings are the cheapest. Booking is not essential, but recommended during peak times.

To drive in Belgium, you must carry a current EU or national driving licence, vehicle registration document, insurance, a nationality sticker fixed to the rear of your car, and a red warning triangle to display in the event of a breakdown. Children under 12 are not allowed in front seats if there is room in the back. Seat belts must be worn. Belgium is crisscrossed by a network of toll-free motorways. However, once you are in Brussels, a car is often more of a hindrance than a help *(see page 212).*

DISTANCES

From other European cities:
Amsterdam 211 km
(131 miles)
Paris 309 km (192 miles)
Calais 200 km (125 miles)
Cologne 220 km (136 miles)
Ostend 114 km (70 miles)
Luxembourg 216 km
(134 miles)

By Train

Belgian Railways (SNCB/NMBS) maintains a well-developed rail network. Several international lines cross Belgium, connecting France and the Netherlands, the UK and Germany with each other.

Trains from Paris take 1 hour 25 minutes; from Cologne 2 hours; from Amsterdam 2 hours 40 minutes; and from the ferry terminal at Zeebrugge about 1 hour. High-speed train services include Eurostar from London; Thalys from Paris, Amsterdam and Cologne; TGV from northern France; and ICE from Germany. Some international trains stop at all three of the city's main rail stations, which are Brussels Gare du Nord (North), Brussels Gare Centrale (Central) and Brussels Gare du Midi (South), but the various high-speed services stop only at Gare du Midi. Both national and international rail information is available on tel: 02-528 28 28.

Eurostar (08701-606600 in the UK; 02-528 28 28 in Brussels; www.eurostar.com) trains run from London (Waterloo) via Ashford and Lille to Brussels Gare du Midi. There are up to 12 trains a day between 6am and 7pm.

GETTING AROUND

From the Airport

A frequent train service (every 20 minutes) connects the airport with Brussels' main railway stations from about 5.30am–midnight. The journey takes 20 minutes.

Orientation

Brussels is easier to negotiate than some other important European capitals. It is not too big – the population is just under 1 million – or spread out. And not only are most of the attractions that people want to visit within the pentagonal-shaped city centre, but many of these are within easy reach of the centre of the pentagon, on or around the Grand-Place. Some other attractions are located in clusters that are easily reached by public transport. Some of these are the Atomium/Bruparck complex, and

the Waterloo battlefield.

But for all its relative compactness, Brussels isn't so small that you can easily walk everywhere. This will work only in the most central zone; beyond this it's best to mix walking with use of public transport.

Public Transport

Brussels has an extensive metro (trains that run underground through the city and partly overground in the suburbs) network, complemented by tram and bus routes, operated by the local public transport company STIB. In addition, there is what's known as the pre-metro – trams that run partly underground. Information is available from STIB at 15 Avenue de la Toison d'Or (tel: 02-515 20 00; www.stib.be), as well as at Porte de Namur, Rogier and Midi metro stations. Public transport runs from 6am–12pm.

Several different types of tickets are issued, including single-journey tickets, multi-journey tickets for five or 10 rides, and a 24-hour ticket, good for all metros, trams and buses within the city limits. Tickets must be validated in the machines at metro stations and on board trams and buses, and are good for multiple transfers within one hour of first validation; you insert your ticket each time you board a new vehicle and the machine automatically either allows you to be in transit or validates a new journey period. Tickets can be bought at metro stations, STIB information offices, and at the tourist offices on the Grand-Place and in Rue du Marché aux Herbes. Passengers caught riding without a valid ticket by the frequent, roaming controls are required to pay a hefty on-the-spot fine.

Metro

You can recognise metro stations by the "M" sign (a white "M" against a blue background). Be sure to validate your ticket at one of the platform machines before boarding the train. Using the metro is the preferred way to get around the centre and out to the suburbs when you are in a hurry, or if it is raining, but of course you do not get to see much, if any, of the city as you travel. Many of Brussels' metro stations have been "decorated" by leading contemporary Belgian artists and are well worth a visit; a leaflet providing details can be obtained from the STIB information office and from the tourist offices.

Trams and Buses

Tram and bus stops are marked with red-and-white signs. All stops are request stops: if you wish the vehicle to stop lift your hand up to the driver. Many stops with shelters have maps of the city's complete public transport network. The trams are somewhat faster and more direct than buses, and are the best way to get around if you have a choice of modes, but buses reach areas that are not covered by any of the other modes.

Trains

These are not as convenient as the city's own public transport for getting around town, but do have some utility for going quickly between Gare du Nord and Gare du Midi (though you can do the same journey by premetro). There are six important railway stations in Brussels. The three main ones are Gare du Nord, Rue du Progrès; Gare Centrale, located underground at Boulevard de l'Impératrice; Gare du Midi, Rue de France; Gare du Quartier Léopold, Place du Luxembourg and Gare Schuman, Chaussée d'Etterbeek, which both serve the European institutions; and Gare de Schaerbeek, Place Princesse Elisabeth, which is also the terminal for car/sleeper trains. Information and tickets for Belgian Railways (SNCB) are avail-

able in the booking halls at all the city's railway stations. For both national and international information, tel: 02-528 28 28.

Taxis

Taxis are plentiful in Brussels but cannot be hailed in the street. There are many taxi ranks in the town centre: outside the European institutions, hotels and railway stations, on Boulevard Anspach and Place de l'Agora. Alternatively, they can be ordered from the following companies: **Autolux**, tel: 02-411 12 21 **Taxis Bleus**, tel: 02-268 00 00 **Taxis Verts**, tel: 02-349 49 49 **Taxis Orange**, tel: 02-349 43 43

Any complaints should be addressed to the Service Régional des Taxis et Limousines, tel: 02-204 1814 or 0800-14 795.

Driving

Driving in Brussels is invariably an unpleasant experience, with the possible exceptions of Sundays, public holidays, and during July and August. At most other times the roads are very busy and progress may be slow; where faster speeds are possible, for instance in the confusing network of underground tunnels, Brussels drivers put their foot down and expect others to do the same. In fact, the city's drivers are aggressive to a fault, and afford no mercy to foreigners or obvious "out-of-towners".

In general, the "priority to the right" rule applies to most situations, meaning that the vehicle to your right has the right of way, unless the road is marked with an orange diamond-shaped sign. If you have priority, be sure to take it – otherwise the driver behind you may go straight into the back of your car. Note that trams always have the right of way.

The maximum speed limit in built-up areas is 50 kph (31 mph), and on country roads 90 kph (56 mph). On motorways and

dual carriageways this limit rises to 120 kph (75 mph). In all cases, lower limits may be indicated. The use of both front and back seat belts is mandatory.

The legal blood alcohol limit is 0.05%. If the breathalyser test is positive, your driving licence will be withdrawn for at least six months. It is illegal for children under the age of 12 to sit in the front passenger seat if there is room in the back seat. Motorcyclists and moped riders are obliged by law to wear helmets, and parking is not permitted in places where the kerb is marked with a yellow stripe. Hazard triangles must be carried in the vehicle at all times. Foreigners caught defying traffic regulations are required to pay any fines incurred on the spot.

Brussels lies at the centre of Belgium, and the motorways radiate from the capital outwards. A motorway (the R0 Ring) runs around the outside of the city, giving vehicles easy access into as well as around the city. There is also an inner ring road encircling the city centre.

Breakdown Services are offered by **Touring Secours**, tel: 070-34 47 77 and the **Royal Automobile Club de Belgique (RACB)**, tel: 02-287 09 11 (8.30am–5pm) or 078-15 20 00.

Car Hire

All the major car hire firms are represented in Brussels; they each have a central reservations number, a desk at the airport and offices in town.
Avis, tel: 070-223 001 (reservations); 2 Rue de France (Gare du Midi), tel: 02-527 17 05; www.avis.be
Budget, tel: 0800 15 555 (reservations); 327b Avenue Louise, tel: 02-646 51 30; www.budget.be
Europcar, tel: 02-348 92 12 (reservations); 46 Avenue Fonsny (Gare du Midi), tel: 02-522 95; www.europcar.be
Hertz, tel: 02-717 32 01 (reservations); Gare du Midi, tel: 02-524 31 00; www.hertz.be

A CCOMMODATION

WHAT YOU SHOULD KNOW BEFORE YOU BOOK THE ROOM

Choosing a Hotel

Visitors to Brussels will find a large selection of hotel accommodation in every price range. As a broad and not infallible rule of thumb, hotels closest to the Grand-Place can charge more for whatever they offer than similar establishments in less desirable locations. In the city's official hotel guide you will find a complete list, including addresses and prices, of the 120 or so hotels in the city. This guide is available at the tourist offices at 63 Rue du Marché aux Herbes and in the Town Hall *(see page 231 for contact details)*.

Although you will find hotels throughout the city, there are two main areas where hotels are located: in the Old Centre, broadly defined, and in the districts on either side of Avenue Louise as well as on this avenue itself. You can choose from the smoothest-run flagship properties of the major international chains, through a few local Art Nouveau gems, to good-quality budget hotels, and the odd fleapit.

Reservations

Resotel (tel: 02-779 39 39, fax: 02-779 39 00, www.belgiumhospality.com; open Mon–Fri

8.30am–6pm) is a free accommodation booking service for Belgium which offers competitive hotel rates. The Brussels International Tourism Office *(see page 231)* does last-minute bookings.

Rates

Brussels is well served by hotels in all price categories, although in recent years the emphasis has been on the top end of the market, as all the big international chains, and many of the smaller ones, have staked their claim to a piece of the action in the "capital of Europe". One result of this is that there is often a glut of rooms in the upper categories, and in order to fill them the hotels may offer steep discounts, which has a knock-on effect all the way down the financial food chain. It's always worth asking about a better rate, unless there's a big convention or political gathering in town.

Many of the larger hotels offer special bargain rates for weekend stays. Hotels must post their room rates at the reception desk and are permitted to charge only these prices on your final bill. All hotels in Belgium are graded from one to five stars according to their facilities (or lack of them). As a general rule, the quality of accommodation

is high, but you get what you pay for. Prices also vary depending on the season. Winter rates are commonly 30–50 percent lower than the published rates. But you need to ask for a discount – it won't be offered automatically.

You can book directly with the hotel; invariably the person who answers the phone will speak English. And at an increasing number of hotels you can book directly through their website. You will often get the best available rate by doing so – but not always. It may be worthwhile to compare the Internet rate with the one you get from a direct call to reception or reservations accompanied by a request for a discounted rate.

BED AND BREAKFAST

These two agencies can book decent guest rooms with local people.

Bed & Breakfast Taxistop
28/1 Rue du Fossé-aux-Loups, 1000 Brussels
Tel: 070-22 22 92
www.taxistop.be
Bed & Brussels
9 Rue Kindermans, 1050 Brussels
Tel: 02-646 07 37
www.bnb-brussels.be

Camping

There is just one campsite in the city of Brussels itself.
Bruxelles Europe à Ciel Ouvert
203–5 Chaussée de Wavre
Tel: 02-640 79 67
Close to the European Parliament *(see page 157)*. Open July–Aug only. Limited caravans and camper vans. Costs €5 per person plus €5 per tent for each night.

The following sites are located in places quite near to Brussels and are within reach by public transport. They are open all year round.
Camping Beersel
75 Steenweg op Ukkel, Beersel
Tel: 02-331 05 61
Camping de Renipont
7A Rue du Ry Beau Ry, Ohain (near Waterloo)
Tel: 02-654 06 70

Youth Hostels

Brussels has a handful of good hostels. These are described in the "inexpensive" category of the area listings below. To stay at a hostel run by the International Youth Hostel Assocation (YHI) , you need to have a membership card issued in your country of residence. Most hostels include breakfast in the price.

ACCOMMODATION LISTINGS

THE GRAND-PLACE, LOWER CITY AND THE MAROLLES

De Luxe

Amigo
1–3 Rue de l'Amigo
Tel: 02-547 47 47
Fax: 02-513 52 77
www.roccofortehotels.com
This already formidable hotel has got even better under its new ownership, adding to a reputation for plush facilities and excellent service that complement a location just behind the Hôtel de Ville, close to many of the city's premier sights.
Radisson SAS Hotel
47 Rue du Fossé-aux-Loups
Tel: 02-219 28 28
Fax: 02-219 62 62
www.radissonsas.com
Impeccable top-flight hotel, a byword for its cool Scandinavian style, incorporating part of Brussels' old city wall. Among its stand-out features are the superb health club, Sea Grill restaurant and sociable comic-strip-themed Bar Dessiné downstairs.
Royal Windsor Hotel
5 Rue Duquesnoy
Tel: 02-505 55 55
Fax: 02-505 55 00
www.warwickhotels.com

A modern hotel with an old-fashioned sense of service and style. Its location close to the Grand-Place adds to the attraction.

Expensive

Astoria
103 Rue Royale
Tel: 02-227 05 05
Fax: 02-217 11 50
www.sofitel.com
One of Brussels' most illustrious hotels, dating from 1909 and still boasting the plush *belle époque* interior. There is a fine French restaurant and the graceful little Pullman Bar, modelled on the old bar aboard the Orient Express.
Le Dixseptième
25 Rue de la Madeleine
Tel: 02-517 17 17
Fax: 02-502 64 24
www.ledixseptieme.be
In a 17th-century town house that was once the Spanish ambassador's residence, this elegant small hotel by the Grand-Place is one of the best small hotels in the city. It enjoys a lot of repeat business

thanks to its refined service.
Métropole
31 Place de Brouckère
Tel: 02-217 23 00
Fax: 02-218 02 20
www.metropolehotel.be
A city classic and rich in tradition, dating from the 19th century. Its French L'Alban Chambon restaurant is among the most highly regarded in town. The stunning Art Nouveau Le 19ième bar and bustling pavement terrace of the Café Métropole are places to see and be seen.

Moderate

Saint Michel
15 Grand-Place
Tel: 02-511 09 56
Fax: 02-511 46 00
www.hotelsaintmichel.be
The only hotel on the Grand-Place. Its once rather tatty and small rooms have been refurbished and upgraded, so location is no longer the sole reason to stay here. They are still somewhat overpriced, but you do get a great view.

Welcome
23 Quai au Bois-à-Brûler
Tel: 02-219 95 46
Fax: 02-217 18 87
www.hotelwelcome.com
This great little boutique hotel on the Marché aux Poissons takes pride in its personal service. Its 15 small rooms are each individually decorated to evoke an exotic country. Sadly, the hotel's excellent seafood restaurant, La Truite d'Argent, has closed.

Inexpensive

A la Grande Cloche
10–12 Place Rouppe
Tel: 02-512 61 40
Fax: 02-512 65 91
www.hotelgrandecloche.com
In this relatively small

budget hotel just off the city centre, the rooms are plainly furnished and some have no bathroom. But the money you save can be put to good use at the Michelin-starred restaurant, Comme Chez Soi across the square.

Arlequin
17–19 Rue de la Fourche
Tel: 02-514 16 15
Fax: 02-514 22 02
www.arlequin.be
A modern and reasonably comfortable hotel in the heart of Brussels' atmospheric (if touristy) city-centre dining area, the Ilot Sacré.

Auberge de Jeunesse Génération Europe
4 Rue de l'Eléphant
Tel: 02-410 38 58
Fax: 02-410 39 05
www.laj.be
This youth hostel is located slightly out of town, but has good facilities: bar, restaurant, garden and barbecue, laundry and parking.

Galia
15–16 Place du Jeu de Balle
Tel: 02-502 42 43
Fax: 02-502 76 19
www.hotelgalia.com
If your style is down-at-heel charm, there can be few more atmospheric locations than this clean little hotel in the Marolles with comfy rooms overlooking the daily flea market held on the square. All rooms have a tiny toilet and shower room.

Jeugdherberg Breugel-IYHF
2 Rue du St-Esprit
Tel: 02-511 04 36
Fax: 02-512 07 11
www.jeugdherbergen.be
Conveniently located hostel in the city centre, close to Gare Chapelle. Parking for bikes and motorbikes, 24-hour access.

La Légende
35 Rue du Lombard
Tel: 02-512 82 90
Fax: 02-512 34 93
www.hotellalegende.com

For a taste of old Brussels in a desirable area just off the Grand-Place and for a reasonable price, it is hard to beat this attractive hotel, which has small but well-kept rooms, built around a central courtyard.

Mirabeau
18–20 Place Fontainas
Tel: 02-511 19 72
Fax: 02-511 00 36
www.hotelmirabeau.be
Small, recently renovated hotel with airy clean rooms, some of which have bathrooms and some of which don't. Rooms at the back are much quieter than those at the front. The Continental breakfast is a treat.

Noga
38 Rue du Béguinage
Tel: 02-218 67 63
Fax: 02-218 16 03
www.nogahotel.com
This wonderful small hotel not far from Place Ste-Catherine strikes the perfect balance

between kitsch, quirky and homely. The rooms are spacious and brightly decorated with a mix of modern and antique styles.

Sleep Well Youth Hostel
23 Rue du Damier
Tel: 02-218 50 50
Fax: 02-218 13 13
www.sleepwell.be
This modern hostel in the city centre has a wide range of facilities including cybercafé, tourist information centre and disabled access.

Vendôme
98 Boulevard Adolphe Max
Tel: 02-227 03 00
Fax: 02-218 06 83
www.hotel-vendome.be
Recently renovated in a cosy English style, this large, modern hotel has good facilities and a central location that is not greatly diminished by being on a busy street. The rooms vary in size, but even the smallest are not cramped.

THE UPPER CITY

Expensive

Hesperia Sablon
2–8 Rue de la Paille
Tel: 02-513 60 40
Fax: 02-511 81 41
www.hesperia-sablon.com
A suave hotel with plenty of modern design sensibility behind its old facade. It is ideally

PRICE CATEGORIES

Price categories are for a double room with breakfast:
De Luxe: over €300
Expensive: €200–300
Moderate: €100–200
Inexpensive: under €100

located in the Sablon area, for those who love to wander around the antiques shops here. 32 rooms.

Moderate

Congrès
42 Rue du Congrès
Tel: 02-217 18 90
Fax: 02-217 18 97
www.hotelducongres.be
Converted from a quartet of refurbished 19th-century neighbouring town houses, this hotel off Rue Royale has modern, comfortable rooms in a variety of sizes and styles.

Inexpensive

Auberge de Jeunesse Jacques Brel
30 Rue de la Sablonnière
Tel: 02-218 01 87
Fax: 02-217 20 05
www.laj.be
Just 15 minutes' walk from the Grand-Place, this youth hostel has 174 beds and good communal facilities. Disabled facilities are offered in some rooms.

Tasse d'Argent
48 Rue du Congrès
Tel/Fax: 02-218 83 75
This family-run small hotel in a converted town house has a char-

acterful public space, and just eight plainly furnished rooms – reached by a steep stairway – decorated in a cosy, old-fashioned style that runs to flowery cotton sheets.

THE LOUISE QUARTER AND SOUTH BRUSSELS

De Luxe

Brussels Hilton
38 Boulevard de Waterloo
Tel: 02-504 11 11
Fax: 02-504 21 11
www.hilton.com
A fairly standard implementation of the Hilton approach defines this hotel, so regulars will know what to expect. The highly regarded French restaurant, La Maison du Boeuf, is open to the public. All rooms have a view of the city and a park.

Conrad Brussels
71 Avenue Louise
Tel: 02-542 42 42
Fax: 02-542 42 00
www.conradhotels.com
Arguably one of the city's finest hotels, set in the heart of the deluxe shopping area on Avenue Louise. The sumptuous decor is elegant and stylish, with lots of marble and huge crystal chandeliers, and the rooms are spacious and lavishly equipped.

Stanhope
9 Rue du Commerce
Tel: 02-506 91 11
Fax: 02-512 17 08
www.stanhope.be
The spacious rooms set in a former convent and a neighbouring cluster of elegant town houses are all individually furnished with 19th-century antiques, paintings and chandeliers, all in a sumptuous English-country manor style.

Expensive

Bristol Stéphanie Brussels
91–93 Avenue Louise
Tel: 02-543 33 11
Fax: 02-538 03 07
www.bristol.be
A modern hotel set amid the town houses of this fashionable avenue. The decor has a definite Scandinavian influence, though it can feel rather stuffy. Plus-points are a heated indoor swimming pool and a fine French restaurant, Le Chalet d'Odin.

Manos Stéphanie
28 Chaussée de Charleroi
Tel: 02-539 02 50
Fax: 02-537 57 29
www.manoshotel.com
It's by no means cheap, but the Manos, a characterful mansion-style hotel near Avenue Louise, is more stylish than many other hotels in this price range. The lavish marble lobby makes an impression and the 55 rooms are equally elegant.

Moderate

Agenda Louise
6 Rue de Florence
Tel: 02-539 00 31
Fax: 02-539 00 63
www.hotel-agenda.com
This fine small hotel, recently renovated, and with facilities aimed at the mid-level business or leisure traveller, is located just off Avenue Louise and close to Place du Châtelain, an area full of trendy bars and restaurants.

Chambord
82 Rue de Namur
Tel: 02-548 99 10
Fax: 02-514 08 47
www.hotel-chambord.be
A hotel in an intriguing location, a bustling little street that links the Royal Palace area with the chic Upper City shopping zones. The rooms are bright, modern and comfortable and the hotel has an attractive bar.

Inexpensive

De Boeck's
40 Rue Veydt
Tel: 02-537 40 33
Fax: 02-534 40 37
www.hotel-deboecks.be
Its big rooms, tolerable comfort and reasonable prices make this hotel in a handsome 19th-century house, conveniently located near Place Stéphanie, a good bet for budget group travellers.

Les Bluets
124 Rue Berckmans
Tel: 02-534 39 83
Fax: 02-534 09 70

www.geocities.com/les_bluets
Set in a quiet street just off Avenue Louise, this friendly, idiosyncratic hotel will suit those who prefer a more relaxed and informal approach. The rooms of the 19th-century house are all individually furnished and full of knick-knacks collected by the owners over the years.

THE EUROPEAN QUARTER AND THE CINQUANTENAIRE

Expensive

Leopold
35 Rue du Luxembourg
Tel: 02-511 18 28
Fax: 02-514 19 39
www.hotel-leopold.be
Though its position in the shadow of the EU Parliament may not be the best, this family-owned hotel has a certain elegance. Inevitably it attracts business

from across the way, and inevitably it has an excellent restaurant.

Inexpensive

Derby
24 Avenue de Tervuren
Tel: 02-733 75 81/08 19
Fax: 02-733 74 75
www.hotel-derby.be
A small budget hotel close to the Parc du Cinquantenaire, the

Derby specialises in personal service, which makes a pleasant change from the usual brisk and business-like approach of your average Euro-district accommodation. The hotel's L'Aurige bar-restaurant is a popular neighbourhood eatery and watering hole. Next to the Mérode metro station, a direct link to the Grand-Place.

ROYAL LAEKEN, HEYSEL AND NORTH BRUSSELS

Expensive

Sheraton Brussels Hotel & Towers
3 Place Rogier
Tel: 02-224 31 11
Fax: 02-224 34 56
www.sheraton.com/brussels
Gargantuan modern hotel close to the Gare du Nord in a busy, newly developed business area. It certainly lacks character, but lies within easy reach of the centre. The hotel itself is an

island of tranquillity, and has a heated rooftop swimming pool.

Moderate

Comfort Art Hotel Siru
1 Place Rogier
Tel: 02-203 35 80
Fax: 02-203 33 03
www.comforthotelsiru.com
The Hotel Siru first opened in 1932 but was transformed in the 1980s, when each of its 101 rooms was fitted

out with a work of art by a contemporary Belgian artist. A good option for a rather bland area.

Inexpensive

Centre Vincent Van Gogh/CHAB
8 Rue Traversière
Tel: 02-217 01 58
Fax: 02-219 79 95
www.chab.be
A 15-minute walk from the Grand-Place, this hostel has a bar, restau-

rant and gardens and offers Internet access.

OUTSIDE BRUSSELS

De Luxe

Château du Lac
87 Avenue du Lac, Genval
Tel: 02-655 71 11
Fax: 02-655 74 44

www.martins-hotels.com
Overlooking the lovely Lac de Genval, the Château is an 1890s copy of an old abbey. The rooms are bright and luxurious and there is an excellent restaurant.

Expensive

Die Swaene
1 Steenhouwersdijk, Bruges
Tel: 050-342 798
Fax: 050-336 674
www.dieswaene.com

Built around an 18th-century guild house, overlooking a picturesque canal, this is a very special hotel, and its few rooms do not stay vacant for long.

Moderate

Kasteel Gravenhof
676 Alsembergsesteenweg, Dworp, Tel: 02-380 44 99
Fax: 02-380 40 60
www.gravenhof.be
This Flemish-style

château set in extensive grounds south of Brussels is reminiscent of a Spanish parador. The interior is as romantic as you would expect, and the price is reasonable.

ACTIVITIES

THE ARTS, NIGHTLIFE, FESTIVALS, SHOPPING AND SPECTATOR SPORTS

THE ARTS

Museums & Galleries

Brussels' 90 or so museums house a huge variety of art, fine arts, natural-history exhibits, machines, curiosities and more. The most important and many lesser ones are described in more detail in the relevant chapters.

Most museums and galleries are open daily except Mondays and public holidays, 10am–5pm, but it is advisable to check first (call the museum or refer to www.brusselsmuseums.be/en); they usually offer reduced admission charges for groups, children and senior citizens. If you intend to spend a large part of your time visiting museums, galleries and other attractions, buying a Brussels Card *(see page 7)* is a worthwhile investment. It affords free or discounted admission to some 30 places, along with free use of public transport.

Music, Opera, Ballet and Theatre

The chief venue for classical music is Bozar (formerly the Palais des Beaux-Arts, *see page 130)*. Opera and ballet produc-

tions are performed at the venerable Théâtre Royal de la Monnaie (Royal Mint Theatre), the most important stage in Brussels. Aside from these large venues, there is a host of smaller ones which stage less mainstream productions.

Belgium has an excellent reputation for modern dance, ever since Maurice Béjart caused a revolution in the dance world with the opening of his Mudra School and Twentieth-Century Ballet Company. Over 50 dance companies work in the Brussels region. Some, including Anne Teresa de Keersmaeker at the Monnaie and Wim Vandekeybus at the Koninklijke Vlaamse Schouwburg, are leading names in the world of contemporary dance.

In Brussels there are theatres which perform dramatic pieces in both French and Dutch. There is a lively English-language theatre scene, with groups specialising in Shakespeare, Irish and American drama and comedy. Check the weekly publication, *The Bulletin*, for details of future events *(see page 229)*.

Big-name rock and pop performers can be seen and heard at the Forest National venue in the south of the city, while less mainstream and up-and-coming artists play at Cirque Royal in the centre and various other venues.

Music & Dance Venues

Théâtre Royal de la Monnaie
Place de la Monnaie
Tel: 070-23 39 39
The Monnaie is the jewel in Brussels' crown, putting on bold and innovative opera and dance performances. This is home to the National Opera and Anne Teresa de Keersmaeker's Group Rosas.

Bozar (Palais des Beaux-Arts)
23 Rue Ravenstein
Tel: 02-507 82 00
This prestigious concert hall is home of the Belgian National Orchestra.

Ancienne Belgique
110 Boulevard Anspach
Tel: 02-548 24 24
Newly renovated venue for a variety of modern music.

Le Botanique
236 Rue Royale
Tel: 02-218 37 32
Three venues in one staging mostly indie rock bands. Joint host of Les Nuits Botanique rock festival with the Cirque Royal *(see below and page 221)*.

Conservatoire Royal de Bruxelles
30 Rue de la Régence
Tel: 02-511 04 27
Houses an intimate concert hall, mostly used to stage chamber music and recitals.

Cirque Royal
81 Rue de l'Enseignement
Tel: 02-218 20 15
Popular music venue in the round

and second stage for the Les Nuits Botanique festival.

Forest National
36 Avenue du Globe
Tel: 0900-00 991/070-34 41 11
Vast, somewhat soulless indoor venue on the outskirts of town, drawing big names (Bob Dylan, Bruce Springsteen, Robbie Williams, Tori Amos and Frank Zappa to name a few) for sell-out concerts.

Theatres

Beursschouwburg
20–28 Rue Auguste Orts
Tel: 02-550 03 50
Beautifully refurbished 19th-century theatre run by the Flemish Cultural Community.

Halles de Schaerbeek
20 Rue de la Constitution
Tel: 02-227 59 60
French cultural centre in a converted market hall with a varied programme of events.

Koninklijke Vlaamse Schouwburg
7 Quai aux Pierres de Taille
Tel: 02-210 11 00
Royal Flemish Theatre with occasional performances in English.

Théâtre de la Balsamine
1 Avenue Félix Marchal
Tel: 02-735 64 68
Brussels' most experimental dance and theatre venue.

Théâtre National de la Communauté Nationale Wallonie Bruxelles
111–115 Bvd Emile Jacqmain
Tel: 02-203 41 55
State-subsidised "national" theatre, for the French-speaking community.

Théâtre de la Place des Martyrs
22 Place des Martyrs
Tel: 02-223 32 08
New productions and modern interpretations of classical plays.

Théâtre Royal des Galeries
32 Galerie du Roi
Tel: 02-512 04 07
Comedy and cabaret in the king's gallery.

Théâtre Royal du Parc
3 Rue de la Loi
Tel: 02-505 30 30 (11am–6pm)
Classical comedy and drama

BOOKING TIPS AND WHAT'S ON

The best source of information in English is *The Bulletin,* a weekly publication with a free *What's On* listings guide. The Brussels-based magazine has a heavy bias towards coverage of the city, though other parts of Belgium are featured too. The cultural pages of daily newspapers such as *Le Soir* and *De Standaard* also contain information about entertainment in Brussels, and even if you have problems with French and Dutch, the listings information is straightforward. Cultural events are also listed on www.brusselsdiscovery.com and www.brusselsinternational.be. There is no central reservation office; contact the individual theatres for tickets, or for bigger events, try FNAC, City 2 Mall, Rue Neuve, tel: 02-275 11 16 (information); 0900-00 600 (reservations).

---

staged in an elegant, long-established Upper City theatre.

Théâtre Royal de Toone
Impasse Schuddeveld,
21 Petite Rue des Bouchers
Tel: 02-511 71 37
Puppet shows in the Brussels dialect have been staged at the Toone Theatre since 1830.

Cinema

Films are generally shown in their original language, which in most cases is English. Several cinemas are multi-screen complexes, the largest being Kinepolis with 24 separate theatres.

Mainstream Cinemas

Actor's Studio
16 Petite Rue des Bouchers
Tel: 0900-27 854

Arenberg/Galeries
26 Galerie de la Reine
Tel: 02-512 80 63

Aventure
17 Galerie du Centre, Rue des Fripiers. Tel: 02-219 17 48

Kinepolis
20 Boulevard du Centenaire
Tel: 0900-00 555

UGC De Brouckère
38 Place De Brouckère
Tel: 0900-10 440

UGC Toison d'Or
17 Galerie de la Toison d'Or
Tel: 0900-10 440

Vendôme
18 Chaussée de Wavre
Tel: 02-507 83 70

Arthouse Cinemas

Cinquantenaire Drive-in Cinema
Parc du Cinquantenaire,
Chaussee d'Alsemberg
Tel: 0900-20 700
Every weekend night in front of the Cinquantenaire arch from late July to the end of August. On Friday and Saturday those who arrive in vintage or classic cars pay less.

Musée du Cinema
9 Rue Baron Horta
Tel: 02-507 83 70

Nova
3 Rue d'Arenberg
Tel: 02-511 24 77

NIGHTLIFE

Brussels' reputation as a dull city is undeserved, especially when it comes to nightlife. The Brussels "scene" is cosmopolitan and eclectic, with varied offerings from a discreet piano bar to a dingy punk venue, from a surreal samba club to a Russian striptease, from boisterous Irish pubs to trendy late-night American bars and fashionable Flemish music venues. In short, Brussels' nightlife can be as exuberant as the night is long. The city's cosmopolitan mix also means that in musical terms, the exotic is commonplace.

The area around the Grand-Place has the greatest concen-

TRANSPORT
ACCOMMODATION
ACTIVITIES
A – Z
LANGUAGE

tration of late-night bars, brasseries and traditional cafés. However, the gentrified Sablon quarter has more elegant pavement cafés and wine bars, ideal for whiling away a long summer's evening. Although nightclubs are scattered throughout the city, the regenerated St-Géry quarter across from the Bourse boasts more than its fair share of funky clubs and bars. Even without the attraction of music or a show, local residents are content to spend many evenings in any number of distinctive bars.

Nightspots

Start your evening's clubbing too early and you'll more than likely find yourself facing locked doors. The majority of clubs and dance venues do not open until at least 10pm.

Bazaar
63 Rue des Capucins
Boasts a "Thousand and One Nights" atmosphere and live acts, from poignant *chanson française* to vibrant World Music. For those who prefer to dance, there is a disco in the cellar.

Cartagena
70 Rue du Marché au Charbon
Only hot-blooded Latin types need apply – along with any cool northerners whose blood could use a little extra heat.

Club 7
20 Boulevard du Centenaire, Bruparck
In the shadow of the Atomium, this place puts out a mixture of house, Latin and R 'n' B.

Dirty Dancing
38 Chaussée de Louvain
Rigorously chic dance-spot in a former cinema.

Fuse
208 Rue Blaes
This is the city's most famous techno club, with house music and jazz-funk featured on different floors. The clubbers are drawn to the celebrity DJs and dancers, as well as the buzz.

Jeux d'Hiver
1 Chemin du Croquet,

Bois de la Cambre
Dependable mainstream club, popular with Brussels' latter-day yuppies. Live music and shows enliven a regular disco, which features a mix of chart hits and old favourites.

Le Claridge
24 Chaussée de Louvain
The rather stiff name belies the fun and frivolous nature of this tongue-in-cheek disco.

Le Sud
43 Rue de l'Ecuyer
This eclectic bar/nightclub started as a squat several years ago but is now well established. The decor is kitsch Eurotrash influenced by the 1001 Nights. Mixed crowd.

Mirano Continental
38 Chaussée de Louvain
Popular dance club. DJ Cosy Mozzy's Dirty Dancing Night is a magnet to the terminally hip.

Recyclart
25 Rue des Ursulines
Pulsing electro-beats dominate the airwaves in this former Marolles railway station.

Why Not
7 Rue des Riches Claires
The trance, house and techno attract a predominantly gay crowd.

You Night Club
18 Rue Dusquesnoy
This nightclub appears to have lost its appeal to Brussels' ultra-chic crowd. Nonetheless, its location near the Grand-Place ensures it remains a popular disco with tourists and is usually crowded. Gay night on Sunday.

Jazz Cafés

L'Archiduc
6 Rue Antoine Dansaert
Cool jazz on Saturday and Sunday.

Phil's Jazz Kitchen Café
189 Rue Haute
Relaxed bar hosting jazz or other music most nights of the week.

Studio Athanor
17–19 Rue de la Fourche
Varied range of jazz, Latin and blues from Tuesday through to Sunday.

Théâtre Marni
23–5 Rue de Vergnies, Ixelles
Top jazz and world music acts, and a great bar.

Pubs and Bars

In addition to the places recommended below, a selection of bars and cafés is listed after the restaurants at the end of each area chapter.

A L'Imaige Nostre-Dame
3 Impasse des Cadeaux, Rue du Marché aux Herbes
Traditional antiques-filled café.

Au Soleil
86 Rue du Marché au Charbon
Fashionable bar-café with Art Nouveau interior, on a street full of good bars and teeming with life on a Saturday night.

Belgica
32 Rue du Marché au Charbon
One of Brussels' best known and popular gay bars; gets very busy after 11pm.

Beursschouwburg
22 Rue Auguste Orts
Trendy late-night venue full of Flemish-speaking creative types and hip foreigners. The funky bar, which is connected with the Flemish cultural centre, hosts dance nights and live music.

Chez Maman
7 Rue des Grands Carmes
Popular, classy-looking gay bar well known for its drag shows, held every weekend.

Chez Moeder Lambic
68 Rue de Savoie
This temple of Belgian beers has over 1,000 varieties on the menu.

Goupil le Fol
22 Rue de la Violette
Sink into the enormous sofas in the recesses of this dimly lit bar on several floors of a rambling old town house. Near the Grand-Place and open until late.

Kafka
6 Rue de la Vierge Noire
Intellectuals and locals gather here to chew the fat over a variety of vodkas and Belgian beers.

La Bécasse
11 Rue de Tabora
Traditional Brussels tavern

specialising in beer (tastings can be arranged); popular with students.

La Lunette
3 Place de la Monnaie
Another old-fashioned café where the speciality beer is served in a cross between a beer glass and a soup bowl.

La Rose Blanche
11 Grand-Place
Great views of the square and a good traditional menu, but tourist prices.

Le 19ième
Hôtel Métropole,
31 Place de Brouckère
An early evening aperitif on the heated terrace of this Art Deco hotel is a Bruxellois tradition.

Le Corbeau
18 Rue Saint Michel
Lively and convivial bar just off Rue Neuve, where you can drink a half-metre of Belgian ale from a *chevalier* (a large glass on a wooden frame).

Le Java
14 Rue St-Géry
Tiny but noisy and popular bar.

L'Espérance
1–3 Rue du Finistère
Wood-panelled Art Deco bar frequented during the day by old and young, but at night a funky place to be with good music.

Le Wine Bar
9 Rue des Pigeons
Romantic wine bar, run by real connoisseurs, with an impressive list of wines and gourmet dishes.

L'Homo Erectus
57 Rue des Pierres
Popular and longstanding gay bar with a good atmosphere in a street full of gay bars and clubs.

Mappa Mundo
26 Rue du Pont de la Carpe
Friendly and trendy bar with good food on Place St-Géry.

P.P. Café
28 Rue Van Praet
Lively bar-restaurant with 1930s decor and good food.

Rick's
344 Avenue Louise
American bar set in a grand neo-classical mansion, serving cocktails, hamburgers and spare ribs.

Tels Quels
81 Rue du Marché aux Herbes
Popular gay bar with helpful knowledgeable staff; the building also houses the gay and lesbian community centre *(see page 228)*. The bar is open daily 5pm–2am, until 4am weekends.

Underground Kafé
45 Rue des Pierres
Friendly gay bar with entertaining drag shows – glamorous on a Friday and Saturday night, comic pastiches every Sunday night.

Zebra
33–35 Place St-Géry
Hip café on a happening square.

FESTIVALS

The city festivals are an engaging mixture of spectacular medieval pageants, cutting-edge drama and dance, populist street festivals, prestigious international events and elitist high jinx. The following events take place at roughly the same time each year:

March
Brussels International Fantasy Film Festival One of Europe's premier fests for science-fiction and fantasy film buffs.

April
Flanders Festival Classical concerts from April–October.
Sablon Spring Open-air baroque-music concerts on Place du Grand Sablon.

May
KunstenFESTIVALdesArts Arts festival covering opera, theatre, dance, cinema, music and fine arts.
Les Nuits Botanique Two-week music festival of independent music and *chanson* hosted by Le Botanique French cultural centre. Concerts are staged in the concert hall under the lovely glass dome and on the grounds. The Cirque Royal is joint host.
Queen Elisabeth International Music Competition Prestigious

musical event alternating between singing, violin and piano, held at Bozar.
Brussels Jazz Marathon Live jazz at cafés and on outdoor stages throughout the city.
Brussels Zinneke Festival A biennial costume parade (next in 2006) to promote Brussels as a multicultural city.

June
Re-enactment of the Battle of Waterloo Large-scale and popular event held every five years (2005, 2010).
Couleur Café World Music festival at the giant Tour et Taxis entertainment complex, Rue Picard.

July
Ommegang The procession, which began as a lavish display by the burghers of Brussels, gained a new lease of life as a tribute to Charles V in 1549, the ruler who declared Brussels the capital of his boundless empire. Today's Ommegang is a carnival-like parade held during the first week of July on the Grand-Place.
Brosella Folk and Jazz Festival Held in mid-July at the Théâtre de Verdure in Osseghem.
National Day Celebrated on 21 July with processions in the city centre and fireworks and festivities in the Royal Park.
Sundays in the Bois de la Cambre Classical and jazz concerts from 11am–1pm throughout July and August.
Brussels Kermesse/Foire du Midi A large, annual funfair near Gare du Midi railway station runs for about a month from mid-July.
City of Brussels Summer Festival Open-air concerts at various places in the city centre.

August
Sundays in the Bois de la Cambre As above.
Foire du Midi As above.
Planting of the Meiboom The planting of the "Tree of Joy" on 9 August is preceded by a folkloric ritual and procession from Rue des Sables to the Grand-Place.

TRANSPORT
ACCOMMODATION
ACTIVITIES
A – Z
LANGUAGE

Carpet of Flowers Every two years (2006, 2008) the Grand-Place is covered in a wonderful display of flowers.

September

Brueghel Festivities Held around the middle of the month in Rue Haute, in honour of the great local artist.

October

Audi Jazz Festival Concerts at venues throughout the city from mid-October to mid-November.
Modo Bruxellae Fashion shows in the city centre.

November

Audi Jazz Festival As above.

December

Christmas Market Craft stalls and ice-skating rink on the Marché aux Poissons.
Crib and Christmas Tree The Grand-Place.

SHOPPING

What to Buy

Brussels is known for its fine chocolate, beer, crystalware, diamonds and the world-famous Brussels lace. You will find souvenir shops just about everywhere tourists tend to visit: around the Grand-Place, the Manneken-Pis, near the Stock Exchange and Opera House. Fashionistas may want to look out for renowned Belgian designers with shops in the Lower City, particularly on Rue Antoine Dansaert.

Where to Buy

There are numerous areas in Brussels where you can shop to your heart's content. The main shopping area in the Lower City is Rue Neuve, a pedestrian street (in more than one sense) with mainly international chains such as C&A, Hennes and Mauritz, and the large City 2 shop-

TAX REFUNDS

Non-EU residents are entitled to a refund of most of the 21.5% value-added tax (TVA) levied on items bought in certain shops above a total value of €125. You'll recognise participating shops by the Tax-Free Shopping stickers in their windows, and they will provide the form that needs to be completed and submitted to Customs before leaving the EU in order to get the refund.

ping mall hosting smaller boutiques. You will find plenty of shops at Place de Brouckère, Place de la Monnaie and along Boulevard Anspach (predominantly fashion boutiques and book stores). The smaller galleries off Rue Neuve, for example the Passage du Nord and the Galerie du Centre, have a wide range of unusual shops.

A good place to go window-shopping is among the glass-roofed arcades of the Galeries Royales St-Hubert, near the Grand-Place: Galerie du Roi, Galerie de la Reine and Galerie des Princes. Built in 1847, as the first covered shopping gallery in Europe, it houses mainly luxury boutiques of leather, jewellery and design both classic and modern. Cheaper casual clothing can be found in the neighbouring Galerie Agora. On the other side of the Grand-Place, in Rue du Midi, are numerous music stores and a few art supply shops. Rue du Beurre is good for sweets and gift shops.

Rue Antoine Dansaert is the place to find ultra-fashionable boutiques such as Stijl, as well as the showcases of Belgium's best designers. Internationally recognised designer names are concentrated in the Upper City around Place Louise and along Avenue Louise, Porte de Namur.

Chaussée d'Ixelles is slightly more downmarket. The most chic

arcades are located in the Upper City as well. You will find both the Galerie Espace Louise and Galerie Louise at Place Louise; the Galerie de la Toison d'Or and Galerie d'Ixelles are located at Porte de Namur. These arcades lead one into the other, forming a huge glittering labyrinth where you can shop till you drop.

Antique lovers should head for the area around Place du Grand Sablon, which is packed with antique shops and has an antique market on Saturdays and Sundays. The Sablon Shopping Garden on the square is Belgium's longest art gallery.

For second-hand furniture and *brocante* take a look in the Marolles district, especially in the streets leading to and around Place du Jeu de Balle.

Beer

Bière Artisanale
174–176 Chaussée de Wavre
Around 400 different beers, and they deliver all over the world.
De Bier Tempel
56 Rue du Marché aux Herbes
Over 400 Belgian beers all with matching glasses.

Belgian Designers

Hatshoe
89a Rue Antoine Dansaert
Designer headgear and footwear.
Modes
164 Rue Blaes
Quality vintage linen and clothes for men and women, at reasonable prices.
Elvis Pompilio
29 Rue des Pierres
He is an amazing hatmaker, of both traditional and eccentric head-gear – and that really is his name.
Christa Reniers
29 Rue Antoine Dansaert
Beautiful contemporary jewellery never short of some humour.
Stijl
74 Rue Antoine Dansaert
This temple of Belgian designers stocks Dries Van Noten, Martin Margiela, Dirk Bikkembergs and many others for men and women.

Olivier Strelli
44 Rue Antoine Dansaert
72 Avenue Louise
Contemporary, elegant fashion
for men and women by one of
Belgium's top designers.

Kaat Tilley
4 Galerie du Roi
Loose clothes in unusual colours
and stunning fabrics.

Nicholas Woit
80 Rue Antoine Dansaert
This young designer uses new
and second-hand materials to
create some fabulous clothes.

Bookshops

Brüsel
100 Boulevard Anspach
Large bookshop selling comic
strips in several languages.

FNAC
City 2, Rue Neuve
Good section of books in several
languages, as well as CDs, maps,
concert tickets and photography.

Sterling Books
38 Rue du Fossé aux Loups
English bookshop.

Tropismes
Galerie des Princes
Elegant bookshop with a good
selection of art books.

Waterstones
71–75 Boulevard Adolphe Max

A good branch of the large British
bookshop chain.

Chocolates, Cakes and Biscuits

Dandoy
31 Rue au Beurre
This delightful old-fashioned
store specialises in biscuits and
other Belgian specialities.

Galler
44 Rue au Beurre
Excellent chocolates from the
Belgian Royal Warrant Holder.

Godiva
22 Grand-Place
47–48 Place du Grand Sablon
Prestigious and attractive chocolate shop, a rival to Neuhaus, producing some of the finest Belgian
chocolates.

Marcolini
39 Place du Grand Sablon
Some chocoholics claim these
chocolates to be the best, but
they are rather dark and serious.
One of four shops in the city.

Mary's
73 Rue Royale
Produces intensely flavoured
dark chocolate good enough for
the Belgian royal family.

Neuhaus
27 Grand-Place
25–27 Galerie de la Reine

The praline was supposedly
invented by Neuhaus, arguably the
most traditional chocolatier. These
shops (two of seven in the city) are
as pretty as their gift boxes and
the chocolates are excellent.

Planète Chocolat
24 Rue du Lombard
Chocolate here really is art.
Frank Duval sculpts chocolates
of the finest quality. You can try
them in the tearoom on the first
floor, which also has tea dancing
on Sunday afternoons.

Wittamer
6 & 12–13 Place du Grand Sablon
Excellent but expensive patisserie with handmade chocolate
pralines, amazing gateaus and
the best sorbet in town.

Spectator Sports

Horse-Racing

Horse-racing and trotting have
strong local followings and take
place at three courses in and
around Brussels: Boitsfort, Groenendaal and Sterrebeek.

Hippodrome de Boitsfort
51 Chaussée de la Hulpe
Tel: 02-533 10 80

Groenendaal
20 G B Charlielaan
Tel: 02-657 30 63

Sterrebeek
43 Avenue du Roy de Blicquy
Tel: 02-767 54 75

Soccer

Stade Roi Baudouin
135 Avenue du Marathon, Heysel.
Tel: 02-475 32 40
The national soccer stadium,
rebuilt in the 1990s to the most
exacting modern standards to
erase the stain of the 1985 Heysel Stadium disaster.

RSC Anderlecht
2 Avenue Theo Verbeeck
Tel: 02-522 15 39
Brussels' crack soccer squad,
dubbed Les Mauves after the
colour of their shirts, has its

MARKETS

If you enjoy raking through markets – whether for kitsch or art,
books or flowers, bric-a-brac or
exotic spices – Brussels is the
place to be. Every day is market
day somewhere in the city. From
cars to canaries, there is little
that can't be found in a Brussels
market. Some of the best are:

Antiques Market
Place du Grand Sablon
Saturday 9am–6pm, Sunday
9am–2pm
The quality here is generally high
and prices are set to reflect this.

Flower Market
Grand-Place
Tuesday–Sunday 8am–2pm
Small but appealing, the market
is a soft-sell service that

enhances its venerable surroundings.

**Marché aux Puces
(Flea Market)**
Place du Jeu de Balle
Daily 7am–2pm.
The city's renowned vieux
marché (old market) is the place
for all kinds of old tat – and
some genuine finds too. At its
best and most atmospheric on
Sunday.

Marché du Midi
Around Gare du Midi
A large and colourful food and
textile market that's like a slice
of a Middle Eastern bazaar and
is a good place to buy all kinds
of exotic foods, herbs and
spices.

moments but has rarely scaled the international heights.

FC Brussels
61 Rue Charles Malis
Tel: 02-411 69 86
The city's other big soccer club, formed from the merger of several small ones.

Participant sports

There are sporting and recreational centres located in all the different districts of Brussels, where non-members will find plenty of opportunities to work up a sweat. The French-speaking sports association ADEPS has a list of sports centres on its website (www.adeps.be; tel: 02-413 23 11). The Flemish equivalent is BLOSO (www.bloso.be; tel: 02-209 45 11). Or consult the city's *Pages d'Or* (Yellow Pages) phone directory for a full listing of private and public facilities.

Bowling

There are two bowling alleys in the city open Mon–Sat 2pm–after midnight, Sun 10am–midnight:
Bowling Crosly
43 Quai au Foin
Tel: 02-217 2801
Bowling Crosly
36 Boulevard de l'Empereur
Tel: 02-512 0874

Cycling

The most popular sport in Belgium is cycling. You'll find avid cyclists everywhere, despite chaotic traffic and inconsiderate drivers. Cycle racing also enjoys widespread popularity. The Forêt de Soignes and Bois de la Cambre both have good cycling tracks.To hire a bicycle and for suggested routes or to join guided tours contact **Pro Vélo** *(see City Tours)*.

Golf

There are many golf courses in and around Brussels. Contact: La Fédération Royale Belge de Golf, 110 Chaussée de la Hulpe
Tel: 02-672 23 89
www.golfbelgium.be

Ice-Skating

The opening hours vary throughout the year and are generally longer during school holidays. Check exact times before setting out.
Forest National
36 Avenue du Globe
Forest
Tel: 02-345 16 11
Poseidon
4 Avenue des Vaillants
Woluwe-St-Lambert
Tel: 02-762 16 33

Riding

Horse-riding is very popular in the many parks and wooded areas. The Forêt de Soignes and Bois de la Cambre both have bridleways and riding schools nearby.
Centre Equestre de la Cambre
872 Chaussée de Waterloo
Tel: 02-375 34 08
Royal Etrier Belge
19 Champ du Vert Chasseur, Uccle. Tel: 02-374 28 60

Rollerblading

Rollerbladers gather in Bois de la Cambre on Sundays, when the roads are closed to traffic and taken over by rollerbladers and cyclists. There is also an open-air skating rink here where you can hire rollerblades (Patinoire Ganzaroller, 1 Chemin du Gymnase; tel: 0495-80 41 04; open Wed, Sat and Sun noon–6pm, school holidays daily noon–6pm).

Sports Centres

The following sports centres offer a wide range of facilities.
Centre Sportif de la Forêt de Soignes
2057 Chaussée de Wavre
Tel: 02-672 9330
Centre Sportif de la Woluwe
87 Avenue Emmanuel Mounier
Woluwe-St-Lambert
Tel: 02-672 9330
Centre Sportif de Woluwe-St-Pierre
2 Avenue Salom
Tel: 02-773 18 20
Complexe Sportif du Palais du Midi
3 Rue Roger van der Weyden
Tel: 02-279 59 54

GUIDED TOURS

Tours vary greatly from classic walks to specialist tours which can be tailor-made to suit you. More specialist tours include those covering **Art Nouveau**, which take a detailed look at the most innovative style in Brussels' architectural history, **comic strip** tours, which visit sites and museums associated with the "Ninth Art", and city walls that have been decorated by comic strip artists, and of course **brewery** tours *(see page 225)*.

ARAU
55 Boulevard Adolphe Max
Tel: 02-219 33 45
Organises tours in English on urban architecture and history, departing from outside the Hôtel Métropole on Saturday mornings at 9.45am.

Brukselbinnenstebuiten
47 Rue du Houblon.
Tel: 02-218 38 78
Tours on foot or by coach to discover hidden aspects of Brussels.

Brussels City Tours
8 Rue de la Colline
Tel: 02-513 77 44
Daily bus tours around the city and to Ghent, Antwerp and Waterloo.

Brussels by Water
2B Quai des Péniches
Tel: 02-203 64 06
Boat trips around the city's waterways for groups and individuals.

Calèches Carlos-Moens-Stassens
1 Watermolen, Aalst
Tel: 053-70 05 04
Old-fashioned horse-drawn traps with driver, usually parked in Rue Charles Buls near the Grand-Place, take you around the city centre.

Chatterbus
12 Rue des Thuyas
Tel: 02-673 18 35
Tours on foot and by bus for adults and children.

The European Information Centre
Info-Point, 12 Rond-Point Schuman
Tel: 02-296 5555
For organised visits to the European Parliament and discussions on the workings of EU institutions

GBB (Guides Bruxelles Belgique)
Town Hall, Grand-Place
Tel: 02-548 04 48
A whole host of tours on offer.

Heli Service Belgium
140 Gaasbeeksesteenweg, Halle
Tel: 02-361 21 21
See Brussels by helicopter.

Pro Vélo
15 Rue de Londres
Tel: 02-502 73 55
Runs guided bike tours through the city and rents out bikes.

Brewery Tours

Belle-Vue Brewery
33 Quai du Hainaut
Tel: 02-410 19 35
For the renowned Kriek cherry-beer, among others.

Cantillon Brewery and Museum
56 Rue Gheude, Anderlecht
Tel: 02-521 49 28
Produces the gueuze, Kriek and faro "champagnes" of Belgian beer.

Oud Beersel
230 Laarheidestraat, Beersel
Tel: 02-380 33 96
A traditional producer of lambic and gueuze beers.

FOR CHILDREN

Here are the best museums and activities for children in and around the city.

Atomium
Boulevard du Centenaire
Tel: 02-474 89 77
This symbol of Brussels, built for the 1958 World Exhibition, represents an atom in the form of an iron crystal, enlarged 165 billion times. It is currently undergoing renovation and will reopen in January 2006. www.atomium.be

Bruparck
20 Boulevard du Centenaire
Tel: 02-474 83 77
This entertainment complex just next to the Atomium should keep children amused for hours. It includes the multi-screen cinema **Kinepolis**, the **Village**, a selection of shops and restaurants, as well as **Mini-Europe**, where you can do a whistlestop tour of all of Europe's famous landmarks in miniature. There's also **Océade**, a water funpark with all the usual slides and wave pools. It is open all year round at varying times.

Centre Belge de la Bande Dessinée (Comic Museum)
20 Rue des Sables
Tel: 02-219 19 80
A wonderful museum, devoted to one of Belgium's passions. It is housed in a magnificent building, the former Waucquez warehouse designed by Victor Horta in 1906. Fun and enjoyment for both the young and the young at heart *(see page 110)*. Open: Tues–Sun 10am–6pm.

Children's Farms
There are three in Brussels. One is just north of the city centre: Ferme du Parc Maximilien, 21 Quai du Batelage, tel: 02-201 56 09. Another is in the northwestern commune of Jette (by arrangement only): 172 Petite Rue Ste-Anne, tel: 02-479 80 53. The third is in the southern commune of Uccle: Ferme Modèle d'Uccle, 93 Vieille Rue du Moulin.

Dierenpark Planckendael
Leuvensesteenweg 582, Muizen (Mechelen)
Tel: 015-41 49 21
A short drive out of Brussels, this is a large animal park surrounded by greenery, plus a mini-farm and adventure playground. Open: daily 10am–between 4.45 and 7pm – varies seasonally.

Musée des Enfants (Children's Museum)
15 Rue du Bourgmestre
Tel: 02-640 01 07
An altogether fascinating hands-on museum for children, designed to make education fun. Open: May–June Wed and Sat 2.30–5pm; July Mon–Fri 2.30–5pm; Aug closed; Sep–end April Wed, Sat and Sun 2.30– 5pm.

Musée du Jouet (Toy Museum)
24 Rue de l'Association
Tel: 02-219 61 68
An interactive museum and playroom containing thousands of toys from 1830 to the present day.

Open: daily 10am–noon, 2–6pm.

Musée Royal de l'Armée et d'Histoire Militaire (Royal Army and Military History Museum)
3 Parc du Cinquantenaire
Tel: 02-737 78 11
Extensive collection of weapons and armaments from the 7th to the 18th centuries. A large hall full of planes traces the history of military aviation and parachuting from 1912 to the present. Open: Tues–Sun 9am–noon, 1–4.45pm.

Museum des Sciences Naturelles de Belgique (Museum of Natural Sciences)
29 Rue Vautier
Tel: 02-627 42 11
Large collections of minerals, fossils and skeletons, including the famous iguanodons, moving dinosaur models and an Arctic and Antarctic section. Note that the museum is undergoing major refurbishment until 2007 so some galleries may be closed. Open: Tues–Fri 9.30am–4.45pm; Sat and Sun 10am–6pm.

National Planetarium
10 Avenue de Bouchout
Tel: 02-474 70 50
Study the night sky, trace the Great Bear and Pole Star, and learn where comets come from. Open: Mon–Fri 9am–4.30pm, Sun 1.30–4pm.

Q-Zar
36 Boulevard de l'Empereur
Tel: 02-512 08 74
Laser-gun fun Mon–Fri from 2pm, Sat from 1pm, Sun from 10am.

Scientastic Museum
1st floor Metro Station Bourse
Tel: 02-732 13 36
Fun museum filled with interactive displays and experiments. Perfect for a rainy day. Open: Sat and Sun and school holidays 2–5.30pm. On reservation during the week.

Walibi
9 Rue J Dechamps, Wavre
Tel: 010-42 15 00
Belgium's biggest and best theme park, featuring a range of white-knuckle rides and other amusements. The adjacent **Aqualibi** (tel: 010-42 16 03) is great for hours of watery fun.

A - Z

A HANDY SUMMARY OF PRACTICAL INFORMATION, ARRANGED ALPHABETICALLY

A dmission Charges

Museums and galleries charge moderate entrance fees, typically between €5 and €10. A few special attractions charge more than this. Most of the larger places and even some of the smaller ones have special deals for families and groups. The Brussels Card *(see page 7)* gives reduced entrance fees to many museums and galleries in the city.

Young people under 24 can invariably get reduced-rate admissions to museums, though they may need to produce a student card or other proof of age. Senior citizens can also get discounts at many places. Some museums and galleries have free admission on the first Wednesday afternoon of the month.

B udgeting for Your Trip

If you're looking for a hotel with an acceptable minimum level of comfort, cleanliness and facilities, a reasonable starting point for the price of a double room is €60; in budget-class hotels, going up from there to around €100 should make a significant difference in quality. Hotels in the centre tend to be more expensive, so you will generally get more for your money elsewhere – but you won't get the convenient location. For between €100 and €200 a whole range of hotels opens up, ranging from bland business-traveller places to character-rich establishments looked after by loving owners. Beyond this, and certainly beyond €250, you're moving into deluxe territory, though you do not really

arrive there in all its genuine-marble glory until €300 and above.

Food costs range from a couple of euros for a perfectly acceptable sandwich, through €10–€20 for a 2–3-course meal at a decent local restaurant, to €25–€50 at a fine restaurant. From there, you can head up to the €100 mark and above, with the extra cost taking you well into Michelin-star territory.

Getting around by tram (and metro and bus where appropriate) costs as little as about €7 a day. Taxi fares around the centre run from about €5–€15.

Business Hours

There are no official closing times for shops in Belgium. Most shops are open between

CLIMATE CHART

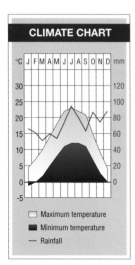

☐ Maximum temperature
■ Minimum temperature
— Rainfall

9am and 6pm; supermarkets and local grocery stores often keep their doors open until 9pm. Some shops close for a lunch break from noon–1pm or 1–2pm. On Fridays, many larger stores and supermarkets in Brussels are open until 8 or 9pm. A few night shops are open around the clock. Apart from those in the city centre, the vast majority of shops close on Sundays and holidays.

Most banks are open Monday–Friday 9am–4 or 5pm, with some closing for lunch between 1 and 2pm. Post offices are generally open Monday–Friday 8 or 9am–5 or 6pm; the office at the Centre Monnaie shopping mall on Place de la Monnaie is also open on Saturday 9.30am–3pm.

Museums and galleries are usually open from Tuesday to Saturday or Sunday. Some have late-night opening on Thursday or Friday evenings. The majority are closed on Monday.

C limate

Belgium enjoys a temperate maritime climate, typical of northwest Europe. Extremes of heat and cold are rare, with summers being relatively cool and winters relatively mild. In summer the average temperature is about 16°C (61°F), in winter about 3°C (37°F). Summer tends to be somewhat cooler and winter somewhat warmer at the coast, a situation that is reversed among the Ardennes hills of the interior.

Brussels, being about equidistant from the coast and the Ardennes, is roughly average in terms of its weather. The warmest months are July and August, and paradoxically this is a good time to be in the city, since many of its permanent residents take their annual holidays during these months and the normally intense traffic is greatly reduced, making the whole experience more pleasant.

In addition, the city's many parks and café and restaurant terraces come into their own at this time. It does not snow too often in winter, and some winters there is no snow at all; when there is, the powdery covering adds an additional romantic touch to places like the Grand-Place.

Crime & Safety

Brussels is generally safe, but crime does exist and is to a degree a growing problem. You should take sensible precautions against becoming a victim of petty crime like pickpocketing, bag-snatching, and theft of and from cars. Keep a careful watch on wallets, bags and other valuables, especially on public transport, at metro stations, and at busy transport nodes like Gare du Midi and Gare du Nord. To guard against theft, many women carry shoulder bags, with the strap crossed over the shoulder and the clasp facing inwards. Less common but more serious are robberies with threats or with violence, and even car-jackings. And exercise some caution in certain areas after dark, and in parks.

Some parts of the centre and many parts of outlying districts can seem like ghost towns at night, and the Belgians practice of closing metal shutters on their windows, fortress-like, can make streets darker than they might otherwise be, which all adds to the potential risk of mugging in these places. The red-light district north of Gare du Nord is a gloomy, sleazy and threatening place that's best avoided, though its extension on the south side of the station is tamer.

In an emergency, call the police on 101. For non-emergencies, there are police stations around the city, the most central of which

BELOW: the Bozar cultural centre is the city's top arts venue.

is at 30 Rue du Marché au Charbon, just off the Grand-Place tel: 02-279 79 79.

Customs

There is no limit to the amount of foreign currency that can be brought in or taken out of Belgium. Items for everyday use and those frequently transported by tourists, such as cameras and sporting equipment, may be brought into the country duty-free.

Visitors over 17 travelling between EU nations are not subject to restrictions on goods and consumable items for personal use. Duty-free shopping is no longer available to travellers within the EU. For travel within the EU, customs restrictions on alcohol, cigarettes and many other items no longer apply, although there are guide levels designed to prevent illegal trading.

Visitors entering Belgium from a non-EU nation are permitted to bring the following items duty-free: 200 cigarettes or 50 cigars or 250g tobacco; 2 litres still wine; 1 litre spirits or 2 litres sparkling or fortified wine; 50g perfume and 0.25 litres *eau de toilette*.

D isabled Travellers

In Britain, the Royal Association for Disability and Rehabilitation (RADAR) has information on planning holidays, transport and equipment for rent, and accommodation. Their address is Unit 12, City Forum, 250 City Road, London EC1V 8AF, tel: 020 7250 3222. Information is also avail-

EMERGENCY NUMBERS

• **Police** tel: 101
• **Fire, Ambulance** tel: 100
• **Doctors**
Médi Garde, tel: 02-479 18 18
SOS Médecins 02-513 02 02
• **Dental Service** (out of hours) tel: 02-426 10 26

able from Brussels International Tourism and the Belgian Tourist Information Centre *(see page 231)*, which can provide advice on the accessibility of hotels, restaurants, museums and other places of interest with disabled facilities.

Most of the major museums and galleries have access for wheelchairs, although the city in general, with its busy streets, cobbled squares, and hills between the Lower City and the Upper City, is not ideal. Public transport is tolerably accessible, in particular the trains, trams and metro trains. Buses are a bit more difficult, but the exit doors double as access doors for wheelchairs, and there is generally someone there to help. Taxi companies have some vehicles able to take wheelchairs.

E lectricity

The standard in Belgium is 220 volts AC. Visitors bringing appliances from countries where the standard is 110 volts may need to bring or buy a voltage transformer and perhaps also a plug adaptor before using them. Hotels may have a 110-volt or 120-volt outlet for shavers.

Embassies

These offices are generally open 9 or 10am–4pm (some consular offices are open only until noon or 1pm), and are closed on the public holidays of their country.
Australia, 6 Rue Guimard
Tel: 02-286 05 00
Canada, 2 Avenue de Tervuren
Tel: 02-741 06 11
Ireland, 50 Rue Wiertz
Tel: 02-235 66 76
New Zealand, 1 Square de Meeûs
Tel: 02-512 10 40
South Africa, 26 Rue de la Loi
Tel: 02-285 44 00
United Kingdom, 85 Rue d'Arlon
Tel: 02-287 62 11
USA, 27 Boulevard du Régent
Tel: 02-508 21 11

Entry Requirements

Citizens of EU countries require a valid personal identity card (or passport for countries that have no identity card). Citizens of some other European countries require only a passport; others need a visa also. Visitors from the United States, Canada, Australia, New Zealand, Japan and most other developed countries need only a valid passport; no visa is required. Citizens of other countries may need a visa, obtainable in advance from Belgian embassies or consulates in their home countries or country of residence. Children under the age of 16 must be in possession of a child's identity card/passport if their names have not been entered in one of their parents' cards.

Travellers bringing in cats or dogs are required to have an official certificate issued by a vet stating that their pet has been vaccinated against rabies. This vaccination must have taken place at least 30 days prior to arrival and be no more than one year old (in the case of cats, six months).

G ay & Lesbian Travellers

The scene in Brussels is a long way from being as developed or open as that in Amsterdam, Paris or London, but it does exist and is a growing phenomenon, with an expanding roster of cafés, bars and clubs; the main streets are Rue des Pierres and Rue du Marché au Charbon. For more information, contact the gay and lesbian community centre Tels Quels, 81 Rue du Marché au Charbon, tel: 02-512 45 87, where there is a bar (open daily 5pm–2am, until 4am on weekends) and friendly staff to help you orientate yourself in the city.

H ealth and Medical Care

No health certificates or vaccinations are required for citizens of the EU and many other countries. EU citizens who have obtained an E111 form from their local post office before departure (note that this will be replaced in 2006 by a European Health Insurance Card) are entitled to free treatment by a doctor, excluding a small patient charge at private practices, and free prescribed medicines. Remember that one form is required for each person/family member travelling. This insurance is not comprehensive and will not cover you, for example, for holiday cancellation or the cost of repatriation. For full cover, you are advised to take out separate private medical and travel insurance. As long as you are insured, treatment will be given and the cost recovered later, by way of a bill sent to your home address or direct to your insurance company.

Medical Services

Health and medical services in Belgium are generally excellent. A well-equipped Brussels hospital, though not in the centre, is the Cliniques Universitaires St-Luc, 10 Avenue Hippocrate, tel: 02-764 11 11, which has a casualty (emergency) department and an outpatient department.

Pharmacies

After regular business hours and during holidays you will find the name and address of the nearest pharmacy on nightduty posted at all pharmacies (easily identified by a green neon cross).

■ nternet

Internet cafes are slowly disappearing from the Belgian capital (even the large easyEverything branch in the city centre has closed down), as demand is decreasing. Your best bet for internet access is your hotel. If they don't offer access, they should be able to advise you on the nearest internet access point in your area. *For useful websites on Brussels see page 231.*

■ ost Property

There is a Lost and Found office for items lost at Brussels airport, tel: 02-753 68 20; to recover belongings left on an aeroplane, or to retrieve lost luggage, tel: 02-723 60 11 or tel: 02-723 07 07. For articles lost or left behind on a train, tel: 02-224 55 91, but enquire first at the nearest train station. Items left on trams, buses or the metro may turn up at the STIB Lost Property Office, 15 Avenue de la Toison d'Or (Porte de Namur metro station), tel: 02-515 23 94.

Lost items may also be reported to the police inspector's office in the relevant *commune*, or at police headquarters, 30 Rue du Marché au Charbon (in the city centre), tel: 02-279 79 79. Report loss or theft of valuables immediately, as most insurance policies insist on a police report.

■ aps

The tourist office's *Brussels Guide & Map*, which costs €3, includes a detailed map of the city centre. Some hotels provide adequate free maps of the centre, and paid-for maps are available from bookshops, newsagents and souvenir shops. Free public transport route maps are available from the main metro stations and from the offices of the public transport company, STIB, 15 Avenue de la Toison d'Or.

Media

Newspapers and Magazines

Because Belgium is composed of three different language communities, you will find numerous newspapers. The three most important French newspapers are the *Le Soir, La Libre Belgique* and *La Dernière Heure*. The three most widely distributed Flemish papers are the *Het Laatste Nieuws, De Standaard* and *De Morgen*.

PUBLIC HOLIDAYS

1 January New Year's Day
1 May Labour Day
21 July National Day
15 August Assumption
1 November All Saints' Day
11 November Armistice Day
25 December Christmas Day
In addition, there are "moveable" holidays: Easter Monday, Ascension Day and Pentecost Monday. If any holidays should fall on a Saturday or Sunday, the following Monday is taken off instead.

The weekly English-language magazine, *The Bulletin*, keeps the many thousand members of the international community in Brussels informed and up to date regarding what is going on in Belgium, and has an excellent *What's On* pull-out section.

Foreign newspapers and magazines, including the main British and American ones, can be purchased at newsagents and bookshops throughout the city.

Television and Radio

RTBF and BRT share the television monopoly, in French and Dutch respectively. In addition, in practically all areas of the country it is possible to receive a huge range of foreign stations by cable and satellite. Aside from the national radio stations – RTBF in French, BRT in Dutch and BRF in German – there are some local stations. The BBC World Service can be picked up.

Money

The unit of currency in Belgium is the euro (€). A euro is divided into 100 cents. Euro notes come in denominations of 5, 10, 20, 50, 100, 200 and 500; coins are 1 cent, 2 cents, 5 cents, 10 cents, 20 cents, 50 cents, €1 and €2. You won't often come across the €200 and €500 notes, and for most purposes they won't be of much use to you, since few busi-

TRANSPORT

ACCOMMODATION

ACTIVITIES

A – Z

LANGUAGE

ABOVE: the main tourist office is in the Hôtel de Ville on the Grand-Place.

nesses or individuals want to take them, partly for practical reasons and partly because counterfeiting is a problem. Some small businesses are even reluctant to accept the €100 notes, for the same reasons.

Changing Money

All banks in Belgium exchange foreign money, and they generally give the best rates of exchange. There are many exchange offices in the city centre, most of them open daily for longer hours than the banks. Those located in the large railway stations offer competitive rates and are open daily, including public holidays, at the following times: **Gare du Nord** Mon–Fri 8am–8pm, Sat 8.30am–5pm; **Gare Centrale** Mon–Fri 8am–6pm, Sat 8am–5pm; **Gare du Midi** Mon–Fri 7am–8.30pm, Sat–Sun 8.30am–7pm. Other exchange offices may not have such good rates, or charge higher commissions, but they are likely to be open when the banks and station exchanges are closed. Beware high commission rates at hotels.

There are automatic cash-dispensers all over the city; you will recognise most of them by

their Bancontact and Mister Cash logos. A convenient one is at the CBC Bank branch on the Grand-Place.

Credit Cards

International credit cards such as MasterCard/Eurocard, Visa, American Express, Diners Club and JCB are accepted by hotels, restaurants, shops, car-hire companies, airlines and many other businesses.

Tipping

Tips are included in taxi fares and prices in restaurants and bars, so all that is required is to leave some small change if you think the service warrants it – but service personnel will not object to receiving a tip and have become used to the fact that many visitors (in contrast to their fellow citizens) do tip. In most restaurants, a tip of 10 percent will be considered generous, or at least adequate. In public toilets and establishments with a toilet attendant, it is customary to leave between 20 and 50 cents.

P ostal Services

Most post offices are open Monday–Friday (except national holidays) 8 or 9am–5 or 6pm (perhaps with a one-hour break at lunchtime); the office at the Centre Monnaie shopping mall on Place de la Monnaie is also open on Saturday 10am–4pm, and the post office at Gare du Midi, 1E/F Avenue Fonsny, is open open Mon–Fri 7am–10pm, Sat 10am–7pm, Sun 11am–7pm. Some shops which sell postcards also sell stamps (but usually only if you buy postcards). Post restante facilities are available at main post offices; you need a passport to collect your mail.

R eligious Services

While Catholic ones are by far the most important, there are places of worship for most religions and

denominations in Brussels. Some venues are:
Catholic Services
Cathédrale des Sts-Michel-et Gudule
Parvis Ste-Gudule (at Boulevard de l'Impératrice)
Tel: 02-217 83 45
Jewish Services
Grande Synagogue de Bruxelles
32 Rue de la Régence
Tel: 02-512 43 34
Muslim Services
Grande Mosquée de Bruxelles
14 Parc du Cinquantenaire
Tel: 02-735 21 73

S tudent Travellers

Students and young people may be entitled to reduced-rate admission to many museums, but a passport or student identity card may be required as proof of age and validity.

T elephones

Brussels fixed-line telephone numbers have a two-digit area code and a seven-digit subscriber number. This format applies also to Antwerp, Liège and Ghent. For all other localities, the format is a three-digit area code and a six-digit subscriber number. The area code for Brussels is 02 (the code for Bruges, for instance, is 050).

TIME ZONE

Belgium is on Central European Time (CET), which is Greenwich Mean Time (GMT) plus one hour. When it is noon in Brussels it is also noon in Paris, Rome and Berlin; 11am in London; 6am in New York, Montreal and Boston; 5am in Chicago; 3am in Los Angeles and San Francisco; and 9pm in Sydney. From the last weekend in March to the last weekend in October, clocks are advanced 1 hour – this corresponds to Daylight Saving Time in the UK and North America.

When you phone a Belgian number from inside Belgium, you must always use the full area code, even if the number is in the same code zone you are calling from. So to call the Brussels international tourism office from inside or outside the city, you would dial 02-513 89 40.

For calling a Belgian number from outside the country, first dial the country code, 32, followed by the area code minus the initial zero, then the subscriber number.

Some public phone boxes take coins of 10, 20 and 50 cents, and €1 and €2 coins, but most take Telecards of €5, €10 and €20, which are sold at post offices, railway stations, newsagents and kiosks. Current calling rates can be found posted in all telephone booths. For national phone information, dial 1207 or 1307.

To use phonecards, dial one of the following access numbers:
AT&T: 0800-010
MCI: 0800-10 012
Sprint: 0800-10 014
British Telecom: 0800-10 024
Canada Direct: 0800-10 019

If you want to place a call outside Belgium, first dial 00, then the country code, and finally the subscriber number (delete the zero in the area code if the code contains a zero). For international information, dial 1405.

If you bring your mobile phone with you, remember that if you are calling a local number you need to dial the international access code (e.g. 00 from the UK) followed by the country code for Belgium (32) and the area code for Brussels (2). Calls are expensive because you are still going through your service provider at home.

Toilets

Public toilets are few and far between in Brussels. But there are plenty of cafés and fast-food restaurants where you can use the toilet facilities either free or for a charge of 20–50 cents. Hotels, in particular those with

TELEPHONE CODES

When phoning abroad from Belgium, some country codes are:
- **Australia** 61
- **Canada** 1
- **Ireland** 353
- **New Zealand** 64
- **South Africa** 27
- **UK** 44
- **USA** 1

busy lobbies (so you won't be recognised as an interloper), are a resource that should not be overlooked, and their toilets are invariably clean.

Tourist Information

The city's own tourist office is Brussels International Tourism, Hôtel de Ville (Town Hall), Grand-Place, tel: 02-513 89 40; fax: 02-513 83 20 (www.brussels international.be), open Easter–mid-December 9am–6pm; mid-December–Easter Mon–Sat 9am–6pm.

Then there is the national tourism office, the Belgian Tourist Information Centre, just a block away at 63 Rue du Marché aux Herbes, tel: 02-504 03 90, fax: 02-513 04 75, (www.opt.be and www.visitflanders. com), open May–Oct, Mon–Fri 9am–6pm, and weekends and holidays 9am–1pm and 2–6pm (July and Aug until 7pm); Nov–Mar Mon–Fri 9am–6pm, Sat 9am–1pm and 2–6pm, Sun 9am–1pm. For hotel reservations, *see page 213*.

Offices Abroad
Belgian Tourist Office
USA
Belgian Tourist Office, 220 East 42nd Street, Suite 3402, 34th Floor, New York 10017
Tel: 212-758 8130
Fax: 212-355 7675
E-mail: info@visitbelgium.com
www.visitbelgium.com
Canada
Same mailing address as USA office.

Tel: 514-457 2888
Fax: 212–355 7675
E-mail: info@visitbelgium.com
www.visitbelgium.com
United Kingdom
Brussels and French-speaking Wallonia: 217 Marsh Wall, London E14 9FJ
Tel: 0906-302 0245
Brochure line: 0800-954 5245
Fax: 020-7531 0393
E-mail: info@www.belgiumtheplaceto.be
www.belgiumtheplaceto.be
Brussels and Flanders: 1A Cavendish Sq. London W1G 0LD
Tel: 0906-302 0245
Brochure line: 0800-954 5245
Fax: 020-7307 7731
E-mail: info@visitflanders.co.uk
www.visitflanders.co.uk

W ebsites

The first place to turn to for information on Brussels is Brussels International Tourism's own comprehensive website www.brussels international.be, which has plenty of information on attractions, sights and places of interest, hotels and restaurants, guided tours, walking routes, shopping, and more. It's all promotional and uncritical, of course, but still full of useful information. For details of the city's museums, try www.brusselsmuseums.be

For a wider vista on Belgium, the Belgian tourist information centre has *two* sites: www.opt.be for Brussels and Wallonia, and www.visitflanders.com for Brussels and Flanders; and www.visit belgium.com, which is their joint face to the world; for British visitors they once again go their separate ways, with www.belgiumtheplaceto.be and www.visitflanders.co.uk respectively.

Some good independent sites are www.trabel.com, from the Belgium Travel Network, and its associated section for Brussels www.trabel.com/brussels; www.xpats .com, for Belgian news, weather, tourism and more. For hotels, visit the comprehensive www.hotels-belgium.com; and for eating out, the equally thorough www.resto.be.

TRANSPORT
ACCOMMODATION
ACTIVITIES
A – Z
LANGUAGE

L ANGUAGE

UNDERSTANDING THE BRUXELLOIS

French

Pronunciation

Learning the pronunciation of the French alphabet is a good idea. In particular, learn how to spell out your name.

a = ah, **b** = bay, **c** = say, **d** = day, **e** = er, **f** = ef, **g** = zhay, **h** = ash, **i** = ee, **j** = zhee, **k** = ka, **l** = el, **m** = em, **n** = en, **o** = oh, **p** = pay, **q** = kew, **r** = ehr, **s** = ess, **t** = tay, **u** = ew, **v** = vay, **w** = dooblahvay, **x** = eex, **y** = ee grek, **z** = zed

Even if you speak no French at all, it is worth trying to master a few simple phrases. The fact that you have made an effort is likely to get you a better response, even though many Belgians speak English. Remember to emphasise each syllable, but not to pronounce the last consonant of a word as a rule (this includes the plural "s") and always to drop your "h"s. Whether to use "vous" or "tu" is a vexed question; increasingly the familiar form of "tu" is used by many people. However it is better to be formal, and use "vous" if in doubt.

It is very important to be polite; always address people as Madame or Monsieur, and address them by their surnames

FLEMISH

Brussels is officially bilingual – both French and Flemish are spoken – although the majority of its population is French-speaking. For more on language in Belgium, *see page 40*.

until you are confident first names are acceptable. When entering a shop always say, *"Bonjour Monsieur/Madame,"* and *"Merci, au revoir,"* when leaving.

French Words & Phrases

What is your name? *Comment vous appelez-vous?*
My name is... *Je m'appelle...*
Do you speak English? *Parlez-vous anglais?*
I am English/American *Je suis anglais/americain*
I don't understand *Je ne comprends pas*
Please speak more slowly *Parlez plus lentement, s'il vous plaît*
Can you help me? *Pouvez-vous m'aider?*
I'm looking for... *Je cherche*
Where is...? *Où est...?*
I'm sorry *Excusez-moi/Pardon*

I don't know *Je ne sais pas*
That's it *C'est ça*
Here it is *Voici*
There it is *Voilà*
Let's go *On y va/Allons-y*
See you tomorrow *A demain*
See you soon *A bientôt*
Show me the word in the book *Montrez-moi le mot dans le livre*
At what time? *A quelle heure?*
When? *Quand?*
What time is it? *Quelle heure est-il?*
yes *oui*
no *non*
please *s'il vous plaît*

thank you *merci*
(very much) *(beaucoup)*
you're welcome *de rien*
excuse me *excusez-moi*
hello *bonjour*
OK *d'accord*
goodbye *au revoir*
good evening *bonsoir*
today *aujourd'hui*
yesterday *hier*
tomorrow *demain*
here *ici*
now *maintenant*
later *plus tard*
right away *tout de suite*
this morning *ce matin*
this afternoon *cet après-midi*
this evening *ce soir*

On Arrival

I want to get off at... *Je voudrais descendre à...*
Is there a bus to the Grand-Place? *Est-ce qu'il y a un bus pour la Grand'-Place?*
What street is this? *C'est quelle rue ici?*
Which line do I take for...? *Quelle ligne dois-je prendre pour...?*
How far is...? *A quelle distance se trouve...?*
Validate your ticket *Compostez votre billet*
airport *l'aéroport*
train station *la gare*
bus station *la gare routière*
Metro stop *la station de Métro*
bus *l'autobus*
bus stop *l'arrêt de bus*
platform *le quai*
ticket *le billet*
return ticket *billet aller-retour*
toilets *les toilettes*
This is the hotel address *C'est l'adresse de l'hôtel*
I'd like a (single/double) room *Je voudrais une chambre (pour une/deux personnes)*
...with shower *avec douche*
...with bath *avec salle de bain*
...with a view *avec vue*
Does that include breakfast? *Le prix comprend-il le petit déjeuner?*
May I see the room? *Je peux voir la chambre?*
washbasin *le lavabo*
bed *le lit*
key *la clé*
lift *l'ascenseur*
air conditioned *climatisé*

On the Road

Where is the spare wheel? *Où est la roue de secours?*
Where is the nearest garage? *Où est le garage le plus proche?*
Our car has broken down *Notre voiture est en panne*
the road to... *la route pour...*
left *gauche*
right *droite*
straight on *tout droit*

far *loin*
near *près d'ici*
car park *parking*
over there *là-bas*
on foot *à pied*
by car *en voiture*
town map *le plan*
road map *la carte*
street *la rue*
square *la place*
give way *céder le passage*
no parking *stationnement interdit*
motorway *l'autoroute*
toll *le péage*
speed limit *la limitation de vitesse*
petrol *l'essence*
unleaded *sans plomb*
diesel *le gasoil*
water/oil *l'eau/l'huile*
puncture *un pneu crevé*
bulb *l'ampoule*
wipers *les essuies-glace*

Shopping

Where is the nearest bank/post office? *Où est la banque/poste la plus proche?*
I'd like to buy *Je voudrais acheter*
How much is it? *C'est combien?*
Do you take credit cards? *Est-ce que vous acceptez les cartes de crédit?*
I'm just looking *Je regarde seulement*
Have you got? *Avez-vous...?*
I'll take it *Je le prends*
What size is it? *C'est de quelle taille?*
Anything else? *Avec ça?*
size (clothes) *la taille*
size (shoes) *la pointure*
cheap *bon marché*
expensive *cher*
enough *assez*
too much *trop*
a piece of *un morceau de*
each *la pièce (e.g. ananas, €2 la pièce)*
bill *la note*
chemist *la pharmacie*
bakery *la boulangerie*
bookshop *la librairie*
library *la bibliothèque*
department store *le grand magasin*

delicatessen *la charcuterie/le traiteur*
fishmongers *la poissonerie*
grocers *l'épicerie*
market *le marché*
supermarket *le supermarché*
junk shop *la brocante*

Sightseeing

town *la ville*
old town *la vieille ville*
abbey *l'abbaye*
cathedral *la cathédrale*
church *l'église*
town hall *l'hôtel de ville/la mairie*
nave *la nef*
stained glass *le vitrail*
staircase *l'escalier*
tower *la tour*
walk *le tour*
country house/castle *le château*
Gothic *gothique*
Roman *romain*
Romanesque *roman*
museum *le musée*
art gallery *la galerie*
exhibition *l'exposition*
tourist information office *l'office du tourisme/le syndicat d'initiative*
free *gratuit*
open *ouvert*
closed *fermé*
every day *tous les jours*
all year *toute l'année*
all day *toute la journée*
to book *réserver*

Dining Out

Table d'hôte is one set menu served at a set price. *Prix fixe* is a fixed price menu. *A la carte* means dishes from the menu are charged separately.
breakfast *le petit déjeuner*
lunch *le déjeuner*
dinner *le dîner*
meal *le repas*
first course *l'entrée/les hors d'oeuvre*
main course *le plat principal*
made to order *sur commande*
drink included *boisson comprise*
wine list *la carte des vins*

the bill *l'addition*

What do you recommend?
Que'est-ce que vous recommandez?

Do you have local specialities?
Avez-vous des spécialités locales?

I am a vegetarian *Je suis végétarien*

I am on a diet *Je suis au régime*

I'd like to order *Je voudrais commander*

That is not what I ordered *Ce n'est pas ce que j'ai commandé*

Is service included? *Est-ce que le service est compris?*

May I have more wine? *Encore du vin, s'il vous plaît?*

Enjoy your meal *Bon appetit!*

Breakfast and Snacks
pain **bread**
petits pains **rolls**
beurre **butter**
sel/poivre **salt/pepper**
sucre **sugar**
confiture **jam**
oeufs **eggs**
...à la coque **boiled eggs**
...au bacon **bacon and eggs**
...au jambon **ham and eggs**
...sur le plat **fried eggs**
...brouillés **scrambled eggs**
tartine **bread and butter**
yaourt **yoghurt**
crêpe **pancake**
croque-monsieur **ham and cheese toasted sandwich**
croque-madame **...with a fried egg on top**

Main Courses
la viande/meat bleu **very rare**
saignant **rare**
à point **medium**
bien cuit **well done**
grillé **grilled**
agneau **lamb**
andouille/andouillette **tripe sausage**
bifteck **steak**
boudin **sausage**
boudin noir **black sausage**
boudin blanc **white sausage**
blanquette **stew of veal, lamb or chicken with creamy egg sauce**
à la bordelaise **beef with red**

wine and shallots
à la Bourguignonne **cooked in red wine, onions and mushrooms**
brochette **kebab**
caille **quail**
canard **duck**
carbonnade **casserole of beef, beer and onions**
carré d'agneau **rack of lamb**
cassoulet **stew of beans, sausages, pork and duck**
cervelle **brains (food)**
châteaubriand **thick steak**
choucroûte **Alsace dish of sauerkraut, bacon and sausages**
confit **duck or goose preserved in its own fat**
contre-filet **cut of sirloin steak**
coq au vin **chicken in red wine**
côte d'agneau **lamb chop**
dinde **turkey**
entrecôte **beef rib steak**
escargot **snail**
faisan **pheasant**
farci **stuffed**
faux-filet **sirloin**
feuilleté **puff pastry**
foie **liver**
foie de veau **calf's liver**
foie gras **goose or duck liver pâté**
cuisses de grenouille **frog's legs**
grillade **grilled meat**
jambon **ham**
lapin **rabbit**
lardons **small pieces of bacon, often added to salads**
magret de canard **duck breast**
moelle **beef bone marrow**
navarin d'agneau **stew of lamb with onions, carrots and turnips**
oie **goose**
perdrix **partridge**
pieds de cochon **pig's trotters**
pintade **guinea fowl**
porc **pork**
pot-au-feu **casserole of beef and vegetables**
poulet **chicken**
poussin **young chicken**
rognons **kidneys**
rôti **roast**
sanglier **wild boar**
saucisse **fresh sausage**
saucisson **salami**
veau **veal**
viande **meat**

Poission/Fish
anchois **anchovies**
anguille **eel**
bar (or *loup*) **sea bass**
barbue **brill**
belon **Brittany oyster**
bigorneau **sea snail**
bercy **sauce of fish stock, white wine and shallots**
brandade **salt cod puree**
cabillaud **cod**
calmars **squid**
colin **hake**
coquillage **shellfish**
crevette **shrimp**
daurade **sea bream**
flétan **halibut**
fruits de mer **seafood**
hareng **herring**
homard **lobster**
huître **oyster**
langoustine **large prawn**
limande **lemon sole**
lotte **monkfish**
morue **salt cod**
moule **mussels**
moules marinières **mussels in white wine and onions**
oursin **sea urchin**
poissons **fish**
raie **skate**
saumon **salmon**
thon **tuna**
truite **trout**

Légumes/Vegetables
ail **garlic**
artichaut **artichoke**
asperge **asparagus**
bolets **boletus mushrooms**
céleri remoulade **grated celery with mayonnaise**
champignon **mushroom**
cèpe **boletus mushroom**
chanterelle **wild mushroom**
cornichon **gherkin**
chips **potato crisps**
chou **cabbage**
chou-fleur **cauliflower**
concombre **cucumber**
cru **raw**
crudités **raw vegetables**
épinard **spinach**
frites **chips, French fries**
haricot **dried bean**
haricots verts **green beans**
maïs **corn**

mesclun **mixed leaf salad**
navet **turnip**
oignon **onion**
panais **parsnip**
persil **parsley**
pignon **pine nut**
poireau **leek**
petits pois **pea**
poivron **bell pepper**
pomme de terre **potato**
pommes frites **chips,
French fries**
primeurs **early fruit and
vegetables**
radis **radish**

Fruits/Fruit
ananas **pineapple**
cavaillon **fragrant sweet
melon**
cerise **cherry**
citron **lemon**
citron vert **lime**
figue **fig**
fraise **strawberry**
framboise **raspberry**
groseille **redcurrant**
mangue **mango**
mirabelle **yellow plum**
pamplemousse **grapefruit**
pêche **peach**
poire **pear**
pomme **apple**
raisin **grape**
prune **plum**
pruneau **prune**
reine-claude **greengage**

Sauces/Sauces
aïoli **garlic mayonnaise**
béarnaise **sauce of egg, butter,
wine and herbs**
forestière **with mushrooms and
bacon**
hollandaise **egg, butter and
lemon sauce**
lyonnaise **with onions**
meunière **fried fish with butter,
lemon and parsley sauce**
Mornay **sauce of cream, egg
and cheese**
paysan **rustic style, ingredients
depend on the region**
pistou **Provençal sauce of basil,
garlic and olive oil**
provençale **sauce of tomatoes,
garlic and olive oil**
papillotte **cooked in paper**

Desserts/Puddings
Belle Hélène **fruit with ice
cream and chocolate sauce**
clafoutis **baked pudding of
batter and cherries**
coulis **purée of fruit**
gâteau **cake**
île flottante **whisked egg whites
in custard sauce**
crème anglaise **custard**
dame blanche **vanilla ice-cream
with hot chocolate sauce**
tarte tatin **upside-down tart of
caramelised apples**
crème caramel **caramelised egg
custard**

Boissons/Drinks
coffee **café**
...**with milk or cream** au lait or
crème
...**decaffeinated** déca/
décaféiné
...**black/espresso** noir/
express
...**American filtered** filtre
tea **thé**
...**herb infusion** tisane
...**camomile** camomille
hot chocolate **chocolat chaud**
milk **lait**
mineral water **eau
minérale**
fizzy **gazeux/pétillante**
non-fizzy **non-gazeux/plat**
fizzy lemonade **limonade**
fresh lemon juice served with
sugar **citron pressée**
fresh squeezed orange juice
orange pressée
fresh or cold **frais, fraîche**
beer **bière**
...**bottled** en bouteille
...**on tap** à la pression
...**from the barrel** au fût
pre-dinner drink **apéritif**
white wine with cassis
(black-currant liqueur) **kir**
kir with champagne **kir
royale**
with ice **avec des glaçons**
neat/dry **sec**
red **rouge**
white **blanc**
rose **rosé**
dry **brut**
sweet **doux**
sparkling wine **crémant**

house wine **vin de maison**
Where is this wine from? **De
quelle région vient ce vin?**
jug **carafe/pichet**
...**of water/wine** d'eau/de vin
mixed **panaché**
after dinner drink **digestif**
cheers! **santé!**

Emergencies

Help! **Au secours!**
Stop! **Arrêtez!**
Call a doctor **Appelez un
médecin**
Call an ambulance **Appelez une
ambulance**
Call the police **Appelez la
police**
Call the fire brigade **Appelez les
pompiers**
Where is the nearest
telephone? **Où est le téléphone
le plus proche?**
Where is the nearest hospital?
**Où est l'hôpital le plus
proche?**
I am sick **Je suis malade**
I have lost my passport/purse
**J'ai perdu mon passeport/
porte-monnaie**

Telephone

How do I make an outside call?
**Comment est-ce que je peux
téléphoner à l'extérieur?**
I want to make an international
(local) call **Je voudrais une
communication pour l'étranger
(une communication locale)**
What is the dialling code? **Quel
est l'indicatif?**
I'd like an alarm call for 8
o'clock tomorrow morning **Je
voudrais être réveillé à huit
heures demain matin**
Who's calling? **C'est qui a
l'appareil?**
Hold on, please **Ne quittez pas
s'il vous plaît**
The line is busy **La ligne est
occupée**
I must have dialled the wrong
number **J'ai dû faire un faux
numéro**

FURTHER READING

General

A Tall Man in a Low Land: Some Time among the Belgians by Harry Pearson, Little Brown (1999). A humorous if often patronising account of the author's travels in Belgium.

Factory of Facts by Luc Sante, Granta Books (1999). A Belgian-born American who never quite felt at home in his new land returns home to trace his roots and rediscover his own country.

The Sorrow of Belgium by Hugo Claus, Viking (1990). A novel charting the effects of the Nazi occupation of Flanders through the eyes of a young boy.

Tintin: The Complete Companion by Michael Farr John Murray (2001). Everything you ever wanted to know about the great Belgian comic-book series.

Art

Bruegel by Gregory Martin, Calman & Cooper (1978). Introduction to the works of great Brussels-born artist Pieter Bruegel the Elder.

From Van Eyck to Bruegel by Max J Friedlander, Phaidon (1969). Definitive account of the œuvre of the great Flemish Masters.

Magritte by Richard Calvocoressi, Phaidon Colour Library (1992). Part of a series on key artists and movements, this handy book is a great introduction to the work of Belgium's favourite Surrealist.

The Flemish Primitives: The Masterpieces by Dirk De Vos, Princeton University Press (2003). More than 200 colour illustrations of works by the likes of Jan van Eyck, Rogier van der Weyden and Petrus Christus, are a feast for the eye.

Victor Horta by David Dernie et al.

Wiley-Academy (1995). A lavishly illustrated book details the artistic vision of the great Belgian Art Nouveau architect and designer.

History

Defiant Dynasty: The Coburgs of Belgium by Theo Aronson, Bobbs-Merril Co. (1968). A gossipy history of the Kings of the Belgians from 1831 to 1950.

Waterloo: Napoleon's Last Gamble by Andrew Roberts, HarperCollins (2005). Exhaustive account of the Battle of Waterloo.

Food & Drink

Belgian Ale by Pierre Rajotte, Brewers Publications (1992). Gets below the foamy surface of the Belgian beers and of a great brewing tradition.

Everybody Eats Well in Belgium Cookbook by Ruth Van Waerebeek-Gonzalez and Maria Robbins, Workman Publishing (1996). A lovingly detailed Belgian cookbook which includes 250 recipes from around the country.

The Great Beers of Belgium by Michael Jackson, Running Press (1998). The author has drunk his way devotedly through the beer rosters of many a land. He came away from his Belgian investigations convinced that it is the proud bearer of one of the world's greatest beer-brewing traditions.

Other Insight Guides

Insight Guide: Belgium covers every aspect of the country: history, culture, people and places. For those on a tight schedule, **Insight Pocket Guide: Brussels** sets out carefully crafted itineraries designed to make the most

of your visit, and comes with a full-size fold-out map. **Insight Pocket Guide: Bruges** does a similar job for the medieval city that is the pride of Flanders. Separate **Insight Compact Guides** to **Brussels**, **Belgium** and **Bruges** are ideal on-the-spot reference guides.

FEEDBACK

We do our best to ensure the information in our books is as accurate and up-to-date as possible. The books are updated on a regular basis, using local contacts and who painstakingly add, amend and correct as required. However, some mistakes and omissions are inevitable, and we are ultimately reliant on our readers to put us in the picture.

We would welcome your feedback on any details related to your experiences using the book "on the road". Maybe we recommended a hotel that you liked (or another that you didn't), as well as interesting new attractions, or facts and figures you have found out about the country itself. The more details you can give us (particularly with regard to addresses, e-mails and telephone numbers), the better.

We will acknowledge all contributions, and we'll offer an Insight Guide to the best letters received.

Please write to us at:
Insight Guides
PO Box 7910
London SE1 1WE
United Kingdom
Or send e-mail to:
insight@apaguide.co.uk

BRUSSELS STREET ATLAS

The key map shows the area of Brussels covered by the atlas section. An index of street names and places of interest shown on the maps can be found on the following pages. For each entry there is a page number and grid reference

Map Legend

▭▭▭	Autoroute with Junction
– – – –	Autoroute (under construction)
▭▭▭▭	Dual Carriageway
▭▭▭▭	Main Road
▭▭▭▭	Secondary Road
▭▭▭▭	Minor road
▭▭▭▭	Track
▬ ▬ ▪ ▪	International Boundary
– – – –	Province Boundary
▬ ● ▬	National Park/Reserve
✚✚	Airport
✝✝	Church (ruins)
✝	Monastery
▰▱	Castle (ruins)
∴	Archaeological Site
∩	Cave
★	Place of Interest
⌂	Mansion/Stately Home
※	Viewpoint
↸	Beach
▭▭▭	Autoroute
▭▭▭	Dual Carriageway
▭▭▭	Main Roads
▭▭▭	Minor Roads
▭▭▭	Footpath
▬▬▬	Railway
▭	Pedestrian Area
▭	Important Building
▭	Park
Ⓜ	Metro
🚌	Bus Station
❶	Tourist Information
✉	Post Office

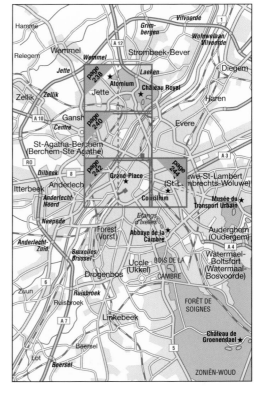

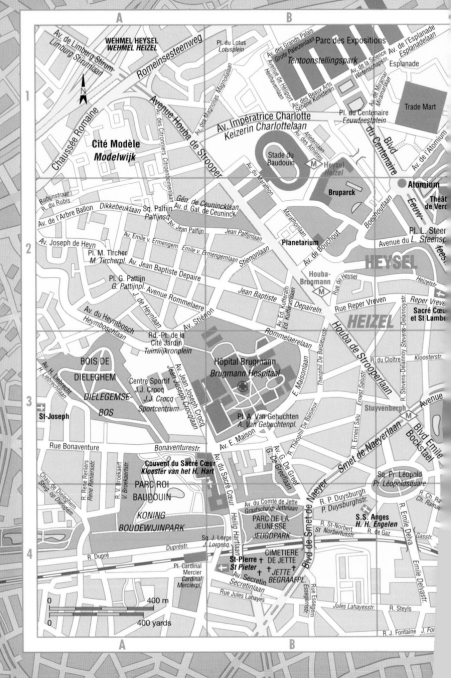

A

B

Av. de Limburg Stirum
Limburg Stirumlaan

WEHMEL HEYSEL
WEHMEL HEIZEL

Romeinsesteenweg

Pl. du Lotus
Lotusplein

Av. des Grands Palais
Grote Paleizenlaan

Parc des Expositions
Tentoonstellingspark

Avenue de Hulpart
Hallhaarlaan

Av. de la Science
Wetenschapsln.

Av. de l'Esplanade
Esplanadelaan

Esplanade

Chaussée Romaine

Av. des Beaux Arts
Schone Kunstenln.

Av. de Miramar
Miramarlaan

1

Avenue Houba de Strooper

Av. des Manolias
Magnolialaan

Av. Impératrice Charlotte
Keizerin Charlottelaan

Pl. du Centenaire
Eeuwfeestplein

Trade Mart

Cité Modèle
Modelwijk

Av. des Citronniers Citroenbomenlaan

Stade du
Baudouin

Aletterlaan
Av. des Athlètes

M   Heysel
Heizel

Blvd
du Centenaire

Av. de l'Atomium

Atomium

Rubijnstraat
R. du Rubis

Gén. de Ceunincklaan
Av. d. Gal. de Ceuninck

Av. du Marathon

Bruparck

Boeghoutlaan

Théât
de Vero

Av. de l'Arbre Ballon

Dikkebeuklaan

Sq. Palfijn
Palfijnsq.

Marathonlaan

Pl. L. Steer

Av. Emile v. Ermengem

Av. Jean Palfijn

Jean Palfijnlaan

Planetarium

Av. de Bouchout

Avenue du L. Steenss
fees.

2

Av. Joseph de Heyn

Pl. M. Tircher
M. Tircherpl.

Emile v. Ermengemlaan

Stienonlaan

HEYSEL

Heizelstr.

Pl. G. Pattijn
G. Pattijnpl.

Av. Jean Baptiste Depaire

Avenue Rommelaere

J. de Heynlaan

Jean Baptiste

Houba-
Brugmann
M

Rue de Heysel

Rue Reper Vreven

HEIZEL

Reper Vreve

Av. du Heymbosch
Heymboschlaan

Av. Stiénon

Rommelaerelaan

Holuba de Strooperlaan

Sacré Cœu
et St Lambe

Rd.-Pt. de la
Cité Jardin
Tuinwijkronplein

E. Maisonlaan

Theophil De Baiseux

Ernest Salustr.

R. du Cloître
Kloosterstr.

Stevens-Delannoy Stevens-Delannoystr.

Kloosterstr.

BOIS DE
DIELEGHEM

H. Liebrechtln.

Centre Sportif
J.J. Crocq

Jean-Joseph Crocqlaan

Hôpital Brugmann
Brugmann Hospitaal

E. Maisonlaan

 Th. De Baiseux

Ernest Salu

Stuyvenbergh
M

Avenue

3

St-Joseph

DIELEGEMSE-
BOS

J.J. Crocq
Sportcentrum

Pl. A. Van Gehuchten
A. Van Gehuchtenpl.

Theophil De Baiseux

Ernest Salu

Smet de Naeyerlaan

Blvd Emile
Bockstael

Rue Bonaventure

Bonaventurestr.

Av. E. Maison

G. De Greefln.

Blvd de Smet de Naeyer

Sq. Pr. Léopold
Pr. Léopoldsquare

Chau. de Dieleghem
Stwg op Dieleghem

R. René Reniers
René Renierstr.

R. V. Broeckaert
V. Broeckaertstr.

Couvent du Sacré Cœur
Klooster van het H. Hart

PARC ROI
BAUDOUIN

Av. du Sacré Cœur

Av. du Comté de Jette
Graafschap Jettelaan

R. P. Duysburgh
P. Duysburghstr.

R. Ch. Ra
R. Ch. Ramae

S.S. Anges
H. H. Engelen

Emile Delva

R. Ch. Ra

KONING
BOUDEWIJNPARK

Heilig Hartlaan

PARC DE LA
JEUNESSE
JEUGDPARK

R. St-Norbert
St Norbertusstr.

R. de Gaz

Gasstr.

4

R. Dupré

Sq. J. Lerge
J. Lorgesq.

Duprèstr.

Pl. Cardinal
Mercier
Cardinal
Mercierpl.

St-Pierre
St Pieter

CIMETIERE
DE JETTE
JETTE
BEGRAAFPL.

Rue Essegem

Jules Lahayesstr.

R. Steyls

0   400 m

0   400 yards

Av. Secretin
Secretinlaan

Rue Jules Lahayes

Rue
Essegem

R. J. Fontaine   J. For

A

B

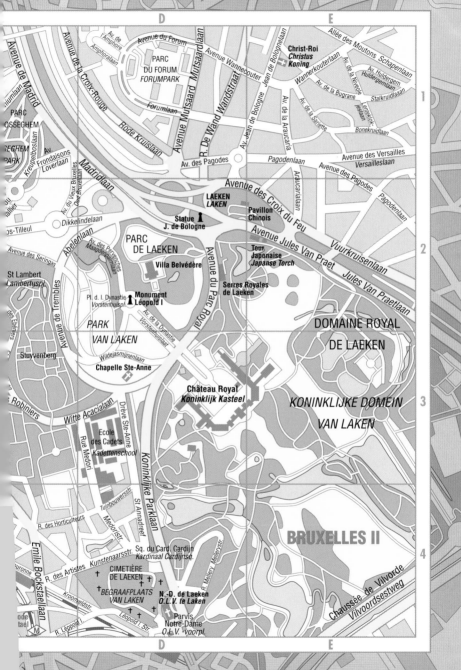

Avenue de Madrid

PARC OSSEGHEM
PARC OSSEGHEM

SEGHEM PARK

Av. Frondaisons Loverlaan

Avenue de la Croix-Rouge

Avenue Mutsaard Mutsaardlaan

Amphoralaan
Av. de l'Amphore

Avenue du Forum

PARC DU FORUM FORUMPARK

Forumlaan

Rode Kruislaan

Madridlaan

Kreupelbostaan

Avenue des Seringas

Abelenlaan

Avenue de Trembles

St Lambert Lambertuspl.

Os-Tilleul

Dikkelindelaan

Av. du Vieux Bruxelles Oude Brusselaan

Av. des Petrolelers Maagdekenstraat

PARC DE LAEKEN

Villa Belvédère

Pl. d. l. Dynastie Vorstenhuispl.

♦ Monument Léopold I

Av. de la Dynastie Vorstenhuisstraat

PARK VAN LAKEN

Wildejasmijnenlaan

Chapelle Ste-Anne

Stuyvenberg

Robiniers

Witte Acacialaan

Drève Ste-Anne

Rue Medori

Ecole des Cadets Kadettenschool

Koninklijke Parklaan

Turnhouwersstr.

St Arnaadreef

Medoristr.

R. des Horticulteurs

Emile Bockstaellaan

Couronne

Kroonveldstr.

ode tael

R. des Artistes

Kunstenaarsstr.

Sq. du Card. Cardijn Kardinaal Cardijnsq.

CIMETIÈRE DE LAEKEN

†BEGRAAFPLAATS VAN LAKEN

N.-D. de Laeken O.L.V. te Laken

Parvis Notre-Dame O.L.V.-voorpl.

Léopold I. Str.

R. Léopold I.

Avenue du Forum

Avenue Wannecouter

Jean de Bologne Jean de Bolognelaan

Christ-Roi *Christus Koning*

Wannerkouterlaan

Av. Huldergem Huldergemlaan

Allée des Moutons Schapenlaan

Av. de la Nucele

Stalkruidlaan

Av. de la Bugrane

Lenteklok-jeslaan

Bonekruidlaan

Av. de la Sanette

Av. Jean de Bologne

Av. de la Araucaria

Av. des Pagodes

Pagodenlaan

Avenue des Versailles Versailleslaan

Avenue des Pagodes

Araucarialaan

Pagodenlaan

LAEKEN *LAKEN*

Statue J. de Bologne

Avenue des Croix du Feu

Pavillon Chinois

Tour Japonaise *Japanse Torch*

Serres Royales de Laeken

Avenue Jules Van Praet

Vuurkruisenlaan

Jules Van Praetlaan

DOMAINE ROYAL

DE LAEKEN

KONINKLIJKE DOMEIN

VAN LAKEN

Avenue du Parc Royal

Château Royal *Koninklijk Kasteel*

BRUXELLES II

R. Mellery Mellerystr.

Chaussée de Vilvorde Vilvoordsestweg

D   E

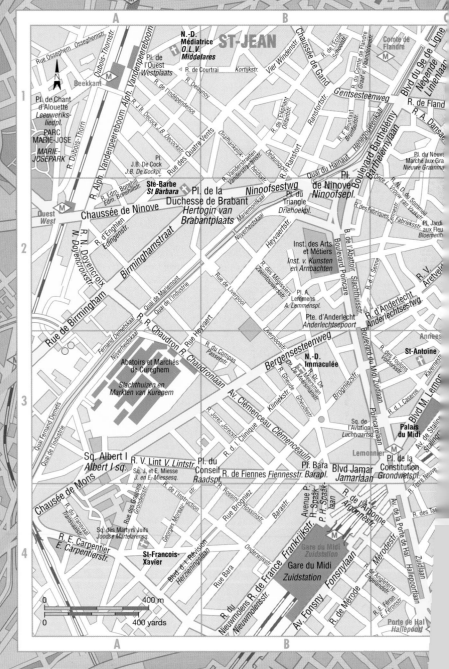

St-Jean

A B C

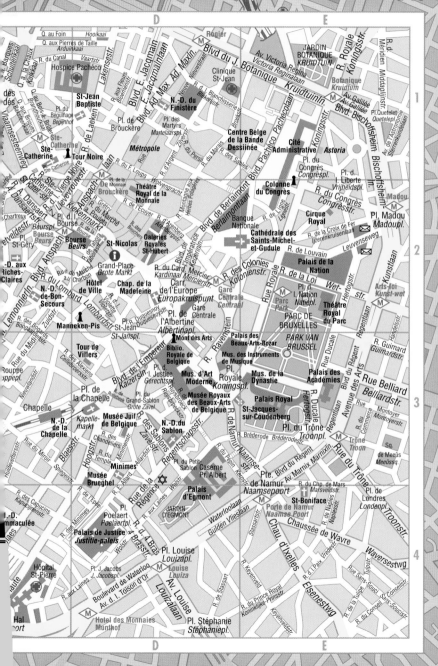

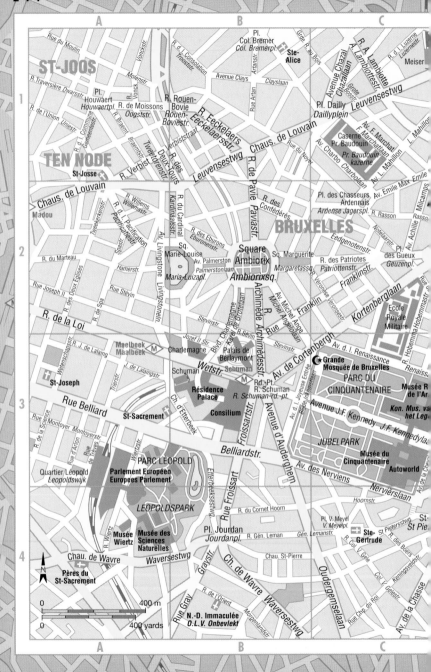

STREET INDEX

French

4 Bras, Rue d. **243** D4
9e de Ligne, Boulevard du **242** C1

A

Abattoir, Boulevard de l' **242** B2
Aerschot, Rue d' **241** E4
Albert I, Pont **241** D1
Albert I, Square **242** A3
Albertine, Place de l' **243** D2
Alexiens, Rue des **243** C3
Allard, Rue E. **243** D3
Alouette, Place de Chant d' **242** A1
Ambiorix, Square **244** B2
Amphore, Avenue de l' **239** D1
Anderlecht, Porte d' **242** B2
Anderlecht, Rue d' **242** C2
Ange, Avenue Michel **244** B2
Angleterre, Rue de' **242** C4
Anspach, Boulevard **243** C2
Anvers, Boulevard d' **241** D4
Anvers, Chaussée d' **241** D4–D3–D2
Anvers, Porte d' **241** D4
Araucaria, Avenue de la **239** E1
Arbre Ballon, Avenue de l' **238** A2
Archimède, Rue **244** B2
Arenberg, Rue d' **243** D2
Aretvelde, Rue V. **242** C2
Argent, Rue d' **243** D2
Argonne, Rue de l' **242** B3
Arlon, Rue d' **244** A3
Armateurs, Place des **241** D3
Artan, Rue **244** B1
Artistes, Rue des **239** C4
Arts, Avenue des **243** E3
Astoria **243** E1
Astronomie, Avenue de l' **243** E1
Ateliers, Rue des **240** C4
Athlètes, Avenue des **238** B1
Atomium **238** C2
Atomium, Avenue de l' **238** C1
Auderghem, Avenue d' **244** B3
Augustines, Rue des **240** B1
Autoworld **244** C3
Aviation, Square de l' **242** B3

B

Banque Nationale **243** D2
Bara, Place **242** B3
Bara, Rue **242** B4
Barques, Quai aux **243** C1
Barthélémy, Boulevard **242** C2–C1
Baudouin, Boulevard **241** D4
Beaux Arts, Avenue des **238** B1
Becker, Rue J de **240** A4–B3

Béguinage, Place du **243** C1
Belgica, Boulevard **240** B2
Belliard, Rue **243** E3, **244** A3
Berlaimont, Boulevard de **243** D2
Berlaymont, Palais de **244** B3
Besme, Rue Jules **240** A3
Bibliotheque Royale de Belgique **243** D3
Birmingham, Rue de **242** A3
Bischoffsheim, Boulevard **243** E1–E2
Blaes, Rue **243** C4
Blanchisserie, Rue d. l. **243** D1
Blindés, Square des **243** C1
Bockstael, Boulevard Emile **238** C3, **240** C2
Bockstael, Place E. **241** C1
Boers, Rue des **244** C4
Bogards, Rue des **243** C2–C3
Bois, Grande Rue au **244** B1–C1
Bois-à-Brûler, Quai au **243** C1
Bologne, Avenue Jean de **239** D1
Bols, Avenue Prudent **240** C1
Bonaventure, Rue **238** A3
Bonehill, Rue Edmond **242** A2
Bouchers, Rue des **243** D2
Bouchout, Avenue de **238** B2
Bourse **243** C2
Bourse, Place de la **243** C2
Bourse, Rue de la **243** C2
Brabant, Rue de **241** E4
Braemt, Rue **244** A1
Bréderode, Rue **243** E3
Bremer, Place Col. **244** B1
Briques, Quai aux **243** C1
Broekaert, Rue V. **238** A4
Brogniez, Rue **242** B4
Brouckère, Place de **243** D1
Broustin, Avenue **240** A2
Brunfaut, Rue F. **242** B1
Bruparck **238** B2
Bugrane, Avenue de la **239** E1

C

Canal, Rue du **243** C1
Capucins, Rue des **243** C3
Cardijn, Square du Cardinal **239** D4
Cardinal, Rue du **244** B2
Carpentier, Rue E. **242** A4
Carton de Wiart, Avenue **240** A2
Caserne, Rue de la **242** C3
Cathédrale des Saints-Michel-et-Gudule **243** D2
Centenaire, Boulevard du **238** C1
Centenaire, Place du **238** B1
Centre Belge de la Bande Dessinée **243** D1
Ceuninck, Avenue du Gal. de **238** A2–B2

Champ de la Couronne, Rue du **238** C4
Chandeliers, Rue des **243** D3
Chapelle **243** C3
Chapelle, Place de la **243** C3
Chapelle Ste-Anne **239** D3
Charbo, Avenue **244** B1
Charbonniers, Rue des **241** D4
Charlemagne, Boulevard **244** B3–B2
Chartreux, Rue des **243** C2
Chasse, Avenue de la **244** C4
Chasseurs Ardennais, Place des **244** B2
Château Royal **239** D3
Chaudron, Rue R. **242** A2
Chaux, Quai a la **243** C1
Chazal, Avenue **244** C1
Chevalerie, Avenue de la **244** C3
Champ de Eglise, Rue du **241** D1
Champ de Mars, Rue du **243** E3
Champ du Roi, Rue **244** C4
Christ-Roi **239** E1
Cirque Royal **243** E2
Cité Jardin, Rond Pont de la **238** A3
Citronniers, Avenue des **238** A1
Claessens, Rue **241** D2
Clays, Avenue **244** B1
Clémenceau, Avenue **242** B3
Cesse, Rue A. **240** C2
Clinique, Rue d. la **242** B3
Cloître, Rue du **238** B3
Colonies, Rue des **243** D2
Colonne du Congrès **243** D2
Combattants, Square d. **241** C1
Commerçants, Rue des **241** C4
Commerce, Quai du **241** C4
Commerce, Rue du **243** E3
Commune, Rue de la **244** A1
Compas, Rue du **242** B3
Comte de Flandre, Rue du **242** B1
Comté de Jette, Avenue du **238** B4
Confédérés, Rue des **244** B2
Congrès, Place du **243** E2
Congrès, Rue du **243** E2
Conseil, Place du **242** B3
Conseil, Rue du **243** E4
Consilium **244** B3
Consolation, Rue de la **244** B1
Constitution, Avenue de la **240** A2
Constitution, Place de la **242** C3
Cornet Hoorn, Rue du **244** B4
Cortenbergh, Avenue de **244** B3
Couronne, Rue du Champ d. l. **239** C4
Courtrai, Rue de **242** B1
Couvent du Sacré Cœur **238** A3
Crocq, Avenue Jean Joseph **238** A3
Croix de Fer, Rue de la **243** E2

Croix du Feu, Avenue des **239** D2–E2
Croix-Rouge, Avenue de la **239** C1–D1

D

Dailly, Place **244** B1
Dansaert, Rue A. **242** C1, **243** C2
Decock, Rue J. B. **242** A1
Delacoigne, Rue F. **240** B4
Delva, Rue Emile **238** C4
Demer, Rue Charles **240** C1
Demets, Quai Fernand **242** A3
Depaire, Avenue Jean Baptiste **238** A2
Deux Eglises, Rue des **244** A2
Deux-Tours, Rue des **244** A1
Dieleghem, Chaussée de **238** A3
Doyencroix, Rue N. **242** A2
Drootbeek, Rue du **241** C2
Dubois-Thorn, Rue **242** A2
Dubrucq, Avenue Jean **240** B3
Ducale, Rue **243** E3
Duchesse de Brabant, Place de la **242** B2
Dupont, Rue **241** E4
Dupré, Rue **238** A4
Duquesnoy, Rue **243** D2
Duysburgh, Rue P. **238** B4
Dynastie, Avenue de la **239** D2
Dynastie, Place de la **239** D2

E

Ebéniers, Avenue des **239** C2–C3
Eburons, Rue des **244** B2
Ecole, Rue de l' **240** B4
Ecuyer, Rue de l' **243** D2
Eeckelaers, Rue **244** B1
Eglise Ste-Anne, Rue de l' **240** B4
Eléphant, Rue de l' **242** B1
Empereur, Boulevard de l' **243** D3
Enghien, Rue d' **242** A2
Epée, Rue de l' **243** C3
Ermengem, Avenue Emile v. **238** A2
Esplanade, Avenue de l' **238** C1
Essegem, Rue **238** B4
Etangs Noirs, Rue des **240** A4
Etterbeek, Ch. d' **244** B3
Europe, Carrefour de l' **243** D2

F

Fabriques, Rue des **242** C2
Féron, Rue E. **242** C4
Fiennes, Rue de **242** B3
Flandre, Rue de **242** C1
Fleurs, Rue aux **243** D1
Foin, Quai au **243** C1
Fonsny, Avenue **242** B4
Fontaine, Rue J. **238** C4
Forum, Avenue du **239** D1
Foulons, Rue des **242** C3
France, Rue de **242** B4
Franklin, Rue **244** B2

Froissart, Rue **244** B4
Frondaisons, Avenue **239** C1
Frontispice, Rue du **241** D4
Fuchsias, Rue des **240** A4

G

Galeries Royales St-Hubert **243** D2
Galilée, Avenue **243** E1
Gallait, Rue **241** E3
Gand, Chaussée de **240** A4, **242** B1
Ganshoren, Rue de **240** A4
Gare Centrale **243** D2
Gare du Midi **242** B4
Gare du Nord **241** D4
Gaucheret, Place **241** D4
Gaucheret, Rue **241** D3
Gaz, Rue de **238** B4
Gehuchten, Place A. van **238** B3
Gele, Rue Col. van **244** C4
Gheude, Rue **242** B3
Giele, Avenue **240** A2
Goujons, Rue des **242** A4
Grand-Place **243** D2
Grande Mosquée de Bruxelles **244** C3
Grands Palais, Avenue des **238** B1
Grand-Sablon, Place du **243** D3
Gray, Rue **244** A4
Greef, Avenue G. de **238** B3
Grétry, Rue **243** D2
Gros-Tilleul, Avenue du **239** C2
Gueux, Place des **244** C2
Guimard, Rue **243** E3

H

Haecht, Chaussée de **241** E4
Haeck, Rue **240** B3
Hainaut, Quai du **242** B2
Hal, Porte de **243** C4
Hallier, Avenue du **239** C2
Haute, Rue **243** C4
Heideken, Rue **240** A1
Héliport, Avenue de **238** B1, **241** D4
Heymbosch, Avenue du **238** A2–A3
Heyn, Avenue Joseph de **238** A2
Heysel, Rue du **238** B2
Heyvaert, Rue **242** B2
Hobemma, Rue **244** C3
Hoegaerde, Place V. **240** B4
Horticulteurs, Rue des **239** C4–D4
Hospice Pachéco **243** C1
Hôtel de Ville **243** C2
Houba de Strooper, Avenue **238** A1–B2
Houwaert, Place **244** A1
Huldergem, Avenue **239** E1

I

Impératrice, Boulevard de l' **243** D2
Impératrice Charlotte, Avenue **238** B1
Indépendance Belge, Avenue de l' **240** A3
Indépendance, Rue de l' **242** A1
Industrie, Quai de l' **242** A3–A2

Flemish

ART & PHOTO CREDITS

GENERAL INDEX

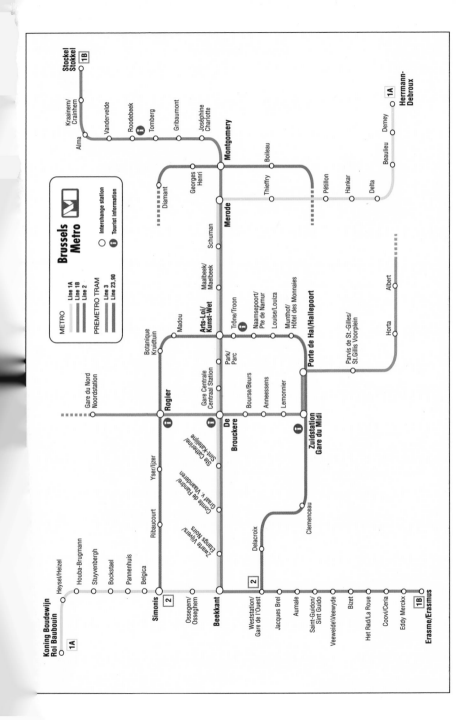

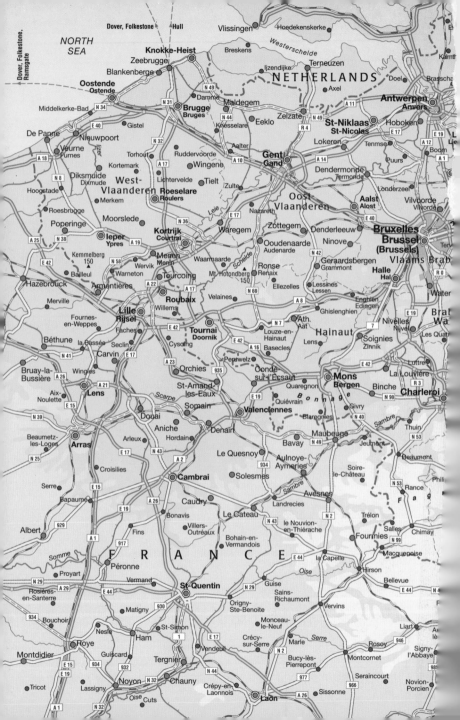